JERUSALEM ON EARTH

JERUSALEM ON EARTH

People, Passions, and Politics in the Holy City

A B R A H A M   R A B I N O V I C H

THE FREE PRESS
A Division of Macmillan, Inc.
NEW YORK

Collier Macmillan Publishers
LONDON

The Free Press
A Division of Macmillan, Inc.
866 Third Avenue, New York, N.Y. 10022

Collier Macmillan Canada, Inc.

Printed in the United States of America

printing number
1   2   3   4   5   6   7   8   9   10

Library of Congress Cataloging-in-Publication Data

Rabinovich, Abraham.
    Jerusalem on earth: people, passions, and politics in the
  Holy City / Abraham Rabinovich.
        p.   cm.
    Includes index.
    ISBN 0-02-925740-9
    1. Jerusalem—Biography.   2. Jews—Jerusalem—
  Biography.   3. Palestinian Arabs—Jerusalem—Biography.
  4. Jerusalem—Social life and customs.   5. Jerusalem—
  Politics and government.   I. Title.
  DS109.85.R22   1988
  956.94′4054′0922—dc19   88-21301
    [B]   CIP

The author thanks the following publishers for permission to adapt work of his that they have previously published: Hadassah, *The Jerusalem Post*, *The New Republic* (reprinted by permission of THE NEW REPUBLIC, © 1987, The New Republic, Inc.).

Contents

JERUSALEM ON EARTH

Prologue
The Neighbors

HAIM MACHSUMI FIRST SAW the old Arab on a summer morning a year before the Six Day War. Haim was standing on the balcony of his house on the Israeli side of Abu Tor, a hilltop village divided by the line of barbed wire and military blockhouses that cut Jerusalem in two. Haim's house lay right on the edge of that line.

The Arab had appeared downslope among the five deserted houses in the narrow strip of no-man's-land beyond the barbed wire. The houses had been abandoned since the War of Independence in 1948, when Israel had captured the upper part of the village to protect the Jerusalem railroad terminus that lay at the western foot of Abu Tor. The old man with the Arab headdress glanced up at Haim, thirty yards away, and hurried down into the Arab part of the village.

He was back a few days later, this time with several younger men. Afraid that they might be Jordanian soldiers in civilian clothing, Haim summoned Israeli soldiers from a nearby blockhouse. The soldiers said the Jordanians were being permitted to reoccupy some of the houses in no-man's-land in return for an agreement that allowed Israel to build a road close to the border on Mount Zion that accommodated Pope John XXIII during his visit to Jerusalem a few months before. It was one of the many gentleman's agreements over the years that Israel and Jordan had quietly arrived at in order to make life in the divided city more tolerable. Nevertheless, soldiers were posted in Haim's garden for a month to ensure that the abandoned house was being renovated as a residence and not as a military blockhouse.

Haim was reassured when he saw the Arabs clearing debris from the yard and planting trees. Women and children appeared after a few days. It was evident that the Arabs had come to live.

1

One Sabbath morning after the soldiers left, Haim was standing on his balcony enjoying the magnificent view of the sculpted hills of the Judean Desert to the east. Arab villages were nestled in the landscape. A mile to the northeast the golden Dome of the Rock dominated the Old City. Suddenly the old Arab came out of the house downslope and looked up at Haim. They had stared at each other often before but had never spoken.

"*Spah'nun*," said Haim, speaking the Arabic word for good morning.

The old man returned the greeting.

They were going to be neighbors, felt Haim, and they might as well be civil. After all, both families had children—Haim had seven and the Arabs seemed to have at least as many—and there was no sense making life uncomfortable for one another.

In the ensuing weeks, Haim and his wife, Rachel, exchanged greetings with other members of the Arab household. One day Haim saw the old man buying yogurt, ladeled out of a large jar, from an itinerant peddler. It was a scene familiar to Haim from his childhood in Iran. "Can I buy some too?" he called down in jest. The old man gestured towards the Jordanian blockhouse fifty yards away and said, "The soldiers are watching." It was the first time they had actually conversed, and they took the occasion to introduce themselves. The old man said his name was Abu Ali.

Haim, who worked as a janitor in the Finance Ministry, had been living in his border house since arriving in the country nine years before. He and his neighbors had been settled in abandoned Arab buildings. Despite the spectacular view, not many Israelis were willing to live on a border that periodically echoed with gunfire. The government had undertaken to fill it in with new immigrants in order to form a living wall against infiltration. At night, Haim would sometimes hear or see movement in the direction of the barbed wire, and it was clear to him that it was a crossing point for smugglers or spies or both.

One day, Haim's elderly mother, who lived with them, chased after a turkey that had escaped from their yard. When she returned, she said there was a girl crying in one of the houses nearby. Taking Haim out to the balcony, she pointed to a house down the slope.

"How did you get there?" he demanded, horrified that the old woman had inadvertently crossed the border. The turkey had gone through a hole in the fence, she replied, and so had she. Haim told her she must never go through the fence again.

"Why not?" she asked. "They're our neighbors."

Haim tried to explain that it was not like it was back in Iran, where they had lived peacefully with their Muslim neighbors. Here, Arabs and Jews were forbidden to pass through the fences that separated them. If they did, they could be shot by the soldiers in the blockhouses.

It was reassuring now to have Abu Ali's friendly family living opposite them rather than to face a hostile void. Nowhere else along the entire four-hundred-mile border between Jordan and Israel did Jewish and Arab families live so close together.

On a Sabbath morning late in May 1967, Haim and Rachel were sitting on their balcony watching Abu Ali cutting weeds behind his house. The pre–Six Day War tension had already started building up. Egyptian troops had moved into Sinai, and Israel responded by ordering a partial mobilization. Nonetheless, all of that seemed remote. Wildflowers, red and white, covered no-man's-land, and on an impulse Rachel called down to the elderly Arab. "Abu Ali. Could I have some of those pretty anemones?" The old man gathered a bouquet, and Rachel climbed down the terraced hillside. All that separated them now was the fence. Abu Ali reached across the barbed wire and handed the bouquet to Rachel.

She had hardly returned to her balcony when Jordanian soldiers appeared at Abu Ali's house and hustled him inside. When they left, he emerged and called up to Haim in a stage whisper from the shelter of a wall. "I can't talk to you anymore." The soldiers had threatened him with three years in jail if they saw him talking or handing things to the Israelis again. The Jordanians were worried about information being passed across. The two men continued to exchange greetings in the coming days, but surreptitiously.

War broke out two weeks later. In the opening hours, Haim took his family to a public shelter on the rear slope of Abu Tor. They remained there for three days. When they emerged, the battle for Jerusalem was over. Arab Abu Tor had been taken by an Israeli infantry battalion supported by tanks. The Arab population was stunned and anticipated a massacre. There was no killing, but as Haim made his way toward his home, he saw youths from Israeli Abu Tor, some of whom he knew to have police records, coming from the direction of the border with booty taken from Arab houses. He telephoned police, who soon arrived on the scene and began arresting looters. An officer suggested storing the booty in Haim's home until the Arab owners had been traced. Haim refused. He did not want the Arabs to think he had had a hand in the looting.

Reaching his house, which was undamaged, he saw Abu Ali

emerging from the house downslope. In the old man's hand was a stick to which was tied a white cloth. Haim scrambled through a breach opened in the barbed wire by the attack force and ran down-slope. Abu Ali stepped back in fright as Haim reached him. The Jew seized the old Arab's hand in a firm clasp and patted him on the shoulder. "At last," said Haim. "We can finally shake each other's hand."

The reunification of Jerusalem in the Six Day War introduced a new and distinct epoch in the four-thousand-year history of the city. The conquerors would settle alongside the conquered as fellow taxpayers even before the dust of battle had cleared. Not since the time of the Second Temple and Jesus two thousand years before would the city witness such intense development as was about to overtake it. Not since the time of the Crusaders would the city become such a focus of world interest.

The universal city symbolized by Jerusalem since antiquity had nothing to do with the dirty Levantine town that had for so long borne its name. Now, from two shriveled towns a great new city had to be built—both physically and in human terms. Jerusalem would become a focus for mystics and madmen as well as for humanists who saw in the united city inhabited by Jews, Arabs, and Christians an earthly symbol no less evocative than the heavenly Jerusalem to which the religious aspired.

For all the glory of its name, Jerusalem had for hundreds of years been a provincial backwater. Now the twentieth century was pre-paring to descend upon it in a rush.

O N E

The Mayor

FOR AN INSTANT AFTER THE GUNS DIED in June 1967, nothing could be heard across the hushed city, but the faint flutter of history. Then it started again—the rumble of heavy vehicles, the unforgiving crump of explosives. This time, however, the sounds were of bulldozers plowing through the concrete barriers and barbed wire that separated the two halves of the city and explosions marking the demise of mine-fields. Within a few weeks, the two Jerusalems were separated by nothing more than a strip of neutered no-man's-land so narrow a child could toss a stone across it, so filled with shadows despite the city's brilliant light that no one could probe its depth.

For nineteen years Israeli Jerusalem had been a sleepy border town virtually cut off from the mainstream of life on the coastal plain to which it was linked by a tenuous territorial corridor. Knesset committees preferred meeting in Tel Aviv rather than making the tedious hour and a half trip up the Judean Hills, and their chairmen periodically had to be reminded that Jerusalem was still the nation's capital. Jerusalemites themselves traveled down to Tel Aviv for serious shopping, major bank loans, or important cultural events.

Located on the crest of a chain of hills that runs down the spine of the country, Jerusalem had been a stony, unkempt warren under the Turks, who had ruled the city, from the sixteenth century. The Brit-

5

ish, who captured the city in 1917, treated it as a much-beloved heir-loom, but their departure three decades later touched off a bitter war that left Jerusalem divided between Israel and Jordan. Many of the 100,000 residents on the Israeli side who had survived the grueling Arab siege in 1948 left Jerusalem afterward. To shore up the popula-tion, the government brought in truckloads of new immigrants, mostly from Morocco and Iraq, and settled them in abandoned Arab buildings or crowded public housing. These Third World immigrants would become the numerically dominant element in a population that also included a large percentage of Hebrew University and gov-ernment personnel as well as the country's major concentration of ultra-Orthodox Jews. No other city in the country had as high a per-centage of both illiterates and university graduates. Jerusalem had become a catchment of the three main streams of the Jewish diaspora: the Islamic world, the West, and the shattered world of east Euro-pean Orthodoxy.

In defiance of the United Nations' call for internationalization of the city, Prime Minister David Ben-Gurion declared Jerusalem the na-tional capital. Aside from its hilltop setting, however, there was little august about the city. Almost all the holy sites and the Old City were on the Jordanian side of Jerusalem. The government in Amman delib-erately restricted development in its half of Jerusalem other than tour-ism in order to assure economic dominance by the East Bank.

The Israeli side had a small-town charm and a distinctive mystique that set it apart from all other Israeli cities, but it possessed few mod-ern amenities. Bars were a rarity; the movie houses were unheated and barnlike; and half a dozen traffic lights were sufficient for the little traffic in town. A resident emerging from a cafe at 10:00 P.M. as it shut down one night in the mid-1960s was confronted on the other-wise deserted street by a tourist. "Excuse me," said the visitor. "Where can I find the nightlife?" The resident pointed up the street to a sign visible in the light of a solitary streetlamp. "That's the office of the burial society. There should be someone on duty till midnight. You won't find anyone else around."

The presence of a tourist after dark was itself a rarity. Almost all tourists stayed in Tel Aviv hotels, coming up to Jerusalem by bus in the morning and returning in the afternoon. The newly elected mayor, Teddy Kollek, ordered the floodlighting of the new Israel Mu-seum in 1965 so that the few tourists who did stay over would have something to see after the sun set. Because of the thirty-dollar nightly electricity bill, however, this could be managed only twice a week.

These problems disappeared in a cloud of smoke—the smoke that covered the city during the Six Day War. In their place came new problems, staggering in scope and complexity.

It was only by remote chance that the person in charge at City Hall when the walls dividing Jerusalem came down was someone whose life had been a preparation for one of the most delicate, urgent, and far-reaching tasks ever to confront a mayor. Kollek was a former gun-runner and intelligence agent with the tastes of a Viennese banker, which he might easily have become were it not for the rise of the Nazis. Born to an official employed by the Rothschild banking interests in the Austro-Hungarian empire, Kollek grew up in a genteel world of spas and pastry but was swept into the Zionist movement in his teens. The handsome, blond youth arrived in Palestine in 1935 on the ship *Gerusaleme* and joined a group of young pioneers in founding Kibbutz En Gev on the shores of Lake Kinneret. His life as a kibbutznik would be regularly interrupted by the Zionist movement, which recognized in the suave, self-confident young man a talent for getting things done. Kollek was thus dispatched to Europe on a series of delicate missions. One of these involved a meeting in Vienna with a Nazi official to obtain travel permits for a group of Jewish youngsters bound for Palestine. The innocuous-looking Nazi who granted Kollek the permits was Adolph Eichmann.

During the Second World War, Kollek was sent on intelligence missions by the Jewish Agency, including an assignment in Istanbul, where he served as liaison with Allied intelligence in that intrigue-ridden city. In 1947 he was posted to New York to head the arms-acquisition mission of the Haganah, the underground army of the emerging Jewish state. From a hotel above the Copacabana night club on the Upper East Side he ran a whirlwind backroom operation, purchasing everything from blankets to bombers. It was a job that kept him one step ahead of British intelligence and the FBI and in touch with scientists, bankers, Mafia mobsters, and anyone else who might help the cause.

With Israel's independence, he took over the American desk at the Foreign Ministry in Jerusalem but he was soon back in the United States as the number-two man at the Israeli embassy. The convivial Kollek established an easy rapport with the top figures in the American political and intelligence establishment and was a frequent guest at the home of Allen Dulles, then head of the CIA.

When Kollek returned to Jerusalem, it was to the nerve center of government as director-general of Prime Minister Ben-Gurion's office. He was to hold the post for eleven years and enjoy the free hand that Ben-Gurion gave his trusted aides. With Ben-Gurion concentrating on foreign affairs and defense, Kollek ran several government agencies and proved himself the epitome of the Israeli *bitsuist*—the executive who gets things done regardless of red tape or ruffled feelings. Among his achievements was the establishment of a tourism infrastructure for the country, the reorganization of radio broadcasting, and the creation of the Israel Museum.

In 1965, following Ben-Gurion's retirement, Kollek went into private enterprise for the first time in his life, becoming a highly paid real-estate executive. For a man who enjoyed fine cigars, wine, and other attributes of the good life, the job seemed to provide a perfect exit from public life. Within six months, however, he was bored and open to new career suggestions. One would soon be put to him by Moshe Dayan, Shimon Peres, and a handful of other Ben-Gurion loyalists who had formed the Rafi Party with Ben-Gurion when the latter broke away from the all-powerful Labor Party. On his way from his Jerusalem home to spend the Succoth holiday with his old comrades at Kibbutz Ein Gev, Kollek had stopped off to have lunch in Tel Aviv with his political cronies and to discuss the upcoming elections. As they dined on the terrace of the new Tel Aviv Hilton looking out over the Mediterranean, someone at the table suggested that Kollek stand for the Knesset on the Rafi ticket. He made it clear that he was not cut out for spending his days listening to and making speeches.

It was then that someone in the group—Peres would later believe it had been himself—suggested that Kollek run for mayor of Jerusalem. Kollek had absolutely no interest in urban affairs and had no intention of beginning to deal at that stage of his life with sewer leaks, illegal building, and the vipers' nest of coalition politics that characterized Jerusalem city hall. Dayan and the others suggested he think about it. Kollek did so on the drive up to Lake Kinneret and at the kibbutz, where he discussed the proposal with old friends, including one who was now a dominant figure in Israel's intelligence community. Driving back to Jerusalem, the decision fell into place. As a gesture of loyalty to Ben-Gurion, Kollek decided, he must run. His one consolation was that while his ticket might win a seat or two on the City Council, there was no chance of its wresting the majority needed for the head of the ticket—himself—to become the mayor. He filed his candidacy on the last possible day for registration.

For campaign manager, he chose Meron Benvenisti, who had worked for him in the Tourism Department. In Benvenisti, Kollek recognized a kindred spirit—an executive who did not permit petty bureaucracy to get in the way of the grand design. "I'm going to tell you something funny," Kollek said to him on the telephone. "I'm running for mayor."

Benvenisti did not treat the campaign as a joke. He had Kollek make speeches from the back of a pickup truck around town, a type of spirited campaigning new to staid Jerusalem. Benvenisti and volunteers descended on florists' shops late Friday afternoons to buy up at cut rate those flowers which had not been sold for the Sabbath. These would be distributed on crowded downtown streets Saturday night with campaign brochures. Kollek's initial lack of enthusiasm gave way as the campaign heated up, and in a major political upset, his party list achieved a tie with that of the incumbent Labor Party. By forming a coalition with smaller factions, Teddy Kollek, at fifty-four, became mayor of Jerusalem. When he entered City Hall with his staff at 6:30 A.M. on December 1, 1965, to assume office, one of his aides would recall, it was like a conquering army entering an empty city.

For Kollek, who had spent decades at the center of events during one of the most dramatic periods of Jewish history, the interest in his new post soon faded before the drudgery of petty routine. Before the year was up, he began wondering aloud to friends whether he would be able to finish out his four-year term. The answer was provided by the Jordanian gunner who fired the first shell into Israeli Jerusalem in the opening hours of the Six Day War. Eighteen months after assuming office, Teddy Kollek had a role to match his vision—to turn an ineffable religious symbol into an earthly city that did not betray its name.

Three weeks after the war's end, the Knesset tripled the boundaries of Israeli Jerusalem by annexing former Jordanian territory. Sixty-five thousand Arabs and 180,000 Jews who had been dodging each other's shells a few weeks before looked out across the broken border fences to find themselves neighbors. The Arabs were stunned and terrified, the Jews stunned and elated. Both recognized that a new and uncharted epoch had begun.

Over coffee on the terrace of the King David Hotel on June 27, Dayan, now defense minister, told Kollek and police officials that the road barriers separating the two halves of the city would be immediately removed and free movement permitted both ways across the former border. The officials reacted with alarm. Murder, looting, and general mayhem would follow such a precipitous move, they warned, but Dayan insisted that if the city were legally joined it must be physically united as well. On June 29, the barriers came down and Jews and Arabs streamed across the former border to look at what had been, until three weeks before, as remote as the far side of the moon.

The annexed area included not only the former Jordanian city but also a large hinterland of Arab villages. It was unclear at first what to call the Arab part of the united city. Jordanian Jerusalem was no longer apt. Occupied Jerusalem had an unhappy ring. Arab Jerusalem smacked of separatism. In the end, a consensus settled on East Jerusalem, a neutral designation that was not entirely accurate geographically but permitted the Arab section of Jerusalem to be distinguished from Jewish "West Jerusalem."

The green line on the map which had delineated the border had been eliminated, but a gray line of mines would continue to divide the city along most of its length for many months. Ninety thousand mines had been planted in a twelve-mile arc in and around Jerusalem by Israel and Jordan during the previous two decades. Most had been sown without designation on minefield maps. Even Mount Zion was mined within a few score meters of the traditional site of the Last Supper. During the War, five Israeli infantry battalions had attacked across no-man's-land without anyone stepping on a mine, many of which had become inactive over time. In the months after the war, however, seventy Jewish and Arab civilians crossing former no-man's-land, as well as a dozen army sappers, had feet blown off.

The medieval ramparts of the Old City were cleared of Jordanian bunkers and the war-battered gates restored by Arab craftsmen under the supervision of Israeli experts in preservation, including Lion's Gate, which had been unhinged by an Israeli tank in the final assault. The authorities decided to leave untouched as an authentic inscription of history the fresh bullet holes pocking the Old City walls.

Water pipes were laid across no-man's-land at the three points where they had been severed during Israel's War of Independence in 1948, providing a round-the-clock supply of water to East Jerusalem for the first time since then. Under Jordan, water had been supplied only on alternate days because of limited facilities, and numerous homeowners who had no water lines at all bought water in five-gallon cans from street vendors. Road connections betwen the two parts of the city were likewise restored.

Only a century before, the entire city, one square kilometer in area, had been confined within the walls of what has since come to be called the Old City. Until 1870, the city's gates were closed every night in order to keep out marauding Bedouins, and it was only in the early 1930s that candlelight began to give way to electricity in Jerusalem.

Now as planners began to sketch massive new housing developments and vast restoration projects, Jerusalem was about to undergo changes greater than any it had experienced since biblical times.

The day after the fall of the Old City, Kollek had driven to the center of the city to buy a newspaper and spotted Meron Benvenisti in uniform. "Come on," said the mayor to his former aide. "I need you."

Four days later, the freshly demobilized Benvenisti appeared in City Hall and was given an office although he still did not know what job Kollek had in mind for him. At the end of the day, the mayor called him in to his office and offered him the most sensitive task in the city administration—responsibility for running the Arab sector of the city.

The Arabs had still not comprehended the fate that had overtaken them. On the eve of the war's outbreak, their leaders had confidently been inviting one another to drinks at the Tel Aviv Hilton in anticipation of speedy victory. Now they found themselves under the occupation of a victorious Jewish army that had needed less than a week to sweep Jordan's vaunted army from the West Bank, while driving the Egyptians out of Sinai and the Syrians from the Golan Heights.

Whether Jerusalem's Arabs would be treated as an occupied people, as equal citizens, or as something in-between depended largely on the decisions of two men—Kollek and Benvenisti. Kollek was a richly experienced man of the world and Benvenisti, in addition to his administrative background, was a promising young historian: he had just finished a book on the Crusader period in Palestine and was preparing for his doctorate. But the pair had no precedent to go by. Nor were there any clear government guidelines except for the bold decision by Dayan to remove the barriers. In place of guidelines and precedent, the two men would rely on their liberal and pragmatic political instincts.

When the first anniversary of the war neared, Benvenisti proposed to Kollek that the Arabs be permitted to put up a memorial to their war dead as the Jews had done on their side of the city. If they were to be regarded as citizens rather than as a conquered population, he argued, they must be allowed the same right to publicly grieve as was granted the Jews. Kollek pushed the proposal through the city council in the face of strong opposition, and a memorial was put up by the Arab community in the Muslim cemetery outside the Old City walls. It would be decked with wreaths every anniversary of the war, as the Jews decorated theirs on the other side of former no-man's-land.

In annexing East Jerusalem, the government offered Israeli citizenship to any Arab resident who applied. Almost all preferred their Jordanian citizenship. By Israeli law, however, residents were considered citizens of the city in which they lived even if they were not citizens of the country and thousands of Arabs exercised their right to vote in municipal elections—the bulk of them voting for Kollek. Although they could legally stand for the City Council as well, the Arabs chose not to field their own candidates in order not to grant legitimacy to Israeli rule over the city. However, Kollek and Benvenisti met regularly with the forty-four mukhtars, or traditional headmen, of the villages and neighborhoods in East Jerusalem and responded to their concerns as if they were a body elected by the Arab citizenry.

The mayor's car was indisposed this day and he had to pry himself out of his aide's Volkswagen by lifting his legs out with both hands, one at a time. His Arab hosts received him, however, as if he were alighting from the rear of a liveried limousine.

Teddy Kollek had come to meet the mukhtars and notables who represented the close to 15,000 residents of Silwan village. It was a routine meeting, the kind Kollek held periodically with neighborhood groups on both sides of the city. He and his aide were ushered into the villa of the mukhtar of upper Silwan, where they exchanged handshakes with the fifteen men awaiting them in the salon.

Everyone settled down in comfortable upholstered chairs, except for the host, who remained on his feet to deliver a formal greeting that was translated by a young Arab seated next to Kollek. It was only a few years after the Six Day War, and not all Arabs in Jerusalem were yet fluent in Hebrew. On the ten-minute drive from City Hall, the aide had briefed Kollek on the problems likely to be raised and the solutions the municipality was offering.

The mukhtar spoke of an open drainage ditch whose runoff in winter "is strong enough to sweep away a camel, let alone a man." Kollek pulled out a large cigar and lit up.

On the walls were framed inscriptions from the Koran and a color photograph of the Dome of the Rock. Through the windows, the bald hills of the Judean Desert could be seen beyond the last house in the village, as the mukhtar reeled off his list of requests. The group paused in their meeting and two men brought in bottled soft drinks and distributed them.

The mukhtar now yielded to a man in a brown business suit and tie who begged Kollek's pardon in Hebrew for exploiting his visit to complain about the neighborhoods's problems but he was sure, he said, that the mayor had Silwan's interests at heart. The street lights on Musatafa Street, he said, had no bulbs in them and there was total darkness at night.

The two men serving as waiters returned with apples and bananas on individual plates, which they distributed to all present. The opening presentations over, Kollek responded. "Today, twenty American state governors came to see me." The men in the room nodded appreciatively and one man said "Ahalan wa sahalan [Welcome]."

The governors, continued Kollek, had asked how contact was maintained with the Arab population, since there were no Arabs on the city council. He had answered, he said, that Arab municipal employees were an important channel to the Arab sector. There were also the heads of the East Jerusalem Chamber of Commerce and businessmen who came to City Hall regularly with their problems. Finally, Kollek said, there were neighborhood groups like this one which had kindly invited him.

"When I come to any nieghborhood in the city, there are always demands, because the municipality is not rich and always does less than enough. I came here to learn what is pressing you. I can tell you ahead of time that we can't solve all your problems. We can solve some of them. But some of them you must solve yourself."

The mayor expressed satisfaction at having learned that the residents might make land available for a girls' school that the village needed. The municipality preferred not to expropriate land. When Kollek concluded, an earnest-looking man in his thirties thanked the mayor for the new street the municipality had built in his quarter and the new street lighting. "But we're uneasy," he continued. "Houses have been built without a permit and with growing families we have to build more."

Kollek puffed on his cigar and nodded as the translation came in. The problem of building permits in the Arab sector was critical, since there was no approved master plan for East Jerusalem.

One of the half-dozen men present wearing a *kheffiya*, the traditional Arab headdress, said he had traveled to Amman to buy building land, because he was unable to build in Silwan, owing to the difficulty in obtaining a permit. Another resident asked for the extension of a road by one hundred meters so that garbage trucks could get in. Kollek's aide intervened. "There are one hundred stretches like this of one hundred meters. If we built half of them, there'd be no money left for sewers, lighting, or water lines."

The coffee arrived now, superb coffee served in tiny porcelain cups. Kollek's aide and an Arab assistant from the village explained what the municipality was planning to do in the neighborhood in the current fiscal year. The plans included installation of more than two kilometers of sewer lines, new roads, and additional street lighting. Under the Jordanian administration, taxes had been minimal and so had the infrastructure.

In summing up, Kollek returned to the absence of Arabs on the city council. He cited the objections recently made by right-wing councilmen to a new mosque proposed for the northern entrance to Jerusalem. They had asserted that it was too large for its location and would give a "Muslim character" to the city at one of its main entrances.

"There was no Arab on the council to say 'We have this coming to us just like any synagogue or church,'" Kollek said.

After a puff on what remained of his cigar, he added: "Still, it was easier getting it through than it would be getting a synagogue built in Damascus." The remark drew a good laugh. The meeting lasted an hour, and it was dark outside when Kollek and his aide left.

"The standard of living on the Jewish side may be higher," said the mayor as they drove off, "but the problems are the same."

The first objective Kollek and Benvenisti set was to bring the substantially inferior services in Arab Jerusalem—roads, utilities, schools—to the level prevailing in Jewish Jerusalem. Politically, they agreed not to work through appointed "uncle Mohammeds," who would sit on the city council in Arab headdress to provide window dressing. The two men accepted the alienation felt by Jerusalem's Arabs as they did the Arabs' need for communal—not just individual—self-expression. When a group of distinguished foreign architects urged Kollek to raze the Muslim Hospital, which they claimed was an eyesore on the Mount of Olives skyline, and build a replacement elsewhere, he replied, "We can't do that because they built the hospital themselves. They infinitely prefer it to anything we can build even if we build it infinitely better."

Kollek and Benvenisti fought the government's plan to hold a military parade on Independence Day a year after the war through the heart of East Jerusalem, claiming it would rub salt in the Arabs' wounds. "This is a parade for Jews, not Arabs," argued Kollek. The route was partially altered. They also attempted to limit the government expropriation of Arab land for Jewish housing developments and to prevent nationalist Jews from settling in Arab neighborhoods.

In their most far-reaching move, they succeeded in persuading the government to waive the Israeli Arab curriculum that had initially been imposed on East Jerusalem schools. The government had maintained that Jerusalem's Arabs must be dealt with as ordinary Israeli Arabs since they now lived within the boundaries of the state. Kollek pointed out that East Jerusalem's Arabs had been given the choice of not becoming Israeli citizens, and the bulk of them had not sought Israeli citizenship. They wished to send their children to universities in the Arab world, where Israeli matriculation certificates would not be recognized. The government finally agreed to permit East Jerusalem's schools to adopt the curriculum of Jordan, an enemy state, and to have their matriculation examination papers processed by Jordanian education officials who entered from Jordan for that purpose. It was a remarkably liberal decision, even if some of the government officials who approved it did so in the hope that many of the Arabs who went abroad to study would stay there.

Addressing a public meeting in 1968, Kollek said: "War and peace is not a city's business, only the process of living. Nobody demands a declaration of loyalty from the Arabs of East Jerusalem." Five years later, he said: "The Arabs will continue to regard themselves as hemmed in, their culture and way of life threatened by our aggressive way of life. You can't change that. But when people ask 'When will there be integration?' or 'Why don't the Jews and Arabs love each other?' they have an absolutely wrong concept of what should be achieved. The Jews and Arabs will not easily love each other in this generation or the next and it isn't necessary. I don't know where in the world different peoples love each other. The question is whether with all the antagonism which exists you can find a way to live together. Can we who run the city be tolerant enough to give others a chance to live their own way of life?"

The two men would come under intense attack by the right-wing. Kollek would be dubbed "Defender of Islam," and Benvenisti, who received several telephone threats, woke one morning to find the word "traitor" painted on his front door.

The relative tranquillity experienced by the city in the postwar years was not won by enlightened policy, Benvenisti would maintain, but by the innate good sense of the Arab population, who chose to refrain from dangerous provocation. Nevertheless, the liberal policies shaped by him and Kollek made life tolerable for the city's Arabs for two decades. By being based on respect rather than power, this policy also laid the foundation for a more durable arrangement in the event of a permanent, negotiated peace.

Kollek's public personality helped him carry through his liberal policies despite strong reservations about these policies in the Jewish sector. His avuncular style, wit, and idiosyncracies headed off charges of softness that would certainly have been hurled at him had he merely been righteous.

"Teddy," as he was called by all, arrived at City Hall at six-thirty every morning and insisted on punching the clock like any municipal employee. Early risers would often see him driving through the city on an inspection tour by seven, sometimes with a visiting journalist for whom he could find no time later in the day. In conspicuous contrast to government ministers, he avoided large cars. By the time his secretaries arrived in the office, they would find notes on a yellow pad about street lights and road signs that needed installing, illegal posters that needed removal, and other observations from that morning's tour. The mayor's work day, including meetings with visiting dignitaries, often lasted past midnight. He never napped at home but he regularly fell asleep on public platforms in the middle of speeches. His own speeches rarely lasted more than two minutes.

Clocks were not the only things the mayor punched. Despite his age (he was seventy-three when elected to his sixth term in 1984) and his girth (he gained an average of four pounds a year while in office) he did not hesitate to take a swing from time to time at citizens whom he thought to have been offensive. Such was his image—a father figure from whom such chastisement was expected—that no one ever filed charges, let alone swung back. The victims, indeed, generally tried to explain to "Teddy" that he had misunderstood them.

Kollek may have been the only mayor of a major city who kept his telephone number listed. An elected official, he felt, should be accessible to his electorate. The electorate would occasionally call after midnight to report the location of a pothole it had run into on its motor scooter. One young man called at two in the morning to report that an emergency city repair crew was using pneumatic drills outside his home. "If I can't sleep, neither will you," he told the mayor.

Although he generally kept his temper with callers, Kollek not infrequently let it go in public. When a demonstrator outside City Hall shouted at the mayor that he would not vote for him in the next elections, Kollek shouted back "Kiss my ass," a remark duly reported in the next day's newspapers.

A unique phenomenon in Israeli politics, the left-leaning Kollek was returned to office over more than twenty years with ever increasing majorities, even though the city's electorate regularly gave a large majority to right-wing candidates in Knesset elections. The right wing found it difficult even to find a candidate willing to stand against Kollek. "I'm running opposite Teddy, not against him," said a candidate in the 1980s who had been pressed by his party hierarchy to enter the race. "Teddy's above politics," explained a blue-collar voter to a journalist outside a polling station. "He cares about the city and he gets things done."

Unification, as the annexation of East Jerusalem came to be called, gave Kollek an opportunity to exercise his talents even more boldly than he had in the past.

He could see the challenges all around him as he moved through the city: alienated peoples who somehow had to find a way to live together, different religious faiths contending with each other for space and status as they contended for souls, an ancient walled city that had to be absorbed into a modern urban framework, a secular population trying to retain its sense of purpose as religious fundamentalism grew increasingly assertive around it, the apathy of less-privileged classes giving way to outrage at the growing gap between them and the more privileged.

The plump, cigar-smoking mayor bore no evident resemblance to the Messiah in whose reign, according to Jewish tradition, Jerusalem was to be rebuilt. But if Kollek was not moved by religious passions, he was passionately inspired by humanistic values. Some would see these stemming from the Central European liberality into which he was born. Kollek himself would call them Jewish values.

One of his major objectives was to devise a strategy to counter international pressure for Jerusalem's redivision or internationalzation. The city since 1967 had come to be the focus of the Arab-Israel dispute. From Morocco to Iraq in the Arab world and as far away as Pakistan in the Muslim world the restoration to Muslim hands of Jerusalem's Temple Mount—third holiest site in Islam—was viewed as a supreme religious duty. To forestall a Muslim military crusade, Western peacemakers had begun to revive proposals to internationalize Jerusalem, a move the United Nations had called for in 1947, when it voted for the creation of a Jewish state. Powerful Christian forces were almost as unhappy as the Muslims about exclusive Jewish rule in the city containing the holiest sites in Christendom. The Vatican, for one, had always pressed for internationalization and some of the major Western powers were inclined in that direction. Others favored some sort of functional redivision that would give the Arabs effective control over East Jerusalem, even if the city were not redivided physically.

To create a buffer against these pressures, Kollek embarked on his own foreign policy, independent of the Foreign Ministry. He initiated a conciliatory policy toward the churches and established an international committee of advisors to give the world a say in the development of the city. He believed that to still the pressures on Israel to relinquish Jerusalem, it had to demonstrate to the world that the city would thrive under Israeli sovereignty as it had not thrived since it was last under Jewish management two thousand years before. To accomplish this, it would be his task to turn an urban minefield into a radiant city.

Before cities came to symbolize crisis, they symbolized culture, and for Kollek the idea of the city as a place of culture still held true. He would make it his task to transform the face of Jerusalem and its cultural ambience. He established the Jerusalem Foundation, which served as a conduit for the more than $200 million that was raised abroad—mostly by himself—to build parks, community centers, theaters, and museums, and to provide cultural activities. This money augmented the scant governmental resources available. Never had Jerusalem known such a cultural flowering. The money came from foreign philanthropists charmed by the combination of Kollek's personality and the name Jerusalem. "He makes them feel he's doing them a favor by letting them give their money to Jerusalem," said an aide. To build a cultural audience for the future, Kollek initiated a program that brought every schoolchild, Jewish and Arab, to a concert or stage performance at least once a year.

The stone-clad Eastern city described a century before by Mark Twain as a rocky wasteland turned green under Kollek's prodding. Each day, he met with the chief municipal gardener to discuss new areas for plantings. Sitting alongside his driver on his daily tour of the city, the mayor would pull a pad out of a shirt pocket to note sites for future planting and of existing plantings that needed watering or trimming. As a result of his efforts, the city is now shaded from the Middle East sun by pine and cypress, and main roads have become lush parkways that burgeon into color each spring.

At the end of the 1960s, disaffected Jewish slum-dwellers—almost all young Sephardi immigrants—burst out of their neighborhoods and held turbulent demonstrations in the middle of Jerusalem against the European Ashkenazi establishment. At the suggestion of American immigrant social workers they called themselves ''Black Panthers,'' a name chosen for its shock value.

Conscious of what the gap between whites and blacks had done to American cities, Kollek gave top priority to providing community centers, as well as parks and other facilities to the underprivileged neighborhoods. The problem in Jerusalem proved small enough and young enough to be manageable. A falling crime rate and a steadily increasing percentage of voters for Kollek in former Black Panther strongholds testify to his success.

He would be less successful in coping with the growing militancy of the ultra-Orthodox Jews, who attempted to impose their worldview on the secular population by demonstrating against Sabbath traffic, blocking plans to build a municipal sports stadium, and burning bus stop shelters for displaying ''unseemly'' advertisements.

Despite this ultra-Orthodox militancy, the greatest contribution Kollek made to Jerusalem in the two decades after the Six Day War was the spirit of tolerance he managed to infuse into a demographic tinderbox. Given the traditions of religious and communal strife in the Middle East, confrontation between Arabs and Jews, Sephardi and Ashkenazi Jews, secular and ultra-Orthodox Jews could have been touched off at any moment. Kollek avoided this partly by preaching and partly by providing the various communities their basic needs, whether these be respect, facilities, or, for the ultra-Orthodox, isolation. His policy in East Jerusalem permitted the Arabs who resided there to follow their own cultural practices in exchange for their patience while the larger political issues were being debated. Despite the occasional terrorist act, Jerusalem would remain a far safer place than almost any major Western city.

As for the Sephardi Jews who made up the bulk of the slum population in West Jerusalem, Kollek upgraded not only their neighborhoods but their sense of ethnic pride by promoting annual ethnic festivals and exhibitions of their rich folk traditions.

The ultra-Orthodox were the most intractable minority but Kollek-managed in some measure to contain them by closing off their neighborhoods to Sabbath traffic, which had always been the most contentious issue.

Even when his party enjoyed an absolute majority on the city council, Kollek preferred to form an all-party coalition that included the ultra-Orthodox and the right wing, in the belief that shared responsibility induced moderation.

Kollek's pace hardly slowed with the years. Even in his midseventies, he would keep going each day until midnight, hours after sending home his exhausted young driver. His attitude toward work was compulsive, and he would regularly descend on aides in their homes on weekends or late at night to dictate letters or discuss business. When he saw the film *Death on the Nile* in 1979, it marked the first time in ten years that he had found time to go to the cinema. Although he generally appeared ebullient and was expansive in good company, he could lapse into dark moods. If asked by interviewers whether he enjoyed his job, he avoided a direct answer. His temper, often unleashed, was gargantuan and left aides shaken, until they learned to regard it as a passing act of nature. He had almost no time for the numerous friends of his youth. Although Kollek was popular in the deprived neighborhoods and had a sincere concern for the welfare of their inhabitants, it was among the worldly and successful that he was most relaxed and able to reach into himself. With a brandy glass in one hand and a cigar in the other—pausing often to stare into the smoke—he could offer a vision of Jerusalem to a group of worldrenown architects and educators in the intimate surroundings of the Israel Museum library with an eloquence the public almost never heard. His one true confidante was his wife, Tamar, with whom he breakfasted each morning at six and upon whose sensible advice he relied. Tamar attempted to set aside Friday evening for themselves and their family.

In his later administrations, Kollek lost nothing of his wit and little of his energy, but he grew increasingly impatient with people and lost some of his bulldog persistence in shaking subordinates until issues were satisfactorily resolved. His unswerving attention to detail and follow-through, even minute detail like deciding the right shape for paving stones or remembering to send birthday greetings to a church leader in the Old City, had made Kollek such an exceptionally effective executive. His long tenure discouraged a series of heirs-apparent whom he had supposedly been grooming, including Benvenisti who quit the municipality after a series of angry quarrels with

Kollek over various policy issues. Long-time associates detected a change in Kollek in his later years in office. "In the old days, Teddy and the rest of us regarded ourselves as representatives of a movement," said one such associate from the Labor Party. "We used 'we' rather than 'I.' Teddy didn't have such a big opinion of himself and saw his shortcomings. Since then he has learned to accept that people regard him as something special, something elevated."

Even his severest critics, however, admitted that he brought a rare stature to the job and displayed a breadth of vision that matched the enormous dimensions of the task. He presided over Jerusalem during one of the most tumultuous periods in its history; that it had not collapsed about his ears was testimony enough to his abilities. The sleepy town he had taken over in 1965 had become a vital city of tremendous complexity and ferment. Whether that ferment would produce champagne or vinegar had depended in good part on him alone.

During his gunrunning days in New York, Kollek recalled one day to a visitor at City Hall, he had sometimes broken the strain of work by traveling uptown at midnight to the Savoy Ballroom in Harlem. He would no longer feel safe to make the same trip today, he noted.

"You have to build a city so that it's safely built," said Kollek, "so that the fire hazard is small. I would like to start building a city that will still be safe years from now."

The formula for rebuilding Jerusalem would not be that of New York or any Western city whose aspiration is to integrate its peoples in order to create a homogeneous society of shared values. The formula would instead be grounded in the basic value of permitting each community to be itself. The Turks had institutionalized this approach through their millet system, which dealt with the individual through organized religious groupings that had their own representatives and their own courts to deal with matters of personal status such as marriage and divorce.

Jerusalem would become unified, but not integrated. Jews, Arabs, and Christians did not wish to be integrated with one another, nor did the numerous subgroups within these major branches wish to surrender their distinctiveness of tradition, dress, language, way of life. If Jerusalem were to remain a universal city spiritually, it had to be ruled as if it were an empire made up of proud and willful peoples representing the divergent spiritual aspirations of half the world. Crammed into the perimeter of a middle-sized city, together with their historical memories, these peoples somehow had to find a way to live together, even while contending for the same holy turf they had warred over in the past. Jerusalem celebrated exclusivity, not brotherly love, and what would hold it together was the creative modulation of tension. During most of Kollek's administration Jerusalem would be a remarkably tranquil city, a place where organized religion in some of its most militant forms and a world-class collection of eccentrics could somehow live in peace. Skirting anarchy, the city constituted a fabulous consortium of religious and ethnic communities that had been evolved by half of mankind over the centuries in its attempt to come to terms with the known and the unknown.

T W O

Heralds of the Messiah

AT FIVE IN THE AFTERNOON, Dennis Rohan climbed the tree on the Temple Mount and settled down to wait for darkness. It would be a long wait, since the August sun did not set until almost eight. Through the branches he could see worshippers coming out of al-Aksa Mosque after the last prayers of the day. The tree was well away from the paths leading them to the gates of the walled compound. As the late afternoon sun illuminated the Mount of Olives across the Kidron Valley in brilliant golden light, the Australian raised the camera dangling from his neck and photographed the scene. The picture would provide proof, if any were needed, that he had been there. With dusk, he slid to the ground and gratefully stretched his limbs. Although he could see no one, he waited three more hours before approaching the main door of the mosque.

From a black bag, he took a length of tubing and pushed one end through the large keyhole in the door. Fitting a funnel into the other end of the tube, he poured into it a bottle of kerosene, which he could hear splashing onto the floor of the mosque. Rohan removed the tubing and inserted a kerosene-soaked rope through the keyhole until he could feel the slack as it coiled on the floor inside. Striking a match, he lit the makeshift wick, picked up his bag, and ran.

The gates to the compound were closed, but he climbed the staircase to the rampart of the city wall and made his way along it until he reached Lion's Gate, one of the seven gates of the walled Old City, and clambered down. It was close to midnight when he neared his hotel, the Rivoli, in the Arab part of the city just outside the walls. The street seemed empty but two policemen suddenly stepped out of the shadows and signaled the hurrying figure to halt.

It was two years after the Six Day War and the security forces were still keeping a close watch on suspicious movement in East Jerusalem. The policemen were one of the Arab-Jewish teams that had begun operating there.

Rohan produced his Australian passport and opened his bag. Stealing a glance behind him, he could see that there was no telltale glow from the direction of the Temple Mount. The Jewish policeman pulled out a whip he saw coiled in the bag. As he touched the haft, it came loose, exposing a dagger. The policeman looked up at Rohan but the Arab policeman told his partner in Hebrew that the whip-dagger was a common tourist item sold in the Old City, a replica of the *korbush* used by riders to coax reluctant donkeys. The policemen handed back the passport and *korbush* and bid Rohan goodnight.

The dagger had been a surprise to the Australian. The only weapon he had intended to acquire was the whip. He might need it to drive the wicked from the Temple Mount as Jesus had driven out the moneychangers.

Post–Six Day War Jerusalem teemed with fundamentalist Christians and Jews for whom Israel's victory heralded the imminent coming of the Messiah. The Bible stipulates the return of Israel to Jerusalem as a harbinger of His coming and Israel's 1967 conquest of the Temple Mount seemed a clear portent. Inevitably, a lunatic fringe would give its own interpretations to events. Bearded and robed figures riding through Jerusalem on donkeys like figures in an Easter pageant became a routine sight in the postwar years. Rohan, however, was not merely awaiting the Messiah's arrival. The twenty-eight-year-old sheepshearer had come to see himself as the builder of the new temple which the Messiah would enter. First, however, it was necessary to destroy the mosque occupying the temple site.

The fire he set this night had gone out even as he was running from the scene, and it left only a stain for the mosque caretaker to briefly puzzle over in the morning. But Rohan would try again. Rarely, if ever, in its eventful history had Jerusalem been so shaken by the act of a single unknown madman as it was about to be.

The first time Rohan had heard a heavenly voice was in the Australian town of Grenfell in March 1964. His wife, Gloria, whom he had met at a country dance, had taken their baby girl and left him two months before. As he lay abed in deep depression in his rented room, he heard a voice say, "Gloria should have married Sandra's father." Sandra was his wife's illegitimate daughter from a previous liaison. "Tomorrow you will be honored and respected," continued the voice. The final "revelation," as Rohan would come to term it, concerned an augur, a thirty-foot-long lift device he had been scheduled to transport the next day from the silo where he was working to another town thirty-five miles away. "Do not take the augur tomorrow," the voice commanded.

Rohan found himself on his knees at the foot of the bed with his hands over his head in a posture of ecstacy as the voice died away. Electriclike shocks pulsed in waves from his head to the tips of his fingers and toes. "Thank you, Father," he cried. "Thank you."

The next day, Rohan tried to avoid taking the augur, but unable to offer a plausible reason for his refusal he finally gave in to the prodding of his fellow workers and hooked up the device to his truck. The men, he knew, regarded him as a fool and laughed at him behind his back. He did not wish to provide them with more ammunition for scorn. Besides, he had begun to think that the voice he had heard might be the voice of Satan.

Two other workers accompanied Rohan as he set out. He could hardly keep his foot on the accelerator and his hands could not firmly grip the wheel. Halfway to his destination he turned back to Grenfell. The agitation forced him to stop at one point but the two men urged him on. As they drove, the augur fell off with a loud clatter. Rohan descended from the truck and managed to hook it back on. Three miles from Grenfell, he could control himself no longer. Jamming the brakes, he flung himself onto the roadway and cried, "Lord have mercy on me." An invisible force struck him and blinded him as he knelt raving. The two men hauled him back to the truck, and one of them drove it back to the silo.

Rohan had quieted down when the silo manager called him into his office. The manager told Rohan to be seated and spoke to him gently. "Dennis, you are mentally sick," he said. "I have just called your wife and father and they want nothing more to do with you. It seems as though I am the only one left to help you. I've made an appointment with a doctor. I want you to come along with me."

With a cry of refusal, Rohan bolted from the office and fled to his rented room. He lay on his bed thinking of the brush fires, among the worst in Australia's history, sweeping the country. Rohan blamed himself for the fires. He thought of himself now as Satan. God was trying to destroy him but would destroy all of Australia in the process unless he killed himself first. He had tried vainly to do so the month before by taking pills. Before he could try again now, a policeman knocked on the door and entered. Leading him down to a waiting patrol car, he drove him to the Bloomfield Mental Hospital.

Rohan was confined for four months and then continued treatment as an outpatient. He was able to function well enough to earn a decent income as a left-handed sheepshearer and at odd jobs in hospitals. In an attempt to understand what was happening to him, he began reading psychology books. He also joined the Church of God, a California-based sect whose brochure he happened to see one day and to which he began to tithe his income by mail. A mail-order religion which did not oblige face to face contact was the perfect vehicle for his dementia, and he avidly read the prophetic visions contained in its brochures.

The wealthy sect, which had founded Ambassador College in Pasadena, California, had a campus in England as well. Four years after his breakdown, Rohan sailed for England with the intention of enrolling. Instead, however, he took a job at a hospital in Middlesex and contented himself with listening to the sect's ''World Tomorrow'' program beamed from Radio Amman in Jordan. After several months, he planned to move on to Canada but the thought of stormy seas and Canadian snows led him to opt for Israel. It seemed a good place to study the Bible and promised clear reception of Radio Amman. A clerk at the Israel tourism office in London told him of the possibility of serving as a volunteer at a kibbutz, where he could work half the day and study Hebrew the other half.

In this offhand way, Rohan arrived in Israel by ship in March 1969 and traveled to Kibbutz Mishmar Hasharon in the Sharon Valley between Haifa and Tel Aviv. Among the forty other volunteers was an American theology student named Arthur Jones, with whom Rohan had long discussions on the Bible. But while Jones stressed Christian love and forgiveness, Rohan spoke of law and commandment. He tried unsuccessfully to persuade Jones to observe the Jewish Sabbath with him.

Their Hebrew teacher was an attractive, willowy brunette named Zipporah. In class, Rohan would stare at her intensely but could absorb little of what she was teaching. After class one day, he boarded the bus she took from the kibbutz to the nearby town of Netanya where she lived. He sat down next to her, but could hardly reply when she good-naturedly asked where he was going.

He heard the voice again one night as he lay in bed at the kibbutz. It said: "Zipporah will be your wife." To his mother, whom he had once beaten and whom he had hardly seen in years, he wrote, "Dear mum. At last I have found her. I hope she will be as good a wife and mother as you have been."

The other volunteers regarded Rohan as weird but treated him sympathetically. He won their respect as a good worker who did not shirk the kibbutz chores. For most of them, life at the kibbutz was a return to the womb of childhood with camaraderie and little responsibility beyond performance of assigned chores. The atmosphere of acceptance was one that Rohan had never experienced. In its warmth, the precarious mental equilibrium he had maintained for the past few years began to dissolve. One day in mid-June, the class sang Hebrew songs with the accompaniment of an accordionist. Rohan was particularly moved by one song "Hinai ma tov" (How goodly it is for brethren to dwell together). That night as he lay alone in his room he began to sing the song to himself but kept breaking into tears. He soon lost control and his wild shouts startled those in nearby rooms. A girl named Mary Ann entered to calm him. She found him sweating and rubbing his face. "What's wrong, Dennis?" she asked, sitting next to his bed.

"I'm Jewish, I'm Jewish," he said.

"How do you know? Have your parents told you?"

"No, they never told me. For the past couple of weeks I've been thinking on this subject. I've been thinking that perhaps I'm Jewish."

Although he could not grasp it yet, something was beginning to take shape in his mind. He spoke to Arthur Jones of the imminence of the Messiah's coming and the construction of a new temple.

"What about the Dome of the Rock," asked Jones, referring to the golden-domed Islamic shrine occupying the site of the Israelite temple destroyed by the Romans in A.D. 70. It was clear that the temple could not be rebuilt as long as the site was occupied by another structure.

"Who knows," said Rohan. "Maybe it will be destroyed by an act of sabotage, maybe the Arabs will do it themselves for political reasons, maybe there'll be an earthquake."

On July 1, he traveled up to Jerusalem for the first time. It was his twenty-eighth birthday. It was also, he noted in the newspapers, the date England's Prince Charles was being invested Prince of Wales. The British royal family, according to the Church of God, was descended from the House of David. Rohan now believed that he was too. In the kibbutz, he had written, but not mailed, a letter to an English firm that checks lineages. In the letter he asked the firm to check his own lineage. The coincidence of the royal investiture and his own birthday he saw as a clear portent, the first of many.

Rohan stayed in Jerusalem a week. The night before he was to leave he moved to the Imperial Hotel inside the Old City walls. As the desk clerk reached back for Rohan's room key, his hand seemed to hesitate. He then detached a large, rusty key and handed it to the guest. Rohan took it and sat down in the lobby to ponder what he had seen. The key, he concluded, was the key of David, and the clerk's hand had been divinely guided to it.

When Rohan returned to the kibbutz, he knew that his fate lay in Jerusalem although he could not yet see its shape. This seemed clearer two weeks later when he left the kibbutz with all his bags for Jerusalem. This time he came not as a humble pilgrim but in royal style, hiring a cab to take him the fifty miles from Netanya. Drawn by the appropriateness of its name, he ordered the driver to take him to the luxurious King David Hotel. When informed that there was no room, he settled for the more modest Kings Hotel, which had room for a few days, and then reluctantly he moved to the Rivoli Hotel in East Jerusalem. Although its name was devoid of symbolism, it was there that Rohan finally discovered who he was and what his mission was.

Leafing through the Catholic Bible, he came upon a passage in Zechariah he had never seen before. "Behold the man whose name is the branch, for he shall grow up in his place and he shall build the Temple of the Lord. It is he who shall build the Temple of the Lord and shall bear royal honor and shall sit and rule upon the throne."

Rohan laid the Bible down as the meaning of his life came flowing in upon him. In one brilliant insight, that whole miserable life suddenly fell into place. The branch was himself. It was he who would build the temple. "I came to understand," he would later say, "that my life would have no meaning if I were not the branch." The agony he had suffered since childhood had been designed to harden him—like passing steel through fire, he felt, or refining gold. He understood why he had been strictly disciplined as a child, why he had been rejected and despised. His past was purposeful and his destiny glowing. He was to build the temple and rule over Jerusalem and

Judea. The beautiful Zipporah would be his queen. Gloria was a Catholic and could not divorce him, but the voice at the kibbutz which informed him that Zipporah would be his wife plainly meant that Gloria was no longer his wife.

As the calmness of certitude settled upon him, Rohan began planning his steps. To build the temple, he must first clear the temple site. The Temple Mount, which occupied a sixth of the walled city, was located on the hilltop site of a Canaanite threshing floor purchased three thousand years before by King David. David's intention was to build on it a sanctuary to house the Holy Ark that had accompanied the Israelites during their wandering in the desert, but his hands had been too bloodied by war for the task. It was his son, Solomon, who leveled the hilltop and built the temple. Almost one thousand years later, King Herod doubled the size of the walled compound and rebuilt the temple and its surroundings into one of the most magnificent architectural complexes of antiquity. Less than a century later, however, in A.D. 70, the Romans destroyed Jerusalem and the temple after a bitter siege and banished the Jews from Jerusalem. The site would remain a desolate garbage dump until the Arab conquest in the seventh century. The Arabs cleaned the vast esplanade, sprinkled it with rose water, and consecrated it as the third holiest site in Islam. The Dome of the Rock, which they built on the presumed temple site in the center of the mount, was an architectural gem polished to even greater brilliance over the course of the centuries by mosaic decorations.

At the southern end of the compound was the al-Aksa Mosque, built early in the eighth century. Capable of holding five thousand worshipers, the mosque was the principal place of prayer for Muslims in Jerusalem. It was the al-Aksa Mosque that Rohan intended to destroy in the mistaken belief that it occupied the site of the temple.

For two weeks, Rohan visited the mount every day, wandering around it for hours, often while muttering to himself. Sometimes he sat in the shade and read a newspaper. Repeatedly, he returned to the mosque. He got to know the Arab guards and made a point of tipping them extravagantly. When the strange, crew-cut Australian would approach, they greeted him with a jaunty *"ahalan"* (welcome, in Arabic). Sometimes he would lie down on the prayer rugs covering the floor of the mosque, something outsiders are forbidden to do. The guards generally refrained from disturbing him unless their own superiors were nearby. Sometimes Rohan even fell asleep on the rugs.

He was still looking for a final, unmistakable sign confirming his mission. He would find it in an eighteen-year-old Arab youth, Munir, who approached him one day and offered his services as a guide. Rohan accepted and paid him fifty Israeli pounds, about ten times more than the going rate, for a brief tour of the mount and its mosques. Thereafter, Munir rushed toward Rohan every time he appeared on the mount and was rewarded with even larger fees. Rohan did more talking than listening on their tours. Some of Munir's friends had begun tagging along on these walks, drawing out the mad tourist. Rohan did not seem to mind. He spoke of his life and cast broad but still mystifying hints about his person and his mission. One day he said to Munir and his friends: ''If you can tell me why I came to Jerusalem I will give you a thousand pounds [about $300].''

Munir copied down some of the things he remembered Rohan telling him, plus some passages in the Bible Rohan had pointed out to him. He also included extracts from a letter sent him by an evangelical American Christian he had guided who urged him to convert to Christianity. Munir went to Rohan's hotel the next day to present him the results. Much of the writing was illegible but Rohan gave him five hundred pounds and told him he would get more if he improved on it. A few days later Munir returned with a more legible version. It contained the sentence Rohan had been looking for—a sentence Munir had copied from the American's letter. ''The knowledge you have of the Temple site should make you a candidate to learn and be protected by the true God through the forthcoming destruction.''

For Rohan, this was the ultimate confirmation: a Muslim was saying that he, Rohan, was destined to destroy the Muslim holy place. Munir, after all, knew where the temple site was, and if he spoke of it in connection with the forthcoming destruction, he must be speaking of the destruction of the mosque that occupied the temple site. Munir could not understand Rohan's excitement but he pocketed the five hundred pounds thrust on him.

The mission decided, there remained only the question of timing. This was determined the next day outside his hotel, when he met the young kibbutz woman in charge of the volunteers at Mishmar Hasharon. She was visiting Jerusalem and would be in the city two more days, she said. Rohan took this as a signal that he had two days within which to do the deed. He bought tubing, a funnel and kerosene, and a camera to photograph these items in his hotel room. He wanted later to be able to prove to the world that it was he who had destroyed the mosque and that he had done it intentionally and not on a whim. This proof would be necessary if he were to be accepted as the man who would build the temple and mount the throne of Judah.

He made the attempt the next night. The normalcy he found in the hotel lobby the following morning indicated that the attempt had failed. Returning to the mosque, he found only a stain on the carpet just inside the door. Walking back to his hotel, he concluded that he had failed because he had not rid himself of his worldly goods and put himself entirely at God's mercy. The $2,000 he had upon his arrival in the country had been going fast in the past few weeks, but he still had several hundred dollars. In the next few days, he spread his money around liberally to children, beggars, mosque guards, and a children's hospital.

Meanwhile, he was planning his next attempt. He spent hours studying the mosque, inside and out. In the huge, almost-bare stone interior, it was not clear how a fire could take hold. A pulpit at the front of the mosque was the only combustible item he could see at floor level beside the carpets. The beautiful pulpit, made of inlaid cedar wood eight centuries before, had been brought from Syria by Saladin after his army had defeated the Crusaders. It was still used every Friday, when the imam would climb its staircase to preach to the masses filling the mosque. One day, Rohan wandered behind the pulpit and saw that its rear was hollowed out. He had found what he was looking for.

Rohan had another brush with the Israeli police during this period, when he attempted one day to pass onto the Temple Mount through Moor's Gate, the only one of the seven gates to the compound whose control was retained by the Israeli authorities; control of the other gates had been turned over to the Muslim Wakf, or religious trust. It was after visiting hours set by the Wakf, and the Israeli guard refused to let him in. When Rohan began shouting and refused to leave, a policeman took him into custody and brought him to police headquarters downtown. The Australian did not have his passport with him, and Sgt. Mordecai Ventura went with Rohan to the Rivoli to retrieve it. The Australian tourist was obviously unbalanced, and the police saw no reason to press charges.

Once again, Rohan began assembling combustibles for his arson attempt, including a gallon of benzine and another of kerosene. On Tuesday, August 19, two days before he would make his final attempt, he drafted a telegram to Ambassador College in Pasadena. "Sorry cannot leave. My father likes Jerusalem now and wishes me to build him a house. Dennis M. Rohan, Nahor." He knew no one at the fundamentalist college but he felt the need to share his mission with someone. He was sure the recipients would understand. In a dictionary of biblical names he had purchased a few days before, he discovered that his name spelled backwards, Nahor, was the same as Abraham's grandfather, a discovery which did much to reinforce his sense of divine destiny.

That same day he wired flowers to his mother in Australia and to Zipporah. To the latter he also dispatched a picture postcard he had bought showing a reconstruction of the temple. In painstaking Hebrew he wrote "Just patience, dear, and everything will be alright." He also drafted a letter to his parents. "There is a lot I would like to say but I cannot at present. I have come to understand a lot of things about my life, so much it would fill a dozen books. So have patience, something I had to have for 15 years. Patience."

The next day, he appeared at el-Aksa at 8 A.M. to talk to the man who guarded the shoes left at the door by persons entering the mosque, Ibrahim Haluani. The guard had been one of the principal beneficiaries of Rohan's largess, and he greeted him with an anticipatory grin. Rohan told him he wanted to take photographs inside the mosque but that there were too many people around. "Between you and me," said Rohan, "I'll give you ten or twenty pounds if you let me come up here tomorrow morning and take some photographs inside the mosque." It was forbidden to take pictures there without special permission from the Muslim authorities. Haluani, however, said it would be alright. Rohan returned later that day and slipped him ten pounds. "I hope there will be no other guards around tomorrow morning so I can take photographs."

"If God wills it," said Haluani, "it will be alright."

In his hotel room, Rohan photographed his arson equipment and asked the desk clerk to wake him at 5:45 A.M. He wakened earlier because of excitement and packed the equipment into a knapsack, with a sweater tied to the outside of the pack to emphasize its innocent character. He was too impatient to wait for breakfast and was out of the hotel by 6:00. To look as much a tourist as possible, he wore sunglasses, a brimless Israeli hat, and the camera slung around his neck.

He had picked this day for his attempt because it was the seventh day of the month by the Hebrew calendar and the 21st of August—a multiple of seven. Rohan knew seven as "the perfect number" and saw this coincidence as portentous.

He reached Lion's Gate at 6:15 and sat down to wait for the gates to the Temple Mount to open at 7:00. At 6:30, Haluani came through on his way to the mosque. "Hello," said the Arab. "Are you coming to the mosque later? I came early especially for you." Rohan assured him he would be along.

Inside the mosque, the night watchman, Haj Russul, opened the front door at 6:45, just as Haluani came up. Haj Russul was surprised to see Haluani so early. The two men chatted awhile, and then the watchman asked Haluani to keep an eye on things while he, Haj Russul, went to the toilet. Instead of returning to the mosque immediately, however, the watchman took advantage of Haluani's presence to go to the watchman's room at the rear of the mosque to tidy up. Haluani, whose official duties went no further than guarding the shoes at the mosque entrance and providing shawls to bare-shouldered women entering the mosque, was thus in sole charge of the mosque when Rohan arrived.

Rohan had entered the Temple Mount promptly at 7:00, when tickets began to be sold to non-Muslims. The mosque itself, however, was not open to non-Muslims before 8:00. The compound seemed empty except for three men sitting under a tree and smoking. As he approached the mosque, he saw Haluani sweeping at the entrance. Rohan paused and pretended to take a picture. Haluani signaled with his head for him to enter.

Before the Australian reached the door, an old Arab woman went in. Haluani pointed at Rohan's shoes and told him to take them off and place them inside the door rather than outside. The guard wanted to shield Rohan's presence from passersby.

Rohan entered the mosque and strode quickly in his stocking feet across the carpeted floor. In the narrow space between the pulpit and the rear wall, he lowered his knapsack and undid its straps. The two containers with flammables were wrapped in old clothing. He set them on the floor and photographed them. Glancing up, he saw someone watching him from the shadows. It was the old woman. She was either praying or muttering to herself, but she was looking straight at him. He pointed his camera at her and she turned away.

Quickly wrapping one end of a scarf around the handle of the container holding the kerosene, he placed it in the hollowed out space at the rear of the pulpit. He unscrewed the cap on the other container and saturated the scarf with benzine. He then took another photograph of the containers. Stuffing the clothes back into the haversack, he struck a match and lit the end of the scarf.

Sheikh Joude el-Ansari, the Wakf official responsible for the mosque's security arrangements, arrived outside the doors at 7:15 wearing his red fez and carrying a walking stick. His family had been in charge of guarding el-Aksa for 1,300 years, and the stout sheikh moved with the majesty of one responsible for what he would describe as "the first light of Islam."

The sheikh was surprised to see Haluani, who normally arrived only at 8:00. "*Salam Aleikem,*" said Sheikh Jouda. "May God give health to all who serve this place." He had expected to be met by the night watchman. Haluani told him where he had gone. He did not tell him of the tourist he had let in. Sheikh Joude looked through the doorway at his domain as he talked to Haluani, who busied himself sweeping. Rohan, who was behind the pulpit, could not be seen in the vast interior divided by lines of columns, and Haluani prayed that he would stay out of sight. He was relieved when the sheikh turned his back on the mosque interior and continued his monologue as he surveyed the Temple Mount, his hands clasped behind his back. Sheikh Joude enjoyed talking, and Halouni had learned not to interrupt him when he was in full stride.

Inside the mosque, Rohan came toward the doorway at a trot, slowing down to a walk as he neared it. He thrust his feet into his shoes inside the door but did not stop to lace them. Looking outside, he was surprised to see the stout Arab with the red fez who had once caught him sleeping inside the mosque. The priest, as Rohan thought of him, had at that time pulled out a pocket watch to indicate that it was closing time and, taking the hint, Rohan had left. Rohan paused for a moment, but with the fire kindled behind him, he had no choice but to step through the doorway.

Sheikh Joude was flabbergasted at the emergence from the mosque of a foreigner with a knapsack on his back. "Why is this man here?" he shouted at Haluani. "Why did you let him in?" He pulled out his pocket watch like a seal of office and again held it up to Rohan. "It's only seven-fifteen," he said in Arabic. "It's not yet time." As he looked more closely at Rohan, he recognized him as the tourist who had been appearing at the mosque every day for weeks. A few days before, Sheikh Joude had said to one of his assistants, "What does this man want here?" Noticing the camera around Rohan's neck now, Sheikh Joude shouted at the stricken Haluani: "This man has been taking photographs from the inside. You know it is forbidden."

Rohan pulled out a ten-pound bill and offered it to Haluani, who stepped back as if horrified. Rohan then offered the bill to Sheikh

Joude, who likewise demurred. Rohan would later contend that he had in previous weeks left gratuities in Sheikh Joude's hand several times. "Thanks for letting me take the photographs," said Rohan. "Goodbye." He moved off toward the Temple Mount gates, trying to restrain himself from running.

Sheikh Joude stepped inside the mosque to see if someone else might be lurking there. Something at the far end caught his eye. It was the glow of a small fire in the pulpit. Turning toward the fast-retreating figure of Rohan, he shouted, "Stop that man, stop that man." Sheikh Joude's cry terrified Rohan, even though he could not understand the words. It was a sound so agonized that he thought it might be the voice of Satan himself. He continued walking for about ten yards and then could control himself no longer. Breaking into a run, he raced to the nearest gate out of the mount compound only to find it closed. He ran toward the gate he had entered twenty minutes before. Covering his face with his arms he dashed past the startled ticket seller and on through Lion's Gate in the Old City wall one hundred meters beyond. He turned left up an embankment into a Muslim cemetery just outside the city wall, where he stripped off his knapsack and threw it behind a cactus bush. At the far end of the cemetery a staircase led down to a main street. Rohan hailed an Arab taxi, which took him to Jerusalem's central bus station on the Jewish side of the city two miles away. From the little money remaining to him, he bought a ticket to Tel Aviv. A bus was just backing out of the bay as Rohan reached it. He rapped on the door, and the driver let him in. Breathlessly, he sank into a seat. As the bus headed down the winding road through the Judean Hills, Rohan leaned back and smiled a beatific smile. He had looked back before leaving the mosque and had seen the flames taking hold. This time, he had done the job.

Sheikh Joude had run to the pulpit to stamp out the flames. He thought the fire small enough to be easily contained but he soon realized he was badly mistaken. Opening the nearby door to the watchman's room, he saw Haj Russul and shouted to him to bring water. As the horrified watchman ran toward the burning pulpit with a jar of water from his room, the sheikh shouted at him: "Why did you leave the entrance? Why weren't you at the door?" The watchman flung the water, but the flames were already out of control. The two men began rolling up the prayer rugs nearby.

Outside, Haluani had ignored the sheikh's order to chase Rohan and had wisely run instead to the Israeli guards at nearby Moor's Gate to call for help. A call was made to the East Jerusalem firehouse.

Its contingent, all Arabs, had constituted the fire department of Jordanian Jerusalem before the war and had been incorporated into the
Israeli fire department serving the expanded city. Although they responded quickly, the fire was already out of control when their vehicles entered the Temple Mount.

Jerusalem Fire Chief Avraham Lieberman arrived and quickly realized that the fire was endangering not only one of the major land-
marks of Jerusalem but the underpinnings of the tenuous coexistence
that had been achieved in the city. He began putting in a succession
of calls for aid—first to the Jewish fire stations in West Jerusalem and
the Arab fire departments in surrounding towns like Bethlehem and
Ramallah. As the fire spread, he issued urgent calls to fire departments as far away as the suburbs of Tel Aviv, fifty miles away. Sixteen
fire companies in all were to become involved.

Arab residents of the Old City poured onto the Temple Mount and
milled in frenzy as they watched smoke and flames coming through
the roof of the mosque with its silver dome. Men, women, and children ran to the mosque with pails of water. A sense of mass hysteria
began to grip the crowd as young men emerged from the mosque
carrying charred pieces of the pulpit and shouting ''Allah Akbar [God
is Great]'' and ''Down with Israel.''

A rumor spread that the Israeli firemen were pouring gasoline onto
the fire through their hoses. Some had the hoses seized from their
hands and some were beaten. The police were hard put to keep the
mob under control. At one of the gates to the Temple Mount, another
mob rushed a small group of military policemen and was stopped
only by shots fired in the air. Shouting Arab youths surged through
the alleys of the Old City.

It was almost noon before the flames were extinguished. Most of
the mosque remained intact but its front was a smoldering ruin. Premier Golda Meir, looking shocked, arrived at the mosque to express
her condolences to Muslim leaders, who received her with frozen
faces. Defense Minister Moshe Dayan said he hoped no human hand
had been involved in the fire, but if the fire had been deliberately set,
those responsible would be apprehended. Later in the day, the cabinet met in special session to appoint a committee to investigate the
cause of the fire.

Even before the flames were extinguished, a special police investigation team headed by Assistant Commander Zelig Meyer had been
set up. The political implications of the fire were enormous, and it

had become a top national priority to establish quickly whether arson was involved and, if it was, to apprehend those responsible.

The Muslim world, and perhaps much of the non-Muslim world as well, would take it as a matter of course that Israel was behind the burning—if not for Messianic reasons, then as a crude attempt to persuade the Arabs to leave. Cries of jihad (holy war) were already being heard from across the borders. To the Israelis, an act of provocation by Arab militants seemed the most likely explanation if arson was the cause, but the involvement of Jewish extremists or madmen could not be ruled out.

Police experts quickly found material impregnated with kerosene behind the pulpit, which had evidently been the focus of the fire. This evidence indicated that arson indeed had been involved. Investigators fanned out across the Old City, and by mid-afternoon Haluani and the ticket seller from whom Rohan had purchased a ticket at the Temple Mount were in police headquarters in the Russian Compound to assist in compiling an identikit portrait of the man that mosque officials said had run away from the fire.

Police Corporal Gabriel Moshez saw one of the portraits being circulated in headquarters that evening at 8:00. The Israeli police were just beginning to use identikit portraits, and he was curious to see one. Slowly, his casual glance took on focus. The portrait strongly resembled the strange Australian brought into headquarters two weeks before, after his altercation with the Israeli guards at Moor's Gate. Moshez had talked to him at the time and found it odd that someone would take a whip-dagger onto the Temple Mount.

The policeman didn't remember the tourist's name and Sgt. Ventura, who had questioned him, was off duty. Moshez took a copy of the portrait and drove to Ventura's home. The sergeant immediately recalled Rohan's name. Back at headquarters, Moshez pulled the file on Rohan and saw the name of the Rivoli Hotel. With three patrolmen, the corporal proceeded there.

The desk clerk was startled when the policemen entered. "Stand here and don't move," said Moshez. "And don't answer the telephone." He showed the clerk Rohan's portrait.

"Is this person staying in the hotel?" asked the policeman.

The desk clerk thought it looked like the guest in room 107 but felt it wiser not to say so. The Arab proprietor likewise feared becoming involved in a police matter; he said he did not recognize the portrait or the name. The policemen carried out a quick search of all the rooms and scanned the faces of guests present. One of the policemen checked the hotel register as far back as the fifteenth of the month, the day Rohan had been arrested at Moor's Gate. When he didn't find the name, he presumed Rohan had registered under an alias.

Having drawn a blank, Moshez drove to Ventura's home and returned to the hotel with the sergeant. Ventura remembered the room to which he had gone with the Australian to get his passport. He asked the proprietor to come along and witness the search. In a drawer, Ventura found several documents with Rohan's name and a small passport photo of him. A policeman checking a closet found two bottles. "Smell these," he said. Moshez smelt a faint but unmistakeable whiff of kerosene. Another policeman held up two stubs of tickets for entry to the Temple Mount mosque.

A policeman was posted in the room and plainclothesmen positioned in the lobby and outside the hotel in case Rohan should return.

Ventura submitted his findings to Commander Meyer. On the reverse of one of Rohan's papers was scrawled the name of Kibbutz Mishmar Hasharon. The investigators sent a telex message to Netanya police headquarters asking whether an Australian named Dennis Michael Rohan could be located at the nearby kibbutz. The officer who received the message decided to wait until morning before dispatching a patrol car.

Arthur Jones heard of the al-Aksa fire from one of the other volunteers, who had picked it up on the English-language news program after their return from a tour of the Jordan Valley organized for them by the kibbutz. It was an incredible piece of news. After dinner in the communal dining room, Jones and his roommate were returning to their quarters when they heard someone approaching fast on the path behind them. Jones turned and saw Rohan emerging from the darkness.

"*Erev tov,*" said Rohan—good evening, in Hebrew. In view of their previous conversation on the subject, Rohan was the person Jones most wanted to tell about the astonishing fire at al-Aksa.

"Did you hear that the mosque burnt down?" asked Jones.

"It did?" said Rohan, who appeared to be in a state of excitement. "Look, I have something to tell you, and I want to talk to you alone."

Jones's roommate excused himself, and the pair went to Jones's room. As soon as the door was shut, Rohan said, "I did it."

"You did what?" asked Jones.

"I did it," said Rohan. "I burnt the mosque."

Jones was stunned. As shocking as Rohan's statement was, he instinctively knew it to be true. "I don't know what to tell you, Dennis," he said.

"You might say I bought if off them," continued Rohan. "You know the thousand dollars I had? It cost me that. I spread it around to guards and to the ones I felt I should."

Rohan told how he had risen that morning with a feeling of excitement. "I knew this was the day; it was finally here." He told of the signs he had received from God and of his previous attempt. He described in detail how he had carried out the burning that morning. "I've got film, I can prove it."

"Do you believe I did it?" asked Rohan eagerly.

"Yes, I believe you," said the American divinity student. "I will remain silent until I have learned what to say and what position to take on this."

Jaunty now, Rohan said he was considering his next move. "I may just walk into the police station in Jerusalem and say 'Boker tov' [good morning] boys." In any case, Rohan would spend the night at the kibbutz.

Before taking the bus to the kibbutz from Netanya that evening, he had waited at Netanya's bus station until the bus that usually carried Zipporah arrived from the kibbutz. He photographed it from a distance—evidence attesting to Zipporah's link to the King of Judah. When he reached the kibbutz, he removed the film and hung the camera on the branch of a tree. He had no more need of it.

Jones woke shortly after dawn as usual and went to work in the fields with the other volunteers for two hours before going to the dining hall for breakfast. Rohan came in shortly afterward and sat down next to him. When someone at the table took out a cigarette and looked around for a light, Rohan took a box of matches from his pocket and offered it to him.

"Funny I should have these with me," he said, with a smile at Jones. "I don't smoke."

The Netanya police arrived shortly afterward and quickly located Rohan. He seemed to be expecting them and went along willingly. Within two hours he was in Jerusalem police headquarters, where Inspector Meyer and the commander of the Jerusalem police district, David Ofer, were waiting for him in an interrogation room. The two veteran policemen started in low gear, avoiding any mention of the fire. They asked Rohan for his passport and then matter-of-factly asked how he had spent his time since arriving in the country. Rohan gave no indication of concern. He described his activities until his stay at the Rivoli Hotel. Finally Meyer asked, ''What did you do yesterday?''

''I got up in the morning and went and set fire to the al-Aksa Mosque,'' said Rohan.

''Stop,'' barked Ofer.

Rohan was asked whether he was prepared to make a written statement. He readily agreed. The statement noted that he had been informed that he was not obliged to say anything unless he chose and that whatever he did say would be recorded in writing and given in evidence. Rohan signed and then began to tell his story to the world through the police stenographer.

The trial got underway less than two months after the fire despite the complex preparations involved. The government saw it as a major national priority to prove to the world that the fire had been set by a demented Christian tourist and not an Israeli.

The fire had fed ingrained fears in the Muslim world that the Zionists were determined not only to conquer Palestine but to build an empire stretching from the Euphrates to the Nile and to displace or subjugate the Arabs. Repercussions had already been widespread. A special summit meeting of twenty-five Islamic nations in Rabat condemned the sacrilege ''perpetrated under Israeli occupation'' and the Arab Defence Council had scheduled a meeting to discuss ''mobilization of Arab resources against Israeli aggression.'' In Saudia Arabia, King Faisal ordered his armed forces to stand by for a holy war to liberate Jerusalem. Widespread loss of life was reported in India in riots set off in the large Muslim community by news of the fire. There had been general strikes in Pakistan to protest the fire and in Manila a crowd of Muslim youths tore down the Israeli flag in front of the embassy. Iraq announced the execution of fifteen ''Israeli and American spies'' in retaliation for the fire. In Indonesia, a former prime minister told the press that Israel had long planned to get rid of the mosque and build a Jewish temple.

The most grievous impact, however, was close to home. East Jerusalem and the other territories captured in the Six Day War seethed with anger certain to vent itself in increased disturbances and terrorist action unless the belief in a Zionist arson plot were dispelled. A significant political setback had already occured in East Jerusalem, where Arabs who had agreed to run for the city council in the upcoming municipal elections renounced their candidacy, establishing a pattern of nonparticipation that would leave the council without Arab representation in the coming decades. Any hope of eventual accom-

modation with the Arab world was lost unless Israel could prove beyond doubt that it was not behind the destruction of Islam's holy
places.

The trial was held in a hall at Jerusalem's convention center in order to accommodate the foreign press and diplomatic corps. The trial
of Nazi war criminal Adolph Eichmann had been held in another
Jerusalem hall eight years before. Like Eichmann, Rohan was seated
in a bullet-proof glass enclosure on the stage with a headset to hear
simultaneous translation from Hebrew or Arabic. The three-man
Jerusalem District Court bench was headed by a crusty British-born
judge, Henry Baker, who handled his court with a firm hand and an
acerbic sense of humor. The prosecution was led by the state's chief
legal officer, Attorney-General Meir Shamgar. Defending Rohan was
the head of the Israel Bar Association, Tel Aviv lawyer Yitzhak Tunik.

The seven-week trial of Dennis Michael Rohan on charges of arson
and violation of a holy place provided a fascinating public insight into
the workings of psychosis. Each of the actors in the drama taking
his place on the courtroom stage was a clearly drawn character: the
imperturbable Sheikh Joude pulling his pocket watch out of his flowing robes at every opportunity to show how he had asked Rohan
what he was doing at the mosque at such an hour; the upright Arthur
Jones declining to be sworn in ("I don't take an oath but I always tell
the truth"); the regal Zipporah, whom Rohan would have made
queen of Judea, wavering between bemusement and bewilderment
as she tried to describe the behavior of her strange student.

For Rohan, the trial was clearly the climax of his life. He sat in
Jerusalem before the judges of Israel with the world's representatives
in the press section hanging on every word. He knew that when the
evidence was laid before them they would recognize who he was.
"My trial is the most important event for the world since the trial of
Jesus Christ," he told a psychiatrist who visited him in his cell. When
his lawyer said something in the courtroom out of hearing, Rohan
would wave him to the microphone so that the remark could enter
the official record. He himself would regularly pause even in the
midst of the most emotional testimony—a searing account of his nervous breakdown, for instance—in order to let the translators catch
up. "I'm not afraid of this trial," he said in court. "I know I won't
be found guilty."

The Dostoyevskian story of his tortured soul was portrayed against
the open landscape of Australia. His father was described by psychiatrists as a stern man free with the strap, his mother as a cold, rejecting

personality who had spent time in a mental home. One of his four sisters was presently in such a home, and his brother had not been seen for many years. A psychiatrist told how Rohan's first-grade teacher would punish him by making him climb into a tall wicker basket and having the other children file by and look at him. Even though he was of normal intelligence, he became the classroom butt and then the village fool.

As an adult, he was not a total recluse. He played cards Saturday nights in the sheep shearing sheds ("I was regarded as a clean shearer but not very fast") and attended village dances. However, Rohan's marriage, which went bad on the wedding night, tipped him over the edge.

His performance on the witness stand was uncanny. Mocked as a fool throughout his life, he stood up to the questioning of some of Israel's best legal minds without faltering. Within his own framework, he was consistent, extremely logical, almost convincing. When Shamgar asked whether he thought God wanted him to commit a crime by burning down a building, he was at no loss.

"What did God tell Abraham to do?" asked Rohan. "Sacrifice his son? Isn't that a crime in today's courts? First degree murder, isn't it?" He displayed total recall of dates and incidents and was never caught out in a contradiction despite the intricate story he told. "My mind has never been as well balanced as it is now," he said. "Satan has no more power over me." He could be objective about himself and admit that "people feel uneasy in my presence." He spoke with animation, and his melodious voice would come to rest on a pitch that expressed his precise meanings.

The tormented figure was at last serene. "I understand why I was born, why I had to suffer strict discipline from my parents, why I was rejected and despised," he told the court. "I did not understand until I arrived in Jerusalem. It all came together in Jerusalem. Satan knew who I was but I did not know." Asked what his attitude would be if found guilty, he said, "I'm still not sorry because I am above earthly courts."

His most revealing testimony, however, came on the last day of the trial when he told of a voice he had heard in his cell. "Because you have obeyed my voice and have done everything I have told you even to your own hurt," he quoted, "I shall exalt you above the whole earth and bring all the maidens of Israel to you to bear forth your offspring to my glory. You shall build the temple and Zipporah will be your queen." Instead of the usual excitement with which he had described his revelations heretofore, Rohan bowed his head this time and had to force himself to describe this ultimate revelation. The psychiatrists who testified were in agreement that the underlying cause for his action had not been religious but sexual.

The trial established clearly that the fire in al-Aksa that had brought the wrath of much of the world down upon Israel had been carried out by a mad Christian exploiting the venality of Muslim guards. Although the al-Aksa fire would continue to be widely portrayed in the official Arab world as a Zionist plot—notably by Jordan, whose government would show extensive pictures of the blaze on television each anniversary—the trial had taken the sting out of these charges and the event would recede into the general turmoil of the Middle East.

Rohan was found guilty and sentenced to life confinement in a mental institution. He was kept at Talbiya Mental Hospital in Jerusalem, where he proved a much sought-after partner in the hospital's Saturday night dances for its patients. In 1974 he was transferred to Australia to live out his life in a mental institution there and to dwell on how close he came to the throne of Jerusalem.

Apart from the loss of the priceless pulpit, al-Aksa would emerge from the fire strengthened and beautified by the work of skilled artisans in a massive restoration project. The fire had warped decorations on the inside of the mosque dome but when these were scraped away by Wakf experts, far more beautiful original decorations were revealed. Egyptian President Anwar Sadat prayed in al-Aksa during his historic visit to Jerusalem and pledged Egyptian assistance in the restoration project.

On the day the Old City was captured in 1967, Defense Minister Dayan had spied an Israeli flag raised over the Dome of the Rock by the victorious paratroopers and ordered it taken down immediately. In the political settlement he envisioned, effective control of the Temple Mount would be retained by the Muslim authorities. Otherwise there was no possible hope of winning Arab acquiesence, however reluctant, in Israeli rule. Within a few days, he had cleared all troops from the mount and handed back to the Muslim authorities the keys to all its gates except one. Israel would retain control over Moor's Gate—and open a small police post on the mount staffed mainly by Arab policemen—to indicate that, while it was relinquishing de facto control and did not flaunt the Israeli flag over the Temple Mount, it was retaining sovereignty.

This pragmatic policy drew important support from rulings of medieval rabbis forbidding Jews from entering the Temple Mount—until the Messiah's coming—for fear of inadvertently treading on the site of the destroyed temple's holy of holies, which only the high priest had been permitted to enter. However, some modern rabbis claimed that it was safe to enter portions of the mount where the temple had plainly not been located.

In post–Six Day War Jerusalem, the Temple Mount became the symbol of the dispute between Abraham's descendants over his heritage. As many as 100,000 Muslims would fill the broad esplanade and mosques on holidays, making a statement that was as much political as religious. In the Jewish camp, a militant fringe group attempted to assert an Israeli presence on the Mount by staging demonstrative prayers. Smaller, but far more militant groups would not make do with prayers. The temple Mount became the target in the 1980s of three bomb plots by Jewish extremists all of them forestalled by the security forces. The plotters, like Rohan, aimed at clearing the site of the Temple but, unlike him, they knew that the site was occupied by the Dome of the Rock in the center of the mount, not al-Aksa.

One group consisted of fringe, drugged-out mystics living in an abandoned village on the edge of Jerusalem. The other two, however, were made up of seemingly stable personalities within the nationalistic religious camp. The plotters included a reserve air force squadron leader from a West Bank settlement, who proposed flying up to Jerusalem during one of his annual stints of reserve duty and leveling the Islamic shrine with bombs. The proposal was rejected for fear of damaging the Western Wall less than one hundred meters away. Others intended to penetrate the mount through an ancient tunnel uncovered by archaeologists. In 1982, a deranged American immigrant doing his military basic training took a bus to Jerusalem on his first pass and rampaged on the Temple Mount with the rifle he had just learned to shoot. He killed a man and nicked the Dome of the Rock with several bullets before being subdued.

These attempts caused deep consternation even within the mainstream Orthodox nationalist camp. Security on the Temple Mount was increased, but it would remain a site where distinction between faith and madness and between politics and religion would continue to be blurred—and would likely remain so until the Messiah's coming.

T H R E E

The Many Faces of Jerusalem

THE *SHTEIBLECH* ARE HOME TO THE OLDEST ESTABLISHED, floating minyan in the Holy City—six adjacent one-room synagogues in the heart
of the Mea Shearim Quarter. *Shteiblech* is Yiddish for "rooms," and
the decor here is strictly functional: peeling walls, a few barebacked
benches, a small Torah ark, a lectern. A bit short on opulence, but
come when you will, before dawn till almost midnight, there will
most likely be a minyan (the minimum quorum of ten males needed
for communal prayer) starting up in one or the other of the small
synagogues. If you don't like the voice of the man leading the prayers, try the *shteibel* next door.

New York City with its 1.2 million Jews has fewer than five hundred synagogues. Jerusalem, with some 350,000 Jews, has close to
eight hundred.

The number reflects not so much the piety of Jerusalem's Jews—
most of whom are seculars who may attend synagogue only on Yom
Kippur—as their diversity. The synagogues are ethnic hearths for the
scores of distinct communities making up the Jewish population, constituting a comforting touchstone of familiarity and communal
warmth. To the outsider, they offer a fascinating glimpse of the rich-
ness and variety of tradition acquired by the Jewish people during
two millennia of exile.

This colorful panoply is best viewed on Simhat Torah when completion of the annual round of Sabbath readings from the Bible is celebrated. In the Bukharan synagogues, women beat tambourines and emit the high-pitched ululation of the East as men in colorful robes and skullcaps dance. In a Sephardi synagogue off Agrippas Street, an elderly man with a good-humored face improvises comic songs in Arabic, the rest of the congregation joining in the refrain. Yemenite Jews sit cross-legged on rugs in their synagogue during prayers, while in the Hassidic houses of Mea Shearim the rafters shake from wild stomping. Jews from Mashad in Iran, whose ancestors had been forced to Islamize but secretly practiced their Jewish faith like the Marannos of Spain, have their own synagogue and customs. So do the dark Cochin Jews from India, the Jews from Afghanistan, and those from the Caucasian Mountains.

There is no sign outside indicating a synagogue but Ezra, who lives in the Ohel Moshe Quarter, leads the way up an exterior staircase and opens the door. "The congregation is Greek," he says. "From Yanina."

Three men are studying the Talmud at a table. The white-haired man in the center is discussing an obscure reference to the Pharaoh. He looks up and smiles. "How are you, Ezra?" His face is familiar. Hot water for tea is boiling on a stove in the corner. Through the window, the Mahane Yehuda open-air marketplace can be seen. It is thronged this Thursday evening with women buying food for the Sabbath.

"That's Judge Cohen," whispers Ezra.

A week before, Judge Moshe Cohen's picture was in the newspapers showing him being sworn in as a Supreme Court justice by President Yitzhak Navon. The president, who had himself grown up in the quarter, noted that the Cohen family's ethnic affiliation had always been a puzzle to the residents, all Sephardim. The founders of the Yanina community had left the Holy Land for Greece well before the destruction of the Second Temple, which had sent the Jews into the great exile in the lands of the east and west two thousand years ago. "They therefore didn't regard themselves as Ashkenazim or Sephardim," said Navon, "and we didn't know how to regard them either."

The benches along the east wall of the Batei Natan Synagogue are empty. In the western Diaspora, the east wall—the one facing Jerusalem—is traditionally reserved for a community's elite. The lack of claimants in this small, ultra-Orthodox congregation is an expression of modesty.

In one corner sits Reb Yosef, the last exorcist in Jerusalem. When someone is ill, a messenger brings a piece of the sick person's clothing to Reb Yosef's home. The white-bearded elder closets himself in his room for several minutes with the apparel and recites a secret prayer. The messenger, after he gets the garment back, is forbidden to speak until he has placed it on the head of the patient. Reb Yosef takes no fee.

In another corner sits Reb Moshe, one of the leaders of the anti-Zionist Neturai Karta. It was he who initiated this second Shabbat minyan in Batei Natan, which begins after the conclusion of the sunrise minyan. He had wanted a minyan with a more *balabatish* (dignified) atmosphere when his own boys began to grow up, one that was more mature than that of a yeshiva synagogue and more stable than a minyan in a *shteibel*.

The Batei Natan Quarter consists of four, two-story row houses built at the turn of the century by a childless American shoe manufacturer and his wife to perpetuate their family name. The leases to the eighty apartments contain a clause obligating all male residents to pray in the quarter's synagogue, which is located on one of the upper stories, slighly higher than the surrounding apartments. Most of the people who live here, preferring to pray in other synagogues, ignore this stipulation, so there is little more than a quorum. On this Saturday, a woman with a prayer book is standing on the balcony outside her apartment across the courtyard. She is following the clear voice of the synagogue reader, Reb Moshe's oldest son.

"There shouldn't be more than fifty synagogues in Jerusalem," says the Jerusalem Religious Council official. "In Paris, which has half a million Jews, there are only fifty-five synagogues. The problem is that everybody here wants to be a *gabbai* [sexton] or a president." In Jerusalem's Baka Quarter, he notes, a Moroccan community of two thousand families is split among twenty-one small synagogues based on towns of origin or family clans. A large synagogue built in the neighborhood by the council in the hope of uniting these dispersed congregations has failed to lead to a single closing. "Why shouldn't Ashkenazim and Sephardim pray together?" he asks. "Why shouldn't Iraqi Jews and Moroccan Jews pray together? Are we or are we not one people?"

The answer, of course, is yes and no. Jerusalem permits men to feel part of a tribal grouping that offers an inner layer of identity and security—without alienating them from the broader national groups to which they belong. In a vast, amorphous world, men come here to huddle with their own God and their own kind.

This characteristic has been recognized over the centuries by the division of the Old City into clear ethnic-religious quarters. Although individuals crossed the line to live in each other's quarters, it was done in the comforting knowledge that the lines existed and their own place in the world was assured. When modern Jerusalem began to be built outside the walls of the Old City, neighborhoods continued to be built as ethnic enclaves—Kurdish Jews here, Turkish Jews there, German Protestant Fundamentalists somewhere else. For several decades, these enclaves were built with walls around them.

This diversity is still reflected each morning in the streets of Jerusalem, as schoolchildren make their way to schools that offer markedly different curriculums, and emphasize different values, often in different languages. In the Jewish sector, two-thirds of the children attend state secular schools, which are like public schools in the United States, except for a dash of Bible studies. Boys and girls here will all go on to army service. Twenty percent of the city's Jewish children attend state religious schools, where the emphasis on religious studies is significant but where national values prevail—boys will do army service and girls will either go to the army or do an equivalent term of national service in jobs like teaching or social work. Twelve percent of the children go to ultra-Orthodox schools, where boys and girls are segregated. The language of instruction is Yiddish, the amount of nonreligious studies is almost nil, and the tone is often antistate. Virtually none of the boys will go on to regular army service, and the girls will do neither army nor national service.

In the Arab sector, the eductional spread is even more diverse. Most study in Arabic, according to the Jordanian curriculum, but the Arabs whose families had been on the Israeli side of the city from before 1967 study according to the Israeli Arab curriculum. Many East Jerusalem Arab youths follow European curriculums in schools run by foreign churches which teach often in foreign tongues.

Mayor Kollek added to the diversity when he prodded leaders of the Syrian Orthodox church to revive one of their schools where instruction had been given in Aramaic, the language spoken in the Holy Land and throughout the Near East during much of the biblical period. The community's two schools had shut down during the previous decades and the children distributed to schools of other churches. With donations raised by Kollek, the church leaders re-opened one of the schools in the mid-1980s. It instructed 150 children and served as a major vehicle for preserving as a living tongue the language which Jesus and his contemporaries spoke and in which the Talmud was written. Apart from three villages in Syria where the dialect is still spoken, and a few other small pockets in the region, the language had virtually disappeared from daily use. Now, in Jeru-salem, where ideas rendered in Aramaic have resounded through the ages, the school is restoring it to daily usage, at least among one small segment of the population.

Kollek did much to promote the self-image of the ethnic and reli-gious communities in Jerusalem in the belief that if people feel good about themselves—and display their pride—they would be less ag-gressive toward others. At his urging, the Armenian patriarchate put on display its extensive artistic treasures normally never seen by the public. Elaborate exhibitions on the folklore of the Moroccan and Kurdish Jewish communities, who make up a substantial portion of the city's population, were mounted at the Israel Museum. When a youth club in the Arab sector could not find someone to teach Arabic folk dancing, the municipality provided a Jewish teacher, who led the course until a qualified Arab teacher was located.

The sheer profusion of religions, sects, and ethnic communities conscious of each other's claims on the city argues against the notion of a dominant culture even though Jews have been a majority in Jeru-salem for a century. Municipal bylaws demand that shop owners close one day a week but this can be either Friday, Saturday, or Sun-day, depending on one's religion.

"Divided we stand" is the way eminent Hebrew University sociol-ogist Shmuel Eisenstadt described the situation in the city. What had spared Jerusalem the explosion that political realities seemed to dic-tate for it, he argued, was precisely the avoidance of Western notions of integration. "The people here demand separation." Jerusalem is set apart from other pluralistic capital cities by the absence of marked social and economic stratification according to community. If Arab workmen collected most of the city's garbage, the Arab elite occupied many of the most opulent villas in town. The economic situation in the Arab sector, particularly for the lower-income residents, im-proved considerably in the post-1967 period, and there was a feeling of expanding economic horizons. If the economic boom was a key, so was the deliberate easing of claustrophobic pressures on the Arabs and the enhancement of their sense of identity by permitting them to retain Jordanian citizenship, travel freely across the Jordan River bridges, and have their children study according to a Jordanian curriculum that opened the way to universities throughout the Arab world.

The tensions that exist among the city's major communities are generally less than those existing within them. In Mea Shearim the tensions are there to be seen on the wall posters that are put up almost every day by one or another subgroup. The posters play the role of the newspaper and electronics media in the outside world, and they reflect the diversity of views and conflicts among the ultra-Orthodox. Allegations of religious or moral impropriety and ideological challenges are supported by learned quotes from the Talmud and Bible.

Even the small and seemingly cohesive Armenian community in the Old City is split into factions. The secular community of some 1,500 persons dates only from the early part of this century, when refugees from the massacres in Turkey arrived in Jerusalem. Before that, there had been only a clerical community maintaining an Armenian church presence going back some sixteen centuries. Although most of the descendants of the refugees today live rent-free inside the walls of the Armenian Quarter—in effect, the grounds of a monastery—there is little contact between the lay residents and the clergy who live there. Students in the church's seminary are never selected from the local Armenian population, only from locations in the Armenian diaspora such as Lebanon or Turkey. The main division is between those who regard their spiritual home as that part of ancient Armenia lying within the Soviet Union and those who do not. These two groups have their own social clubs. Personal divisiveness among the Armenian church leadership also split the community. Intergroup tensions in the mid-1980s led to the murder of a resident in the quarter by a fellow Armenian.

It is not only clerics in the numerous religious orders who follow separate codes of behavior. Ultra-Orthodox Jewish women living in the Shomrei Emunim block of housing adjacent to Mea Shearim are, in the interests of modesty, obliged by their apartment lease never to venture outside their homes without stockings. The laymen living in the Armenian Quarter must be inside the compound before its doors are closed at 9:00 P.M. if they wish to sleep in their own beds that night.

Segregated neighborhoods are a basic planning premise in Jerusalem. When municipal planners were assigned the task of devising a new master plan for the Abu Tor Quarter, which had been split into Jewish and Arab sectors by the War of Independence, they weighed the possibility of attempting to promote integration or at least contact by siting facilities like parks or supermarkets between the Arab and Jewish parts of Abu Tor. They quickly came to the conclusion that both sides preferred to live with their own kind. This meant not only separate dwelling areas and separate schools but separate community centers and medical facilities. Polarization of Arab and Jewish neighborhoods became even more pronounced after 1967 than it was before 1948, when there were some mixed Arab-Jewish neighborhoods. The municipality felt the need to provide some points of contact if only to change the demon image each side might have of the other. Small children's playgrounds were built at several points on the line that separated Arab and Jewish neighborhoods but these became either the scenes of scuffles between the two sides or were used almost exclusively by one or the other.

If parks did not work, municipal planners believed that shopping facilities would. Since antiquity, the marketplace has been the place where even alienated peoples suspend tribal sentiments to buy and sell. The major point of contact after 1967 had been indeed the colorful Arab bazaars of the Old City, which is thronged by Israelis and foreign visitors. In drawing up plans for northern Jerusalem in the 1980s, the municipality laid out two parallel meganeighborhoods—one Arab and one Jewish—separated by a wide strip of land but linked at several points by roads. The primary object of these roads was to serve as commercial arteries that would draw clientele from both the Arab and Jewish quarters. This would be done gradually, tentatively, as both sides were ready for it.

In the Jewish sector, the ultra-Orthodox remained in separate enclaves of their own choosing, but the sharp divisions between Sephardi and Ashkenazi neighborhoods were blurred after 1967. Ashkenazim began to "gentrify" some of the older neighborhoods in which poor eastern Jews had been settled in the early 1950s, and Sephardim who had achieved economic success began moving into former Ashkenazi strongholds. The main venue for mixing of Ashkenazim and Sephardim were the large new neighborhoods built after 1967, where young couples could find modern housing at relatively low cost. These neighborhoods also accommodated new immigrants from around the world, but the housing authorities soon learned that random integration, even of Jews in a Jewish neighborhood, did not always work.

Reservists returning to their homes in the Neve Yaacov Quarter in northern Jerusalem after months of duty following the Yom Kippur War discovered that large numbers of Bukharan and Georgian immigrants from the Soviet Union had been settled in the neighborhood during their absence. The veterans soon found the way of the life of the newcomers backward and disturbing—including the scent of wine being made in bathtubs and basements—and demanded that the proportion of such immigrants in the neighborhood be thinned out. Mayor Kollek proposed that all-Bukharan or -Georgian enclaves be formed, thus isolating them from ongoing contact with the rest of the neighborhood while integration took its slow course in schools and shopping centers and army reserve duty. However, the Housing Ministry sociologists developed their own formula: buildings averaging sixteen apartments would have one or two "weak" families, including welfare families—a small enough percentage to permit them to eventually adapt their behavioral standards to those of the veteran population.

Although cultural pluralism would be given broad rein, the national interest demanded certain common goals and duties. The main vehicle for propagating these would be the school system.

The children of modern Israel are a feisty breed whose educational experience is of a different order from that in other countries. Theirs is a lively, indeed raucous, youth but real life is a close and sobering escort. At the Masorati elementary school on Jerusalem's French Hill, three of the students lost their fathers in the Lebanese war, another lost his father to a terrorist attack after that war, five of the students were slashed by an Arab who went beserk in downtown Jerusalem, and a girl student in 1985 was sheltered beneath her dead mother on a sand dune at Ras Burka in Sinai when an Egyptian soldier deliberately fired into a group of Israeli vacationers. A small terrorist bomb went off one day opposite the school, but fortunately caused no casualties. American-born Barbara Levin, the school principal, recounts these details calmly. "The teachers discuss these things with the children when they happen and encourage them to talk about death and about their fears. The children draw pictures about it and write out their thoughts. After the Ras Burka incident, one little girl would come with her chair for awhile at the beginning of every day and sit just inside my door. She would say, "I just feel sad and want to sit here awhile."" Looking out her office window, Mrs. Levin nods at a cluster of Arab houses less than one hundred yards away and notes that three of the Arab terrorists released in 1985 in exchange for Israeli prisoners of war live in those houses.

"These kinds of things create a different reality for kids here," she says. "When I talk to elementary school kids in the States they're all-powerful and nothing's ever going to happen to them. Here, I don't think a child's so secure, I don't think he thinks he's all-powerful and that nothing is ever going to happen to him and those he loves. I think he confronts the reality of life very early.

"When I was in the States with my family on a visit a couple of years ago, my son and daughter went to school with my niece and nephew, and they both came back tremendously impressed by the lack of maturity among the kids there in comparison with kids of the same age here. The American girls were wearing makeup and fancy clothes and looked more mature and sophisticated, but their relationships with each other, my daughter said, was two or three years behind, everybody acting like fifth and sixth graders. One of the American girls she said this to answered, 'Wait, when we get older we'll have dope and beer parties.' That was their idea of maturity. My daughter spoke of the awkwardness between boys and girls, the superficiality of their relationships. Boys and girls here talk about movies too, but they discuss issues, discuss people, discuss things that are going on. They're concerned with each other and they're concerned with life."

The rigid demands of the matriculation examinations and the emphasis on Jewish studies makes education in Israel narrower than in the United States. Academic demands in the upper grades combined with the prospect of looming military service creates a forced maturity. "Normally, part of growing up is refusal to conform and just mucking around," says education writer Susan Bellos. "There's not time for that here. It's a pressure cooker."

There is an enviable camaradarie to Israeli school relationships that in a small country often extends into adulthood. It is promoted by frequent overnight class trips as well as participation in the scouts and other youth movements. This camaradarie may account in part for the widespread phenomenon of cheating on exams that shocks Western immigrants. "Americans call it cheating," says a prominent Israeli journalist. "We see it as mutual help."

The values inculcated by the schools include a patriotism that teenagers abroad would likely find embarrassing. "I'd say eighty percent of the kids want to go to the army," says a high school junior who like her classmates is just two years away from the army herself. "Kids here don't rebel, not about this. They realize it's got to be done if the nation is to survive, even if they don't happen to agree with the government's policies. Since the Lebanese War, many of the boys are frightened. They see the possibility of war with Syria as something real. They are trying to finish up things before they go to the army as if they don't expect to come back. But they understand the necessity of going."

The Rehavia Gymnasia, founded in 1909, is the second oldest high school in the country and until recent years, one of its most select. Its graduates have helped form the elite of the country's public service and professions. A grimmer reflection of its status is the memorial plaque on the second floor, which lists the names of 126 students and 4 teachers killed in Israel's wars. A large percentage were officers and members of elite units drawn from volunteers that schools like the gymnasia produce in high percentage.

The school's academic posture changed significantly in the 1980s, when it was designated a regional, rather than citywide, school. Instead of drawing students from all of Jerusalem on the basis of stiff entrance examinations, the gymnasia was obliged to accept, without examinations, all students from two elementary schools in Rehavia and one "weak" school in the nearby Baka Quarter, inhabited mostly by immigrants from Morocco and Iraq. The gymnasia was one of the last strongholds of elitism to bow to pressures for integration—in Israel a term meaning integration between Ashkenazi and so-called Sephardi youth, whose parents or grandparents came from Arab countries. (The true Sephardim are those who trace their ancestry to the Jews expelled from Spain in the fifteenth century.)

There was considerable fear of what the influx of these children would do to a school tailored for achievement-oriented Ashkenazim. "The change was not simple," said gymnasia principal Shmuel Michaeli. "There is a lot of frustration when children from homes that are crowded with people and almost empty of books find themselves together with children from uncrowded homes with lots of books and lots of help from parents with studies."

In the sixth grade, where integration begins, there would be frequent outbursts of fighting because of this frustration and a bit of scuffling in the seventh grade as well. After that, things would go smoothly. To overcome the vast disparity between the Rehavia children and the Baka children, the latter are provided with tutoring—some of it by teachers as part of their regular workload and some by upper-grade students who must provide two hours of "volunteer work" each week.

In the years since integration, the percentage of students from Baka who have passed matriculation exams has increased dramatically. Vetern teachers, however, warn against drawing a too optimistic conclusion from such statistics. "The cultural differences are deeper than the figures suggest," says a woman who has been teaching history for more than twenty years. "We've come a long way but we've got a very long way to go and it won't be easy. But, listen, Moses knew you had to wait a long time too before bringing the children of Israel out of the desert."

The heroic burden of the schools not only involves integrating children from scores of different cultures behind a collective vision but integrating them with four thousand years of history, with the notion of the God who played such a prominent role in that history, and with a contemporary world in which the danger of war or terrorism is a seemingly permanent feature.

The plagues of Egypt were upon them but the third graders in the classroom did not seem intimidated.

"So far it's tied one to one," said one boy, mocking the breathless chant of a sports announcer as the teacher drew a vertical line on the blackboard to separate a column marked "Moses and Aaron" from the column marked "Pharaoh's sorcerers." Moses and Aaron had turned the waters of the Nile into blood but the Egyptian sorcerers had shown they could do it too.

"That's right, Ro'i," said the teacher. "We've got two sides and so far they're even. On one side we've got Moses and Aaron and on the other side we've got the Egyptian sorcerers. Of course, Moses and Aaron have the God of Israel behind them." She said it offhandedly, as if He were another one of the players.

When the teacher asked for the second plague, all hands went up almost before the answers were shouted out. "Frogs."

"What's so bad about frogs?" asked the teacher.

Ro'i, tilting back in his chair, was first again. "You put your hand into your pocket to take out money and there's a frog there. You open your drawer to take out socks and there's a frog there. Everywhere you look there are frogs." All the children, particularly the girls, were now doing mock hysterical reactions to discovering frogs in their bed, in their bath, on their plates. The teacher let them run on a few seconds and then brought them back to order.

To the children sitting in small groups around tables, the players and the landscape of the Bible story were as familiar as the newspaper their parents read every morning. Egypt was always being talked about in the news and some of the children had even been there. The Israelites, well, that of course was themselves. Even the God hovering ambiguously in the background was the one to whom they made secret prayers while wondering about his existence. The language of the Bible, while antiquated, was still clearly like the Hebrew they spoke among themselves.

The teacher deftly kept the discussion moving forward while overcoming pockets of intellectual resistance and incipient anarchy. ''Maya, I haven't seen your hand yet today. That's not usual. Amnon, cut that out.'' Some of the children called her *hamorah*—teacher. Others called her by her first name, Leah. From time to time a child would rise and leave the room without first having to ask permission.

About half the class was made up of Ashkenazi children, and the other half were children whose parents had come from Arab countries. To an outsider, it was virtually impossible to guess which was which. The school, Yad Hamoreh, was in the comfortable middle-class quarter of Ramat Eshkol, which was a mixture of Ashkenazis, upwardly mobile Sephardi families, and blends of the two.

A pretty girl with pigtails sitting opposite Ro'i, fed up with the way he kept pushing the table toward her in order to tilt back in his chair, got up and shoved the table back toward him, almost knocking him over. She sat down with a satisfied expression.

''These first two plagues have been unpleasant,'' said Leah. ''But what haven't they been?'' Not even Ro'i understood her drift. ''They haven't yet been dangerous,'' she said. On that ominous note, the Bible period ended. The children were sufficiently aware of ''the situation'' in the region to find even this suggestion of vague menace familiar and not particularly disturbing.

Yad Hamoreh lies on what had been until 1967 a Jordanian minefield. Two hundred yards away, on Ammunition Hill, the fiercest battle of the Six Day War had been fought. That war, and all the other wars Israel has fought since 1948, had been only a brief interregnum for the nation's schools, which are engaged in a six-day-a-week extended struggle to shape the character of an immigrant nation with an ancient memory. It is an attempt to meld the Third World with the First, East and West, religious roots with modernity.

The struggle is epic and its outcome far from certain.

F O U R

Mea Shearim
The New Shtetl

THE LATE AFTERNOON SUN sending its beams straight down Jerusalem's
Mea Shearim Street washed the scene like a warm memory as thousands of black-clad figures hurried past and disappeared into the golden
haze. For a moment, squinting up the narrow, winding street at the
crowds of Hassidim on their way to greet the new Satmar Rebbe, one
was in the universal shtetl, vibrant with life before the great darkness
blotted it out.

Jerusalem had not seen a reception like this since the visit of Egyptian
President Sadat in 1977. In Shabbat Square, where a platform had been
erected for the visitor, the white bearded rebbe looking out expression-
less at the multitude projected no visible charisma, and his high-pitched
voice carried no sense of urgency as he made his first address to his
followers in Israel.

Brooklyn-based rabbi Moshe Teitelbaum had inherited the Satmar title three years before upon the death, at age ninety-three, of his remarkable predecessor, Rabbi Joel Teitelbaum. The new rebbe's credentials as
a scholar and his personal magnetism were trifling compared with those
of the previous Satmar Rebbe, and the aura of otherworldliness demanded by his new post was strained by his reputation in the recent
past as a shrewd player of the stock market. He was said to have had
a telex link to Wall Street in his Brooklyn basement before assuming the
mantle of the rebbe. (Not so, said a Satmar aide when asked by a journalist; and, continued the aide, even if it were true, so what?)

57

The fact that such an unimposing figure could be the subject of such adoration illustrated the vitality with which the Hassidic movement, born in backward villages of eastern Europe two centuries before, has survived, indeed thrived, in the modern era. Hassidism had proved a phenomenon that transcended personality and time.

The founders of Hassidism were radiantly spiritual figures around whom rallied initially the poor, superstition-prone Jews of southeast Poland, who had become increasingly alienated from the scholarly, Jewish elite disdainful of their boorishness. The Hassidic leaders, by virtue of their piety and capacity for ecstacy, were regarded by their followers as having unique access to the divine spirit. The leader, or rebbe, served as an intermediary between his followers and God, as well as a wonder worker and oracle. Emotional fervor and religious joy, rather than scholarship, were the distinctive attributes of Hassidism.

The Hassidic world was virtually wiped out in the Second World War. Although a small number of Hassidic groups had moved to the West before the war and a number of Hassidic leaders escaped the holocaust alone or with a handful of followers, the movement appeared to postwar observers to have become an anachronism as the East European shtetl Jew gave way in Jewish demography to the city Jew of the industrialized West.

Instead of shriveling into a quaint historical footnote, however, Hassidism would experience a remarkable flowering, suggesting that the need for an intermediary between man and God has increased rather than diminished in modern societies. The Brooklyn-based Lubavitcher Rebbe alone reportedly has scores of thousands of followers around the world. Other Hassidic groups have prospered in the United States, from the ultraconservative Satmar, with his anti-Zionist stance, to the liberal Bostoner Rebbe, with his outreach policy toward non-Orthodox Jews in his New England bailiwick. In the case of the Bostoner, the rebbe's very title indicated the roots put down by Hassidism in the New World.

It was, however, in Israel that Hassidism experienced its main resurgence. Great Hassidic houses borne on generations of tradition and still carrying the names of the European towns in which they were founded have been established in Jerusalem, Bnai Brak, and other cities. No mere transplants from a world that is no more, these Hassidic sects are infused with a vitality that an occasion exploded into fraternal violence.

The knock on the door came close to midnight. Rabbi Aharon Moshe Schwartz looked through the peephole and saw a crowd of Hassidim he did not recognize. He had already been alerted by the shouts that had broken out moments before on the quiet street where a group of yeshiva students had been posted to guard him. Their attention was apparently being ocupied by a diversionary force while the men now at the door had approached the ground floor apartment via a back alley.

Rabbi Schwartz, a man in his early forties, bolted for a side balcony as the door behind him began to splinter under the force of crowbars. As he leaped into the courtyard, a group of burly young Hassidim was waiting for him. He had time to note that they carried wooden rolling pins that looked as if they came from a bakery. Wordlessly, three of them beat him to the ground, ripping off part of his beard and an earlock, knocking out several teeth, and inflicting head wounds that required 40 stitches.

The rabbi's wife, mother of nine, was knocked aside by the men who crashed through the door as she attempted to telephone the police and the instrument was ripped from the wall.

The assailants worked with smooth professionalism, faultlessly executing a carefully worked out plan with diversionary, mainforce, and backup teams, and quickly retreating in waiting vans. The initial assumption by Rabbi Schwartz's circle was that they were "hit men" imported from out of town—most likely Hassidim from Bnai Brak—but the attackers were in fact Jerusalem-based Hassidim, followers of the Belzer Rebbe.

The incident in Jerusalem's Geula Quarter electrified the city's black-clad, ultra-Orthodox community known as Haredim, literally "God-fearers," a term embracing the entire ultra-Orthodox community, which is generally distinguishable by its black garb. (The commonly used designation, Hassidim, is inappropriate since only about half the Haredim are Hassidim—that is, followers of a charismatic rebbe. The remainder are *mitnagdim,* whose spiritual leadership is drawn from the scholars of the yeshiva world.) The repercussions would also be felt in New York where Hassidim affiliated with the two opposing camps clashed the next day in a bloody brawl.

A Jerusalem journalist probing the incident was startled to discover that the seemingly otherwordly, seemingly passive Haredi community was seething with passions, human drama, and ideological ferment about which the secular community was totally unaware.

To follow the goings-on in this turbulent world, one first has to understand the Hassidic houses as royal courts focused on the majesty of the rebbe, whose title is generally passed on by inheritance.

The Hassidic groupings are indeed called "courts," and the power of the rebbe as a divine agent over his constituency is far greater on a day-to-day basis than an absolute monarch's. Hassidim seek the rebbe's agreement before they open a business, name a child, move house, choose a mate for their children or take any other significant step in their lives. They will not even submit to an operation ordered by a doctor unless the rebbe had concurred.

The rebbe's major deviation from the practices of ordinary royalty is his accessibility. The rebbe must make himself available to his followers several days a week as a mystic intermediary with heaven, a problem-solving godfather, a master social worker, and a bottomless receptable for the outpourings of the human heart.

Looming over the 1978 eruption in the Hassidic community was the enigmatic figure of the Belzer Rebbe. At 31, he was admor (Hebrew acronm for master, teacher, and rabbi) of one of the strongest Hassidic courts in the world—five thousand families and individuals in Israel, ten to fifteen thousand in North America, Europe, and Australia. The group constitutes a dynamically growing empire, and the rebbe is both its lofty spiritual focus and its down-to-earth chief executive.

The admor, Issacher Dov Rokeah, had been groomed for his position from childhood, even though he was not a direct heir to the Belzer throne. The previous admor, his uncle Aaron Rokeah, had lost his own children and grandchildren in the holocaust, from which he himself escaped with his brother, Issacher's father, through Turkey in the middle of the war. When his brother died, Aaron personally undertook the education of his nephew. The boy was only nine when his uncle died.

The Belzer community, through its elders, chose the boy, known by the nickname Berele, as the heir apparent. His mother objected, even going to court to accuse the community of kidnapping her son. "She knew the burden of the position and she wanted to spare him," a member of the Belzer council would later explain.

Under intense pressure from the community, Issacher's mother finally bowed to her son's fate. Berele's bar-mitzvah was an occasion for Belzer Hassidim to gather from all over the world. The event was described in a contemporary account: "Berele, a thin boy with his brown hair falling in long sidelocks, dressed in a black satin buttonless robe, mounted the dais to deliver his first sermon but was rudely interrupted halfway through and told to 'save his wisdom for later on.'"

In the royal manner of Hassidic courts, a suitable bride had already been selected for him by his thirteenth birthday. The bride-to-be was the nine-year-old daughter of the rebbe of Klausenberg. But royal interests change, and when he finally did marry five years later it was to the daughter of another renowed Hassidic leader, the Vizhnitzer Rebbe. After his marriage, he was formally crowned admor of Belz.

Issacher Dov's ancestor, Shalom Rokeah, had founded the dynasty in the small Galician town of Belz more than 150 years before, and it had become one of the most important Hassidic groups in Poland. Thousands of Hassidim made pilgrimmage to the rebbe's court each year. The Belzer were known for their Orthodox militancy and their opposition to innovation, even rejecting an electrical connection to their yeshiva because the cable touched a church. Change began to come with the reign of Issacher Dov's uncle, who dropped his anti-Zionist stance after reaching Palestine. Upon assuming the mantle, Issacher Dov would prove innovative and ambitious, greatly extending the Belz network his uncle had started to build up. The community grew rapidly, with new yeshivas, elementary schools, synagogues, and its own welfare system for members of the community.

"Nothing happens, not even the hiring of a new teacher in one of our schools in Australia, without the rebbe knowing about it," says an aide.

Several nights a week, the rebbe receives petitioners and it is usually well past midnight before the last one has been heard. The petitioners submit their question in writing—a *kvittle*—to a beadle, usually accompanied with a gift offering. These offerings are a principal support of Hassidic houses. Ushered into the rebbe who has had a moment to read the *kvittle,* the petitioner repeats his request for advice or assistance. The rebbe will sometimes close his eyes and commune with himself before responding. Periodically, he will meet with medical specialists, social workers, and psychiatrists in order to butress his own instincts with professional opinion.

"It's much more difficult to be a rebbe now than it was in Europe," says one of the Belzer Rebbe's principal aides. "It's not just the people who come to see him. There are telephones now and they're constantly ringing with calls from abroad. Now there are also many institutions to run."

When the last caller has departed, the rebbe will summon an aide and hand him a list of things to be done—money to be sent to a family, a young man finishing yeshiva to be sent to an established businessman for possible employment, a visit to a religious social worker to be arranged for a couple having marital difficulties.

The constant exposure to other people's problems—problems he is expected to solve—would tax even a saint. "Once, just before Yom Kippur, when the demands for blessings and advice are especially great," recalled one of the young rebbe's aides, "he said to me: 'I wonder how much I can take before I become indifferent to other people's pain.'" That moment of self-doubt passed and the rebbe resumed his burden.

The Belzer Rebbe's empire building brought him in head-on collision with the Haredi establishment in Jerusalem. The ultimate arbiter for most of the Haredi community in Israel had long been the Eda Haredit (Haredi Community). This organization represents the body of ultra-Orthodox who believe that the Jewish state will be restored by the Messiah and that the Zionist enterprise which dared to establish a "secular Jewish" state was a sacrilege. Apart from its political-religious stance, the Eda Haredit provides services such as a religious court in which civil matters are heard and kashruth supervision. Even many Haredim who do not subscribe to the Eda's political views seek out its widely respected religious services and will not, for instance, purchase food that does not carry its kashruth certificate.

In 1979 the Belzer established their own kashruth certification service, thereby directly competing with one of the Eda's principal sources of income. Soon thereafter, it established its own religious court. "We're not deliberately trying to compete with the Eda," said a Belzer official. "But we're big enough to have our own facilities."

These moves caused a strain within the Haredi camp but were not a cause for open warfare. The explosion came with the decision by the Belzer and other Haredi institutions to accept funds offered by the Israeli Education Ministry for Haredi elementary schools. These schools, which comprise some twelve percent of the Jewish elementary students in the city, are outside the state system and derive their income mainly from donations and school fees. Their study regime is grueling—schooldays from 8:00 A.M. until 5:00 or 6:00 P.M., no summer holidays, just a few days vacation around the major religious holidays. It is a regimen that has effectively implanted love and awe of the Torah in generations of young Haredim, who are as animated and mischievous looking as their peers in regular schools.

Only one hour a day is devoted to secular subjects—a bit of arithmetic and Hebrew writing. Hebrew is not taught as a spoken language—Yiddish is the language of instruction.

One of the Eda's prime ideological planks has always been refusal to accept funding from the Zionist authorities so as not to acknowledge the legitimacy of the state. Acceptance of education funds could possibly open the way to state interference in the Haredi education system itself. "We feel that a donor-recipient relation inevitably makes the recipient liable to influence," said an educator in the Eda camp. "They might begin by seemingly benevolent steps like requiring us to give the children summer vacations. Then they might say 'Why don't you teach Hebrew? It's useful for the children to know.' Little by little, things would be altered until the whole frame of our pedagogy is changed."

When the Likud government headed by Menahem Begin made large sums available to these schools in order to win the support of those Haredim who do participate in the Israeli political process, many of the hard-pressed schools succumbed to the temptation. The Eda's supporters reacted sharply. Loudspeaker vans circulated in Haredi neighborhoods, naming schools that had accepted government funds and urging parents to remove their children. Posters denouncing the schools went up on the walls of the religious neighborhoods. A number of school principals were beaten or threatened.

Some schools gave in to the pressure and stopped taking the money. Most of those that continued to accept money were defensive about it. The Belzer, conscious of their growing strength, felt no need to apologize. "There's a right-wing government giving money to left-wing universities and to Arab schools without these institutions being expected to accept the government's ideas," said a Belzer official. "Neither do we."

As Eda pressure continued against the institutions accepting funds, it suddenly found itself being subjected to anonymous counterpressure directed mainly against the Eda's venerable leader, Rabbi Yehuda Yitzhak Weiss. Ads were placed in the matrimonal columns of newspapers giving his home phone number. Numerous tradesmen, including a diaper service, responded to phone calls summoning them to his address. A funeral wreath was delivered to his door. Late one Friday afternoon, the phone in his house began ringing the instant that candles were lit marking the onset of the Sabbath. Since religious law forbade touching the phone on the Sabbath it would continue to ring until sunset Saturday.

The word on the street in Mea Shearim was that the Belzer were behind it all. Belzer officials met with Eda leaders and promised that if evidence could be furnished against any specific Belzer Hassidim, they would be thrown out of the community forthwith. The next day, the Belzer were taken aback to see two of their leaders named on an

Eda poster put up on the walls of the Haredi neighborhoods as owners of a post office box that had served as "the focus of activity" in
the harassment campaign. The youth wing of the Eda came out the
same day with a poster of their own, which directly accused the two
of responsibility for the campaign. There were some who believed
that the poster's real target was the admor himself. The man the Belzer suspected of inspiring the poster was waylaid as he left his home
and beaten. A senior Belzer official admitted to a reporter that Belzer
Hassidim had carried out the attack. "They just gave him a few
slaps."

The same official also admitted responsibility for the attack on
Rabbi Schwartz. The rabbi, a school principal, had been the guiding
force behind the intimidation against schools accepting government
monies, he said. "We decided to teach him a lesson he'd never
forget."

The ferocity of the attack on Rabbi Schwartz, however, appeared
to have had a more pointed motive. The rabbi, an eloquent public
speaker, had reportedly made slighting allusions to the rebbe himself
while addressing the Committee for Pure Education, one of the many
ad hoc organizations that spring up in the Haredi community as new
issues arise.

Had the admor himself ordered the attack or had he been aware
of it beforehand? "Not only was he not involved," said an aide, "He
told us that violence is not the way of the Belzer and never has been."
The men who carried out the attack had not received orders, he said.
"They just felt what had to be done."

Eda sources ridiculed the notion that the rebbe had not known.
"He has his finger in everything," said one. "It's inconceivable that
a large group of his Hassidim would carry out an action like this without his knowledge."

In the wake of the beating of Rabbi Schwartz, both camps began
to organize themselves for street battles. The Belzer called in reinforcements from its yeshivas around the country, students in their
early twenties, who were bedded down in Belzer institutions in the
city. A news photographer passing the main Belzer yeshiva at the
foot of Agrippas Street at 2:00 A.M. one night was startled to see a
large group of young Hassidim deployed in front of the building. As
he stopped to speak to one, a taxi passed slowly and two black-
garbed men could be seen inside. "Scouts from the other side," said
the Hassid to the photographer. "We want them to see us." The Hassid seemed to be clutching something under his coat. When the pho-

tographer asked him what he was holding, the Hassid drew out a large white stave. The other Hassidim did likewise and posed menacingly as the photographer took pictures. The next day, a delegation of Belzer "executives" visited the photographer and asked him to hand over the photographs, saying that "the other side" was capable of taking reprisals against the families of those shown, including students from the United States. When the photographer suggested that they were exaggerating, a Belzer official said, "You don't know these people. They're capable of burning someone's apartment or factory." The photographer, impressed as much by his visitors' bulk as their arguments, handed over the photographs.

Meanwhile, in the Mea Shearim Quarter a mile away, adherents of the Eda—mainly militant Satmar Hassidim—maintained all-night vigils in anticipation of a Belzer attack. A driver passing through the quarter late at night could see figures beneath lampposts or in the shadows watching the passage of his car. In Brooklyn's Williamsburg section, where the Satmar are the dominant Hassidic force, their followers had stormed through a Belzer synagogue in the wake of the beating of Rabbi Schwartz, beating up Hassidim they found there and breaking windows and furniture. In Jerusalem, however, the balance of forces was more even. What promised to be large-scale bloodshed was finally headed off at the very edge of confrontation by the intervention of a rabbi who was a Belzer Hassid and also a relative by marriage of the Eda chief, Rabbi Weiss. He brought about a meeting of the two sides, in which formal agreement was made to desist from provocative actions. The agreement would hold, both sides having recognized where the confrontation was leading.

The Belzer had emerged strengthened from these events, having boldly challenged the Haredi leadership and survived with their integrity intact. The confrontation had not merely been over status but over the new approach to the modern world that the Belzer Rebbe represented. It was not the openness of the modern Orthodox, but it breached the high walls that the traditional Haredi leadership had created around their camp. The rebbe traveled one day to Tel Aviv to visit the Diaspora Museum in order to see models of old synagogues displayed there. He was planning to have similar models built of the institutions in the *shtetl* of Belz, which he had never seen. The visit to the museum was an unusual excursion for a cloistered, Hassidic rebbe, and it had been sharply attacked—before the truce with Satmar—in wall posters in Mea Shearim. A Belzer aide told a journalist that the rebbe had actually visited on a day when the museum was closed to the general public, an arrangement made with the management. "But we're not going to apologize to the Eda Haredi about this," he said. "We don't share their conservative view of things."

Together with other Hassidic houses and yeshiva leaders, the Belzer had come to view themselves as spearheads in the revival of Jewish religious life while the Eda had sat fast behind its walls. "In our lifetimes, European Jewry was wiped out," said the Belzer aide. "Something miraculous has happened since. Hundreds of yeshivas and schools have been built. Tens of thousands of students have been trained. All of us have built this with our own initiative and our own money. The Eda never had a hand in it. They didn't bear the burden.

"The men on the Eda who are against us are just a few frustrated souls. We have no time for this. We need millions of dollars a year to run our own institutions. Our problem is that we kept quiet all these years."

Shocking as they were, these violent episodes were for the Hassidim only passing diversions from a rich inner life nourished on tales of rebbes whose lives were a miracle and whose wisdom a legend. Each court has its own distinctive traditions, history, and dress.

The Karlin Hassidim are known for shouting when they pray. The Amshanov Rebbe in Jerusalem begins Sabbath prayers in his synagogue at 11:00 A.M., long after most others have finished, and concludes at 5:00 P.M. Bratslav Hassidim take taxis one night a week to the hills outside the city, where they scatter among the trees and commune with themselves and with their Maker at the top of their voices. The Bratslav Hassidim have not had a new rebbe since the founder of the house, Reb Nahman, died at the beginning of the nineteenth century, but the chair on which he sat, smuggled out in pieces from the Soviet Union, has pride of place in the Bratslav synagogue on Mea Shearim's main street. On Purim, the puritan fervor of Reb Arele's Hassidim—the most militant in Mea Shearim and known from their frequent clashes with police as Reb Arele's commandos—gives way to alcoholic drink and rousing dancing on table tops.

Hassidim believe that music is a way to the heart of man, and many houses have court composers who set to music liturgical texts suggested by the rebbe. These songs will be sung at the rebbe's *tish* (table) on the Sabbath when the faithful join the rebbe after their own Sabbath meal at home; the Hassidim look on as he partakes of his late night meal and sing rousing Hassidic songs between courses. The Moshnitz Rebbe himself was considered a great composer, and

houses like the Vizhnitz and Gerrer have produced notable reper-
toires.

Knowledgeable Jerusalemites can distinguish between the Hassidic groupings by their dress, which are often based on the styles
worn by eighteenth century Polish nobility. The Gerrer, the largest
Hassidic court in the country, wear their trousers tucked into the
socks just above the ankle. The Belzer wear theirs tucked higher up
on the leg, and instead of conventional shoes wear laceless mocas-
sins. The Belzer's hat appears identical to that worn by the Vizhnitz
Hassidim, but the Belzer's bow is on the left side while the Vizhnitz
bow is on the right. On Shabbat, the Gerrer wear *spodiks,* high conical
fur hats said to have been inspired by cossack headgear. When traveling out of town, the Gerrer remove their long sidelocks from sight by
tying them over their head and tucking them under their hat. This
apparently stems from a European practice when Gerrer Hassidim
doing business with the gentile world sought to diminish somewhat
the strangeness of their appearance.

The most distinctive Haredi dress in Jerusalem is the golden silk
kaftan with dark vertical stripes worn on the Sabbath by those tracing
their heritage not to the European Hassidic houses but to the veteran
Haredi nucleus that had lived in Jerusalem for centuries—the Old Yishuv (settlement). Gray-striped kaftans are worn by a group known
as "the outcasts," who had rebelled against the Vizhnitz Rebbe for
being too cooperative with the Zionist establishment. Students in the
Mirrer Yeshiva, whose forerunners had spent several years in Shang-
hai during the Second World War after escaping the Nazis via Siberia,
wear a tuxedolike coat on Shabbat.

When rebbes meet, protocol is observed as carefully as at any past
assembly of continental monarchs. A delicate question of status arose
over how the new Satmar Rebbe, during his visit to Israel, was to
meet with the head of the Eda Haredit, Rabbi Weiss, who had in
effect challenged the new rebbe's supreme authority on the right-
wing of Israel's ultra-Orthodox, a position the rebbe's prestigious
predecessor had enjoyed. Who was to be considered senior to whom
and who, therefore, was to host whom? In a brilliant solution worthy
of a Hapsburg royal chamberlain, it was decided that Rabbi Weiss
would be "vacationing" in an ultra-Orthodox suburb on the road
from the airport at the time of the Satmar Rebbe's arrival. The Satmar's party duly stopped off at Rabbi Weiss's retreat, where the two
men drank a toast, neither of them the host. Rabbi Weiss then joined

the Satmar on the ride into Jerusalem. It was a meeting devoid of one-upmanship, and respect was accorded to each man's honor.

With a truly princely view that acknowledges another royal presence even across the field of battle, the Satmar called on the venerable Gerrer Rebbe, the principal Hassidic leader on the political left wing, who accepted state funds for his schools and indeed participated in Israel's political life through his key role in the Agudat Yisrael Party. The visit lasted only several minutes and was followed by an even shorter return visit by the Gerrer. Despite the evident tension, the latter, as a matter of respect, asked for *sherayim*—a portion of some food from which his host has already partaken. The Satmar bit into an apple after making the appropriate blessing and then handed it to the Gerrer who did likewise.

In the wake of the beating of Rabbi Schwartz, the black curtain of the Haredi world had parted to permit outsiders a glimpse of a multifaceted world alive with ambition and passion. Visible too was the urgency of growing empire and threatened tradition. A great Hassidic house had risen out of the ashes of the holocaust and was feeling its way with increasing confidence through a new world. The pale boy shouted down at his bar mitzvah had grown into young manhood and taken on the elders whose word had been law. Men of God sought vengeance with rolling pins. Above it all was the image of a young admor, alone in the silent center, contemplating heaven and earth.

F I V E

Made in Heaven

The Matchmaker

IN THE MARRIAGE MARKET OF MEA SHEARIM, Taub works the margins that heaven itself seems to have overlooked.

"I specialize in problems," is the way he puts it.

His days are spent in the study hall of a *kollel*, or advanced yeshiva for married men whose lives are devoted to studying Talmud. They receive a small stipend, which often is supplemented by working wives and sometimes by generous in-laws. Many, however, find other supplementary forms of income, often by tutoring. Taub's main sideline is money-changing, but he has also established a small reputation as a *shadchan* or matchmaker specializing in finding mates for men and women against whom the Almighty has stacked the odds.

"The Haredim I handle—how shall I say it—don't adjust well to society. They pray too much or pray too loud or study too much or fast too much. They're people who have had breakdowns or have emotional problems or have a bit of a peculiarity. I don't want you to think my work is easy."

He has slipped out of the study hall into a side room where he often takes a tea break. There is a samovar on a table. Here he receives clients who want to buy or sell dollars or to find a mate for their children. In the intimate world of Mea Shearim life is not compartmentalized.

Taub's face is framed by a black, broad-rimmed hat and sidecurls. He has luminous, slightly Oriental eyes that shift from cherubic glint to a trader's wariness as the occasion warrants. He is about forty-five but looks younger.

Besides the emotionally disturbed, says Taub, he also handles Haredim born of mixed marriages—that is, a marriage in which one of the parents is Sephardi. He also deals with pure-blooded Sephardim who have studied in Haredi yeshivas in Mea Shearim and have gone "black"—they not only dress in the dark garb of the Ashkenazi Haredis of European extraction but want to marry an Ashkenazi girl schooled in Haredi ways. From Taub's intonation one gathers that a somewhat addled Ashkenazi rates higher in the Mea Shearim marriage mart than a stable Sephardi trying to "marry in."

What kind of girls does he find?

"I look for a girl who has a problem, but not with the head." This problem could be physical—something wrong with a hand or leg—or a matter of *yikhus* (family heritage) or the girl's personal situation—"she may have no family or want to get away from her family."

It is a delicate balance matching handicap with handicap but basically no different from the ones struck in the free market outside, a mutual calculation of assets and alternatives.

"I make it clear to both sides what the problems are."

An old woman enters and asks Taub in Yiddish how much she can get for a dollar check. Taub pulls a slip of paper out of an inside pocket and checks the day's black market rates, which are a bit higher than the banks'. There is a bit of haggling leavened on Taub's part with good humor and the exchange is made. As the woman gathers up her shekels she asks Taub whether he can find anybody for a nice "Morocconer" girl who comes into her husband's shop. "*Ah gitte meidele* [a good girl]," she says. Taub evinces no interest. His clients, both Ashkenazi and Sephardi, are not interested in Moroccan girls, no matter how nice.

His problem-clients are all male, he explains, because there are no known emotional problems among Mea Shearim females before marriage. "The girls here are not known in the community, and if there's a problem the family doesn't talk about it. The boys are seen every day in synagogue and the yeshiva and the street and are known but the girls are seen maybe once a year outside the synagogue."

Moshe, a handsome young student who married just two months ago, has ambled in and joined the conversation. He lived for six years across the street from his future wife, he says, but never saw her before the matchmaking. "Not even on the street?"

"Well, maybe once."

The young couple meet for the first time in an apartment in the presence of both sets of parents. After the introductions and some general conversation, the elders go into another room and leave the young couple to talk. The door between the two rooms remains slightly ajar. It would not be seemly to leave an unattached young man and woman alone in a closed room.

What do they talk about?

"Well, the girl will probably ask what he's studying," says Taub. "Sometimes they don't say anything. The girl is usually shyer."

Moshe, the young groom, thinks about something and smiles. Sometimes, not always, the couple will meet on their own again before marriage.

Does an option exist for the boy or girl at this point to say no?

"Not really," says Moshe. "We know that our parents have looked into it and we trust their choice." Taub demurs. The young people have the right to turn down the offer and that right is sometimes exercised.

A youngish man wearing the striped caftan of a Hassidic sect enters. He is David, Taub's partner in the *shadchan* business. David has just been checking out a prospective bride. "She's looking for someone *gur frimme* (strictly religious) who wears a caftan," he reports. Dress in Mea Shearim is a clear indication of religious style.

What percentage of marriages in Mea Shearim are arranged by *shadchanim*? "One hundred percent," says Taub. "Even if the parents know each other well and think that their children are a wonderful match for each other they will want to arrange it through a *shadchan*. This way, terms are worked out through a middleman without embarrassment."

Where the parents do not know the prospective bride or groom, they will make inquiries. The girl's father, for instance, may want to *farher* (examine) the prospective groom's talmudic learning or he will go to the head of the boy's yeshiva to inquire about him. The boy's parents will make inquiries about the girl among those who know her family.

Scholarship is a prime attribute among the boys. As for the girls, says Taub, "they should have common sense and good values and should not be stubborn." Beauty, too, is an asset, he says. "The Talmud advises that the man should see the girl before the match and not rely only on a *shadchan*."

The boys are usually eighteen or nineteen, and the girls perhaps a year younger. After marriage, the girls usually work at teaching, accounting, or some clerical job until the first child is born.

The marriage terms include an apartment for the couple. Despite
the low income of most Mea Shearim families, they manage to raise
the money with the help of relatives, friends, and loans.

The two sides normally split the costs of the wedding, apartment,
and furniture evenly. In cases where the groom has an emotional
handicap, his side is often willing to cover all costs. There is also
sometimes a stipulation in writing that if the young man suffers a
breakdown, his family will cover all medical expenses.

"The doctors say that marriage is often the best medicine," says
David, flicking cigarette ash on the floor. "It creates a different atmosphere." As for the girl in such a mating, says David, "It gives a
framework of home and family. It gives fulfillment. The man may
have a problem but he's not a bad man and he can make a good
husband."

If the young men discover after the wedding that they have acquired somebody impossible to live with they generally hunker
down, entrust their fate to the Almighty, and produce heirs in fulfillment of the religious edict to "be fruitful and mutiply." The girls,
however, for all their sheltered upbringing, often assert themselves
in such circumstances and go for divorce.

Enter Reb Simha Gottleib. He has asked Taub, an old friend, to
find a match for his son Aaron, who is not a hard case but, on the
contrary, a young *talmid khochem* (scholar). Taub says he has found a
very good prospect but the girl's parents insist on a *beit*, or double
exchange, which would also involve linking their available son with
Reb Simha's daughter, Chava. Taub says he doesn't know anything
yet about the boy. Reb Simha is leery. "I'm not going to marry off
one at the expense of the other," he says.

Reb Simha is a worldly man who knows how the mating process
works in the Haredi world abroad. It costs more to marry off a child
in Israel than in the United States, he says, because in that land of
rental apartments an apartment purchase is not part of the arrangement. In Israel it is the general practice to buy an apartment.

Reb Simha also disagrees with Moshe about the young man or
young woman not being in a position to say no after they have seen
each other. "It's true that the option is not exercised very often but
it's available. The young people understand that their parents have
chosen the other family on the basis of compatibility, a similar outlook
on life, and that the young person will have that outlook too. But
they can always say no. Only in the case of marriages between the

offspring of Hassidic leaders is there no choice. It's a marriage between dynasties, not between a young man and a young woman.''

All things being equal, the numerous subgroups within Mea
Shearim marry their own kind. Thus members of the various Hassidic
houses will find mates for their children within their own camps.
Hassidim will not usually marry their children to those of *mitnagdim*
from the traditionally anti-Hassidic yeshiva world, and Lithuanians
will usually not marry Hungarians. It is when there is a special
problem that matches may be sought outside the community. The
standards in such cases may be altered somewhat but they are not
abandoned. And in the end, a match is almost always found. ''Ninety-five percent of the people here are married off,'' says Taub. ''It
isn't right for someone to be alone.''

He leans toward a visitor and the cheerful glint shades into confi-
dentiality. ''You don't by chance happen to know of a suitable girl,
do you?''

Returning to his Mea Shearim home from the yeshiva study hall
one day, Reb Simha found Pinhas the *shadchan* waiting for him.

''What are you selling today?'' asked Reb Simha.

He knew that the matchmaker would likely be offering a prospect
for either Reb Simha's twenty-two-year-old son, Aaron, or nineteen-
year-old Chava. There had been such feelers for some time, although
Chava had made it clear she was not interested in a match until her
older brother was married off. In ultra-Orthodox Haredi circles in the
United States girls of marriageable age are often paired off before
older brothers because of social pressures on them, but in Mea
Shearim girls might wait until they were twenty-six or so if an older
brother were slow in fulfilling the commandment to ''be fruitful.''
Pinhas had even invested in telephone calls to New York and London
on prospects for Aaron but nothing had yet worked out.

This time the matchmaker had a surprise. He was offering a double
match with another brother and sister. Reb Simha had been uninter-
ested when the prospect was raised by Taub but time was passing
and he would now not dismiss the idea out of hand. Pinhas had come
to the apartment early to sound out Reb Simha's wife, Ruth, who
had power of veto in the matter. She had expressed interest and Reb
Simha after hearing the identity of the other prospective family—the
Katz family—agreed to let Pinhas proceed. The Katzes had fourteen
children. Simha did not know the children being proposed, but he

had heard of the father who, like himself, was a full-time scholar who received a small stipend from the *kollel* where he studied.

Pinhas, an energetic man in his thirties, himself spent his days in yeshiva study, but like many of his fellow married scholars pursued a sideline that earned him a livelihood of sorts. His father had been a *shadchan* too and had matched Reb Simha and Ruth. Matchmaking is a hardnosed, grueling business that Mea Shearim residents realize is best left to professionals like Pinhas and not to kindly uncles. A matchmaker's fee is fixed by the local rabbinic court at $500 from each side for every successful match, or $1,000 total. In Haredi communities abroad the *shadchan's* fee is higher, a percentage of the cost of the wedding. For a *beit* in Mea Shearim it would be double—he is marrying off twice as many people—but, experience had shown, so would be the *shadchan's* aggravation.

Pinhas had wasted little time after mutual friends mentioned that the Katz brother and sister might be on the marriage market. Without informing Reb Simha, he knocked on the door of the Katz apartment across town the next night and introduced himself. Reb Reuven Katz knew of Reb Simha and indicated interest in the proposal. At Pinhas's request, he spelled out the support he would be willing to offer the two young couples toward the cost of their apartments and furniture and toward the cost of the wedding itself. Reb Reuven's wealth was not in worldy goods and his financial offer was modest. Too modest, suggested the matchmaker. Could he supplement it somehow? Reb Reuven said that one of his married sons would be able to offer an additional sum if his initial offer were unacceptable to Reb Simha. But this possibility was to be spelled out to Reb Simha by the matchmaker only if he rejected the initial offer.

It was the next day that Pinhas confronted Reb Simha with the possible double match and described the brother and sister involved. When asked what financial conditions were being offered, Pinhas as an honest broker mentioned only Reb Reuven's initial proposal.

"Not enough," said Reb Simha.

"Well, he can add a bit," acknowledged Pinhas, spelling out the proposed supplement.

That was still not enough, but Reb Simha, after mulling it over, suggested a possible solution to Pinhas—that the matchmaker himself attempt to elicit a certain sum from one of Ruth's relatives, who had the means of raising money but with whom Reb Simha was not on good terms. Pinhas readily agreed. A few hours later he was back at Reb Simha's apartment.

"He's agreed."

Reb Simha looked at the matchmaker with a new respect and agreed to begin formalities by receiving Chava's prospective groom Moshe, the next evening. It would be on relatively neutral grounds—the apartment of Reb Simha's married son, Haim—rather than Reb Simha's own apartment, since it was necessary to maintain formal distance as long as nothing had been concluded.

Summoned from his yeshiva bench and informed by his father that a possible match had been found for him, nineteen-year-old Moshe Katz was visibly taut when he entered the apartment for his meeting with Reb Simha. Accompanying the youth was a married older brother and Pinhas the matchmaker.

The main purpose of the meeting was for Reb Simha to test the youth's grasp of the Talmud. Moshe had prepared a brief talmudic dissertation, but he appeared so nervous that his brother, a yeshiva headmaster, headed him off and said to Reb Simha, "Let's you and I have a *dvar torah* [learned discussion] first." The brother expanded on a talmudic passage and Reb Simha responded with his own observations. For five minutes the two men engaged in a high-level intellectual exploration and then, in the hope that the digression had permitted the young man's tension to ease, they turned to Moshe. The young man took a deep breath but his mouth shut again.

"*Nu,*" prompted Pinhas the Matchmaker.

Fixing his gaze on Reb Simha, Moshe began his dissertation. From time to time, Reb Simha quietly interrupted to challenge a point or ask for clarification. The youth responded well. After ten minutes, Reb Simha nodded to indicate that he was satisfied. Moshe had displayed a clear mind and a good grasp of his subject. As Moshe rose, Reb Simha shook his hand and wished him a formal "gutte nacht." After the young man and his brother had gone, the matchmaker turned to Reb Simha with another "Nu?"

"I'm willing to consider him," responded Reb Simha, "but I'd like to meet with him again for '*mili d'alma*' [a talk on worldly matters]."

"It will be arranged," said Pinhas.

The next day, Shabbat, it was Aaron Gottleib's turn to unveil his scholarship before Reb Reuven. Reb Simha's son went to the prearranged meeting place accompanied only by the matchmaker, and by all accounts performed brilliantly before his prospective father-in-law.

Now it was the turn of the prospective brides. Each was to meet with her prospective mother-in-law for a general conversation. This occured Saturday night at two different meeting places in Mea

Shearim. Like Henry Kissinger, Pinhas believed in pushing negotiations without leaving time for second thoughts. Instinctive first thoughts, after all, are usually more reliable than calculating second thoughts.

Aaron's prospective bride, Ruchele, came to the apartment of Haim Gottleib accompanied by the matchmaker and her mother. Haim's young wife—who herself had undergone the same ordeal just a few years before—sat with Ruth and attempted to put eighteen-year-old Ruchele at her ease. The girl, who had studied to be a seamstress, proved to be lively and self-confident. The report to Reb Simha afterward was that Aaron would be getting *"ah metsiya,"* a catch.

Later in the evening, Ruchele's mother was the hostess in a nearby apartment as Ruth brought Chava for introductions. A devout girl, nineteen-year-old Chava Gottleib was a *"balabusta"*—a homemaker who cooked well and sewed and worked as a kindergarten teacher in a Haredi school.

Pinhas saw immediately that Mrs. Katz was impressed. There were still, however, some loose ends to be tied up and such loose ends, Pinhas well knew, had lost many a *shadchan* his commission. Reb Simha was at that very hour supposed to meet with his prospective son-in-law in a local yeshiva for their worldly chat. Reb Simha found Moshe going over a Talmud in the rear of the nearly empty study hall.

Walking with the young man through the alleys of the Bait Yisrael quarter, his hands behind his back and still wearing his Shabbat *shtraimel* (a round fur hat). Reb Simha began seemingly idle conversation about mutual acquaintances, about the yeshiva where Moshe studied—Reb Simha himself had studied there at one time—and about Moshe's family. Gingerly he let drop more weighty subjects like political attitudes. Reb Simha had been making his own inquiries about the boy in the past couple of days and knew from mutual acquaintances that Moshe was largely apolitical. This was confirmed in the conversation. It did not trouble Reb Simha. What would have troubled him, even to the point of barring Moshe from the family, would have been the youth's entertaining political convictions directly contrary to his. In the holy land, Reb Simha liked to say, politics is not irrelevant to religion, it *is* religion. Moshe's mind worked well and he was able to unbend somewhat as they talked. When they parted, Reb Simha permitted himself a smile as he said *"gutte nacht."*

Reb Simha had also asked for a meeting with Ruchele Katz. Although the common practice in Haredi circles is for this end of a match to be looked after by the mother-in-law to be, Reb Simha told Pinhas, "I don't want to meet her for the first time after the wedding and say 'I'm your father-in-law.'" The meeting was arranged the next night at Haim Gottleib's apartment and Reb Simha was delighted by the girl. When Pinhas had initially mentioned the Katz children to Reb Simha, he had described the boy as "a *lamden*" (scholar) and the girl as dutiful and "*shain*" (pretty)—her physical beauty was quite striking. He had not, however, touched on the girl's quicksilver charm.

Meanwhile, Ruchele's father has asked for another meeting with his prospective son-in-law after learning that his own son had been invited to meet Reb Simha a second time. However, this was not a worldly conversation but another talmudic examination. "*Zug eppis*," say something, Reb Reuven had said, meaning expound on any learned subject you choose. The scholarly Aaron had no trouble in fulfilling the request.

Pinhas, who had been dashing between the various venues to collect the reactions of all concerned, found almost all systems go. Only one hurdle remained—the youngsters who were to be married off now had to meet each other.

The first encounter the following night was to be between Aaron Gottleib and Ruchele. Reb Simha and his family were waiting in his elder son's apartment when the matchmaker arrived with the Katz family. Watching Ruchele enter the room behind her parents and warily scanning the faces around the long table, Reb Simha could almost feel the click as her eyes met Aaron's. Leaving the young couple sitting opposite each other at the table, everyone else repaired to the large kitchen, where Haim's wife offered tea and cake. She had deliberately left no food on the living room table to emphasize the businesslike, noncommittal nature of the meeting between the two young people. The door to the living room was left slightly ajar for form's sake but the conversation could not be overheard.

What became apparent as time passed, however, was that the conversation was animated. Every once in a while, one of the fathers would look in too see if the youngsters had finished but would be waved off by his respective child. After forty-five minutes, Reb Simha opened the door and, with a smile, said "I think you've talked long enough." Pinhas did not have to wait for the parents' report to know that at least this match had been made in heaven.

Heaven was more circumspect about the other half of the *beit*. When Chava met her prospective groom later that night she found him tense and shy. He avoided her eyes and his head was bent. "I'm not sure," she told her mother afterwards. "I'd like to meet him again."

Reb Simha, who knew Moshe's nervousness to be a transitory thing—but probably unlikely to give way in another meeting with a girl—suggested to Chava that her older brother have a conversation with Moshe instead. Chava agreed. Since they were small children, Chava had looked up to Haim and respected his opinion—even more so, Reb Simha knew, than she respected his own.

The conversation between Moshe Katz and Haim Gottleib, a gentle person and a scholar just a few years Moshe's senior, took place the next day. The young man was able to unbend and speak freely. When it was over, Haim gave his sister a very favorable report. Chava was totally assured. When Haim reported this to their father, Reb Simha asked, "Is she certain?"

"Certain," said Haim.

All the pieces had now fallen into place.

The following night, both families gathered in Haim's apartment, the womenfolk assembling in the kitchen while the men sat around the living room table for *der vort*—the word, or the drawing up of the formal document committing the parties to the marriage of Moshe and Chava. The prospective grooms and brides stole glances at each other through the open kitchen door. The main element in the document drafted by Pinhas was the financial undertakings of the two fathers, and it quickly transpired that there was a difference of opinion as to what had been agreed upon. Voices were raised before Pinhas' deft interjections produced a satisfactory formula.

Haim, who wrote in a beautiful script, made a copy of the document for his side of the family and one of Reb Reuven's sons did likewise. Two yeshiva students living in a next-door apartment had been called in as witnesses. One of them handed a towel to each of the fathers in turn. In accepting the towel—it could just as well have been any other object—the parents were committing themselves to the marriage and the *tnaim* (terms of the memorandum). Moshe and Chava were then asked if they accepted the document and each replied affirmatively, "*Hain*," Chava responding from the kitchen doorway. The fathers and witnesses signed both copies of the memorandum. The two mothers then entered the room with an earthenware dish and together flung it to the floor, shattering it in small pieces as all present shouted *"mazal tov."* The act signified the wish that, as the pieces of earthenware could never again be joined, so might this wedlock never be sundered.

The families then piled into a minibus to make the trip to another apartment to repeat the ceremony for Aaron and Ruchele. The bus made separate trips for the men and women. With the breaking of the second earthenware dish, a mighty round of *"mazal tovs"* went up. Remaining modestly in the background with a weary, reflective smile was Pinhas. One week had passed since he had first knocked on Reb Reuven's door, and two new families were on the way to being created in Israel.

The prospective grooms received complete sets of the Talmud as gifts from their fathers-in-law and the brides-to-be received watches. Haim inscribed the Talmud set given to his brother-in-law with elaborate calligraphy. Although the two brides were forbidden to converse with their grooms again before marriage, they quickly became close friends with each other.

The young men, as their weddings approached, were fitted with *shtraimlach* with the wide brims of the old Yishuv—veteran Jerusalem families—to which their families belonged (distinguished from the narrow-brimmed *shtraimlach* of the Hassidim). They were also provided with *djubes*, brown capes to be worn as a Sabbath garment above their caftan. The brides were also provided with wardrobes.

Chava and Moshe married before the next Passover, Ruchele and Aaron before the High Holidays. Ruchele's father had died a week before the wedding and her eyes under the wedding canopy were moist with tears. Under a verbal agreement stipulated by Reb Simha, apartments were found for both couples within the walled compound of Mea Shearim where he and his other son resided. Although poor as a churchmouse, he had never had doubts about being able to raise his half of the money among family and friends.

"In America," Reb Simha would say later," even in Haredi circles, when a couple meet they want to know how they will live for the rest of their lives. They go out one hundred times for coffee to talk and assess each other. Here in Mea Shearim the future is not discussed at all. Only the past. How they were brought up and how they conducted themselves and how they lived. From this we determine the future."

Are the results any different? "Are they ever!" says Reb Simha.

"Check the divorce rates among Haredim in America. You don't have that here.

"In Mea Shearim, the match is the culmination of an open life style and education which has shaped the young people for everyone to see. The future we leave to God."

S I X

The God Fearers

MAYOR KOLLEK HARDLY NOTICED THEM when he entered the synagogue, but the group of boys with earlocks watching him go in from across the street were swallows that signaled the storm. For months, Kollek had been the target of verbal attacks in the ultra-Orthodox community over a series of disputes in which the mayor had supported the secular population against the Haredim. He had been invited this Sabbath to address the congregants in the Persian Synagogue after morning prayers. The subject of his "sermon" was the growing violence in the ultrareligious camp emanating from the adjoining Mea Shearim neighborhood.

A crowd of more than one hundred ultra-Orthodox men were waiting when he emerged. Sensing trouble, half a dozen members of the Persian congregation, still wearing their prayer shawls, accompanied the mayor as he started to make his way down the street. The area was closed to Sabbath traffic and the mayor's car was parked half a mile away. The crowd began to follow, and the men in front shouted epithets at Kollek. The shouts grew louder as the pace quickened. Suddenly a bottle was thrown, shattering against a stone wall above Kollek's head. A broad-shouldered man in black Haredi garb pushed through the protective ring and knocked the seventy-two-year-old mayor down with a blow. Others rushed in and began kicking him and beating at him with sticks. The mayor rose and hurried

81

on but the crowd caught up with him and knocked him down again. A bottle thrown by a youth skipped off the pavement and caught him in the forehead. Three more times, the mayor was knocked down and kicked before two policemen summoned by telephone came running up the street, the mob scattering before them.

The savage beating of Mayor Kollek in 1983 was the most brutal expression of a dark new spirit that emerged within the city's ultra-Orthodox community after the Six Day War. Seemingly the least likely sector of the population to turn violent, the ultra-Orthodox displayed a fanaticism fed by a sense of growing demographic strength. Producing twice as many children as any other sector of the population including the prolific Arabs, the "ultras" began to sense that the future was theirs. The "Arab problem," on which Jerusalem focused in the first decade after the Six Day War, had given way to the "ultra-Orthodox problem" as the city's major demographic concern.

In the Jerusalem Theater, filled as usual for its Saturday-morning forum on current events, the voice of one of the participants on stage grew faint as he leaned back in his chair.

"Talk into the flowers," came the cry from the audience.

The speaker leaned forward and spoke directly into the large bouquet on the table, his voice reverberating clearly in the hall.

The burial of a microphone within a spray of gladiolas is one of the ways the secular Jewish population copes with the Sabbath in Jerusalem in the face of increasingly powerful and intimidating nature of the ultra-Orthodox community. Use of a microphone is a desecration of the Sabbath, according to the ultra-Orthodox, who would make a holy row if it were openly permitted in a public building. The solution was the hidden microphone—hidden at least from sight even if everyone knows about it.

Such mild subterfuges are regular Sabbath fare for the city's secular Jews—a majority that increasingly feels itself a beleaguered sect. Even visiting the Israel Museum on the Sabbath with one's family requires a slight dodge. The box office selling tickets is closed, but if one has not had the foresight to purchase tickets the day before, there is a pickup truck parked alongside the box office from which an Arab gentleman will sell a ticket at the regular price, unofficially of course.

It would be an exaggeration to say that the secular Jews of Jerusalem feel like the early Christians hiding in the Roman catacombs but at least one day a week, the seventh, they must acknowledge that they do not set the rules. To drive from north Jerusalem to central

Jerusalem entails a wide swing around ultra-Orthodox neighborhoods whose streets are protected from traffic for the day by police
barricades at the direction of the city council. Already on Friday afternoons, well before sunset ushers in the Sabbath, ultra-Orthodox vigilantes descend on the Mahane Yehuda marketplace to demand of any
stall owners still hawking vegetables that they shut down immediately. Before the sun goes down on Saturday afternoon, other
bearded vigilantes patrol downtown streets to ensure that cinemas
and fast food shops do not open before the Sabbath has officially
ended.

Up to a certain limit, most secular Jerusalemites find a definite
charm to living in the Middle Ages—living in a city where at least
one day a week one is spared the sound of buses and the clamor of
commerce. There is no city in the world where one feels the tranquility of the Sabbath, indeed its holiness, as tangibly as in Jerusalem.
On the seventh day, Jerusalem truly rests, and it is a blessing appreci-
ated by the secular almost as much as by the Orthodox. Driving a few
extra minutes to avoid the ultra-Orthodox neighborhoods and similar
inconveniences are a small price to pay for this respite.

The situation, however, is far more serious than an accumulation
of inconveniences. The seculars feel threatened by the growth and
increasing militancy of the Haredim. For decades, Jerusalem has been
developing as an ultra-Orthodox citadel at odds with the liberal spirit
prevailing in the rest of the country. In Tel Aviv, it is almost impossible to find a seat at an outdoor cafe at two o'clock on a Sabbath morning. In Jerusalem, the streets are as silent as a monastery well before
midnight, and for the seculars "going out" means to visit friends. A
journalist who moved to Tel Aviv after years of living in Jerusalem
felt suddenly light to the point of giddiness as if some heavy spiritual
burden that had lain upon him without his being aware of it had been
lifted. Although neither he nor his friends were religious, he had kept
a "semi-kosher" kitchen because Jerusalem seemed to demand it.

Long regarded as a picturesque anachronism on the fringes of Jerusalem society, the Haredim have become the most dynamic element
in the city. Strong convictions and special demands they have always
had. Now they also have numbers.

According to municipality figures, Haredim constitute 27 percent
of the Jewish population of Jerusalem. While some authorities put the
figure at 20 percent, all agree that the Haredim are growing more
than twice as fast as the rest of the population.

The prospect of a Haredi takeover of Jerusalem, which in the past had been a fanciful notion raised by secular circles to amuse or frighten themselves, has come to be seen as a demographic possibility. Indeed, if one is slave to demographic clocks, it would seem a near certainty.

Two striking demographic developments were marked in Jerusalem in the two decades after the Six Day War—the Arab birthrate fell by more than half while the Jewish birth rate rose. Despite the determination with which East Jerusalem's Arabs sought to maintain their separate national identity, more than twenty years of proximity to Israeli society has induced a change in the most intimate aspect of their lives—the rate at which they have children. The average Muslim woman in Jerusalem had 9.7 children in 1967 (an average that included women who did not bear children at all). By 1983, this figure had fallen to 4.5, and it has continued to fall as Arab society emulates the Western standards it has been exposed to. Although the fertility rate among Sephardi Jews from Arab countries countrywide also declined, from 6 to 2.8, the Ashkenazi rate moved in the opposite direction, rising from 2.5 in the 1960s to 2.8, the same as the Sephardim. By comparison, the average among white American women since 1973 is 1.7. There is no separate figure for American Jewish women but demographers believe it is even less than 1.7. The Ashkenazi growth in Israel, which has bucked the broader Western trend, was seen by demographers as an expression of a life force, a clear desire to propagate a society.

Nowhere was this life force more clearly expressed than among the Haredim, almost all of them of European origin, who produced more than twice as many children as the national average. This growth was most significant in Jerusalem, the main Haredi center in the country, where the demands for expansion of Haredi living space created a permanent source of friction between the ultrareligious and the rest of the population.

Even before the Six Day War, the Mea Shearim Quarter, where Haredim first settled a century before, had burst its bounds. A new "Bible belt" was created along the northern edge of the city. The Haredim preferred this border zone, despite its potential dangers opposite Jordanian military positions, because it was isolated from the rest of the city and permitted Sabbath to be marked without interruption by traffic or other secular incursions.

The Six Day War shattered this tranquility. In the early 1970s, violent Haredi protests along the road to one of the new neighborhoods in East Jerusalem, Ramot, became a regular Saturday feature in Jeru-

salem. The road passed just below the "Bible belt" and infringed on
its Sabbath peace. For many months, these protests were marked by
violence, with young Haredim throwing stones at cars and scattering
before charges by mounted police. In time, the protestors confined
themselves to shouting and eventually this too died away.

It was not, however, the silence of surrender. As the residents of
Ramot watched in dismay from their hilltop in the late 1970s, black-
clad residents from the inner city began in ever increasing numbers
to drive out on the Ramot Road themselves—not to protest, but to
move into the new neighborhood.

Reluctant at first to leave their self-made ghettos in the inner city,
the Haredi community had come to realize that the new neighborhoods were the answer to their most urgent need—adequate housing.
Young couples, whose numbers were growing at a fast pace, need
not content themselves anymore with a dismal one-room flat on the
edge of Mea Shearim but could obtain for a reasonable outlay modern
three-room apartments being built by the government in the new
neighborhoods.

The Housing Ministry made a conscious decision not to build separate neighborhoods for the Haredim. The inclination of the Haredim
is to insulate themselves as much as possible from the influences of
the secular world, particularly since such influences could affect Haredi youth and tempt them from the way of their fathers. The ministry
could not ignore the desire of the Haredim to live together in homogeneous communities, but it preferred directing them to enclaves
within larger secular neighborhoods. Thus, they would enjoy their
own ambience but would, in their daily comings and goings, at least
brush up against the broader community and sense that they themselves were part of it. It was an admirable intention but, as the ministry itself would eventually acknowledge, it proved a failure.

It was again at Ramot that the first signs of Haredi indigestability
were perceived. In a near repeat of the fracas over the Ramot Road,
the Haredim now living in Ramot protested at the plan to build a
large public swimming pool in the neighborhood, on the grounds
that the idea of men and women bathing together offended religious
laws of modesty. Once again, after a long and bitter fight, the secular
community won and the pool was built. By this time, however, the
seculars had learned that winning a battle against the Haredim did
not mean winning the war.

As the quarter assigned to them in Ramot filled up, the Haredim
began buying apartments in adjoining quarters as they came on the

market. The appearance of the first black-garbed Haredi on the block was often sufficient to start secular residents thinking about moving. Jews they might all be, but Jerusalem had supplied the seculars sufficient evidence that once the Haredim comprise a large enough percentage of the population they become so assertive that there is literally no living with them.

On Shmuel Hanavi Street on the fringe of the Mea Shearim Quarter, for instance, a number of so-called secular families constitute an enclave within an ever-expanding Haredi tide. Like most of Jerusalem's seculars, almost all light Sabbath candles, go to synagogue at least on the high holidays, and follow a traditional Jewish life-style. They also, however, drive their cars on the Sabbath. After repeatedly finding their tires slashed on Sunday mornings, the residents learned to park their cars well away from the neighborhood during the Sabbath if they intended to use them. There and in other mixed neighborhoods, secular residents lower their radio and television on the Sabbath so they cannot be heard outside—partly as a courtesy to their Haredi neighbors, partly out of fear of militant Haredi passersby.

In several cases in recent years, apartments of seculars on the fringe of Mea Shearim have been firebombed or vandalized when objection was taken to the residents' ''Bohemian'' lifestyle or the presence of single women. Even conventionally Orthodox Jews, including rabbis, have moved from their old neighborhoods when ultra-Orthodox, with their uncompromising views on religion and politics, began to move there. In extreme cases, Haredi militants have threatened seculars with bodily harm or arson if they refuse to sell their apartments on the fringe of the inner city ghettos. In one year, police reported ten such threats.

Although this element of thuggery might be marginal to Haredi society, it has become a persistent feature. The Haredim themselves use the word *kana'ut*, jealousy, to describe this zealotry. The term derives from the Biblical story of Pinhas, the grandson of Aaron, who impaled with his spear an Israelite who had intercourse with a woman of Midian in the sight of all the congregation in an evident challenge to Moses' moral leadership. ''And the Lord spoke unto Moses saying: Pinhas . . . hath turned away my wrath in that he was very jealous for my sake so that I consumed not the Children of Israel in my jealousy.'' It is the duty of the faithful to draw their brethren's attention to their transgressions, say Haredi leaders. The *kana'im*, however, choose to cast a spear rather than an imploring glance. They divide the world between believers and *freierim*—free ones, a pitying or derogatory term for nonbelievers who are "free" of any religious sustenance. Even young children among the *kana'im* speak of the nonreligious as a doomed and dissolute race, not as fellow Jews who have not yet seen the light.

Mayor Kollek's severe beating was one of the more notable examples of this streak of Haredi violence. There were many others. A paint store next to a large yeshiva was gutted after some of the students had warned the owner to get rid of a pretty young saleswoman who was apparently too distracting an influence. In one year, the windshields of seventeen cars passing the fringes of the Haredi quarters were shattered by rocks and eight persons injured. One of them was a Hebrew University geneticist who suffered temporary speech difficulties and loss of memory. "There's a reluctance to move against the Haredim because they all look like our grandfathers," said Mayor Kollek. "But when stones are thrown and people are hit and the mayor is beaten up, things are getting out of hand."

The secular residents of Ramot where well aware of this history when their Haredi neighbors started spilling out of their quarter. Ramot was planned for 10,000 apartments, of which some 1,200 had been slated for Haredim. By 1987, some 7,000 had been built and Haredim occupied 1,300–1,500, according to the Housing Ministry. With 10 percent of the Haredi families in Ramot having eight or more children, the figure was considerable. "Within a few years," said Rabbi Menahem Porush, head of the ultra-Orthodox Agudat Yisrael party in Jerusalem, "Ramot will be 50 percent Haredi or more."

Ramot's seculars were determined that this would not happen. For the first time in Jerusalem, a secular community attempted in an organized fashion to divert the seemingly organic growth of the Haredi enclaves in order to preserve their own way of life. "We're here and we're going to stay here," said Lou Gelehrter, an architect who was one of the leaders of the Ramot seculars. "This is a strong population, and it's not going to run."

The seculars succeeded in blocking rezoning that would have permitted the Haredim to build additional synagogues, ritual baths, and yeshivas in the non-Haredi sections of Ramot—facilities essential to Haredi communal organization. At the same time, the seculars lobbied for pools, tennis courts, horseback riding, and other facilities in these areas, not only as an attraction for seculars but to repel the Haredim, who prefer to distance their youth from such distractions. At the same time the Ramot seculars pressed the authorities to provide the Haredim with alternative housing elsewhere to meet their legitimate needs.

On this point, the national government and the municipality split on a fundamental issue—should the Haredim be regarded as Jews or as anti-Zionists? Esoteric as this point may sound, it would ultimately affect the physical planning of Jerusalem and its metropolitan region.

Haredim had historically opposed the Zionist enterprise. After the state's founding, the bulk of Haredim came to accept it, but conditionally. The Agudat Yisrael grouping agreed to send representatives to the Knesset but not to sit in the government. The bulk of Haredi men avoided full military service: those who entered the army did so only after years of yeshiva deferment. They often served in reserve auxiliary units such as the chaplaincy after minimal basic training. The Haredim operate an independent school system that takes no note of Israel's Independence Day or of national issues more contemporary than those discussed in the Bible.

The problem confronting the authorities is that the Haredim are not just part of the Haredi-secular demographic equation in Jerusalem but part of the politically more important Jewish-Arab equation. Should they, as Jews, be encouraged to live in Jerusalem by specifically allocating them housing in order to maintain the Jewish-Arab ratio at roughly seven to three, or should they, as non-Zionists, be encouraged to live outside the city in order to leave room for Zionists—both secular and religious nationalists—so as to have a more meaningful Arab-Zionist ratio?

The municipality adopted the former attitude—that the Haredim, whatever their beliefs, constituted warm Jewish bodies which could maintain the Arab-Jewish ratio. With the slowdown of secular Jewish immigration, municipal planning officials argued, there was no other source to draw from. The municipality proposed that the Haredim be directed to a new development at Ras Amar in northeast Jerusalem. The site is located on an isolated hill set back from road arteries, permitting the residents to seal themselves off on the Sabbath.

However, the Housing Ministry wanted the Haredi overflow to be directed outside the city. It began constructing a satellite town at Betar a few miles southwest of Jerusalem, which it designated as an entirely Haredi town. Haredi leaders said emphatically that they wanted Ras Amar, not the periphery of the metropolitan region. The ministry remained convinced that in the early 1990s, when there is no more room for Haredi expansion inside the city, they would be happy to move to Betar.

Mayor Kollek and others have warned that if present trends continue, Jerusalem will have a non-Zionist majority consisting of Haredim and Arabs within a few years. This could happen by the year 2000, when even by conservative figures, Haredim are expected to constitute 18 percent of the citywide population, and Arabs are expected to constitute 30–32 percent. A possible portent of things to come was the announcement, just before the Palestinian uprising in 1987, by an East Jerusalem newspaper editor, Hanna Seniora, that he intended to head an Arab list in the next municipal elections. The bulk of East Jerusalem's Arabs have chosen to retain their Jordanian citizenship rather than adopt Israeli citizenship but under Israeli law they are eligible as residents of the city to vote and to stand for office in municipal elections. It is well within the realm of political possibility to envisage a Haredi-Arab coalition on the city council in the future, particularly since the Arabs are also religiously conservative. The amiable Seniora, in fact, has been a guest along with other Arab personalities at Haredi weddings held by antistate Neturai Karta families in Mea Shearim. (A PLO-linked Palestinian from Gaza attending a Mea Shearim wedding smiled when he saw the groom being lifted on a chair by dancing Hassidim. "When I visited my relatives in the Galilee after 1967," he told an Israeli at his table, "I was puzzled at seeing the bride and groom being lifted on chairs at Arab weddings. It hadn't been a custom when I grew up there before 1948. Now I know where it came from.")

However likely or unlikely this future possibility might be, the Haredim pose a problem in the here and now for Jerusalem's secular residents. Scores of bus shelters around the city have been gutted by Haredi arsonists protesting against what they termed "pornographic" advertising. While some of the ads indeed offended even secular citizens, Jerusalemites forced to wait in the rain for buses unprotected had few words of understanding for the Haredi cause. The city's numerous sports fans were deprived of a decent field where they could watch their local soccer heros after the Haredi community, in a major effort, succeeded in blocking construction of a modern stadium on the grounds that it was too close to their neighborhoods. They then attempted to block plans for its construction well away from their neighborhoods—this time on the grounds that such "Hellenistic" innovations are unseemly for the holy city. The Haredim, in short, are still battling against the Hellenizers, who, more than two thousand years ago, propagated the splendid culture of the pagans from the western sea.

The battle being waged between the seculars and Haredim is part of a battle for Jerusalem's soul that is little less significant than the battle between the Jews and the Arabs in 1967 for Jerusalem's body. The struggle is between ultras confident that the future is theirs and moderates, including the modern Orthodox, increasingly concerned about their place in a holy city that grows ever holier.

"The authorities have to decide what kind of Jerusalem they want," said Ramot activist Gelehrter, "a saintly city or a pluralistic city. *La patrie est en danger.* We must save Jerusalem."

From the middle distance, the distance from which most communities view each other, the split between Haredi and secular Jews seems as basic and unbridgeable as the split between the twentieth and eighteenth centuries or the split between Arab and Jew. Sometimes, however, an individual is able to make the crossing and return—marked forever by the passage.

S E V E N

The Police Spy in the Yeshiva

FROM THE COMMANDER'S WINDOW on the second floor of Jerusalem police headquarters, vans full of arrested Haredim could be seen driving into the courtyard entrance to the lockup. Ranks of police reinforcements, wearied by weeks of intermittent skirmishing, were getting their final briefing before moving off again to Mea Shearim, where they would be sent into action behind water cannon. The commander, however, was not looking out. He had seen the scene often enough as the city's ultra-Orthodox community regularly erupted into violence.

The growing militancy of the city's ultra-Orthodox had culminated in 1972 with acts of arson against a sex shop in downtown Jerusalem and other targets, as well as the desecration of the graves of Zionist leaders—including the grave of Theodor Herzl, visionary of the Jewish state. The Hebrew word *keshet* (rainbow) had been painted at the site of these attacks, indicating that a single organization was behind them. Until now, the police had been dealing with a known quantity—a population responding to leaders of their community whose calls for demonstrations were openly broadcast in public speeches and wall posters. Now the police found themselves up against a secret organization whose strength, objectives, and ultimate level of violence was unclear. Would they stop with arson? Anything was conceivable.

It was imperative that the police find out who these people were and what they were up to. Could an agent be slipped into Mea Shearim to find out? This was what the police commander and his intelligence chief were discussing as the men below moved off toward the ultra-Orthodox quarters. Such an infiltration had apparently never been accomplished before. In a notorious case in the early 1950s, when a nine-year-old boy had been abducted by Haredi zealots from his secular father, Prime Minister David Ben-Gurion had ordered the Shin-Bet, Israel's vaunted Security Service, to devote the bulk of its resources to his recovery. Several months later, the boy was tracked down in Brooklyn, but the task had been accomplished by external sleuthing, not by infiltration of an agent into the Haredi community. Although Israeli agents had penetrated the Arab world with great success, there had been no known deep penetration of the Haredi world by the security services. Only recently, a Neturai Karta activist from the Tora V'yira Yeshiva had told a reporter that the police could never plant an agent in Mea Shearim. "Everyone here knows everyone else—where he comes from, who his father is, how he grew up, what he thinks. There's no one here who isn't what he's supposed to be."

The police commander believed that an infiltration plan now on the table could work. It would require an agent young enough to be a yeshiva student, someone who spoke passable Yiddish, someone with the wit and resilience needed to make the difficult crossing. A likely candidate had been identified and he was now ushered into the room.

Curly-haired and with a good-humored, impish air about him, Hanan was twenty-three but looked younger. He sat down opposite the senior officers and at the gentle prodding of the commander described his background. Born in the Tel Aviv area, he had been raised in a religiously traditional home. His father did not wear a hat during the week but often went to synagogue on Saturdays. Hanan himself spoke a broken but serviceable Yiddish. He had joined the police as an investigator the year before, after receiving his B.A. from Hebrew University, and was now studying for his law degree. What did he think of the Haredim? He did not despise them or think they were criminals. They contained the same elements of black, white, and gray as any other community, he said. This broad attitude, unshared by most of his colleagues in squad room debates, had reached the ears of the senior command and was one of the reasons Hanan had been selected. The task could be accomplished only by someone who could identify with the people he was being sent to spy on. When the mission was proposed to Hanan, he accepted it immediately. Apart from any effect on his career, it promised to be immensely interesting. Virtually all he knew about the Haredi world was what he had read of it in the works of S. Y. Agnon, Israel's Nobel Prize–winning novelist. Mea Shearim was only three hundred meters from Jerusalem police headquarters in the Russian Compound, but for Hanan it would be a long-range, possibly hazardous reconnaissance into uncharted territory.

The penetration was cleverly conceived and swiftly executed. Dressed in jeans, Hanan presented himself at a yeshiva outside Mea Shearim specializing in *ba'alai teshuvah*, (penitents)—nonreligious Jews seeking to "return" to religion—and was taken to see the principal. Hanan described himself as the son of Israelis who had emigrated to America. Tired of the fleshpots, he had come back to Israel on his own in order to search for his roots. Since the Six Day War, "penitent" yeshivas in Jerusalem had been awash with young men and women from abroad and from Israel searching for spiritual meaning. Hanan was welcomed like a returning son and by the next day was devoting himself intently to study.

At the end of the first month, he requested another meeting with the principal. He was thankful beyond words for the world of the Torah that had been opened to him, he said, but he felt himself ready now for even more demanding study—at one of the yeshivas in Mea Shearim. The principal, who had seen this process of intensifying religiosity among the born-again often enough, wrote a note of recommendation to one of the "black" yeshivas in Mea Shearim—the designation deriving from the color of the clothing worn by the Haredi ultra-Orthodox. The note praised Hanan as a diligent student with a quick grasp. In swift succession, he maneuvered himself from the recommended yeshiva to other yeshivas in search, he said, of the right one for him. With his tracks thus blurred, he arrived at Tora V'yira, the bastion of the militant Neturai Karta in the heart of Mea Shearim, and was duly accepted. The Neturai Karta activist who had said "There's no one here who isn't what he's supposed to be" would spend months in the same small yeshiva study hall with a police agent without the slightest suspicion.

In the coming four months, Hanan lived his role to the full. At the usual pace of the penitent, he had gradually shed his "American" clothing and taken on black dress. A beard soon made him unrecognizable to those who knew him in his other life. Rising before dawn, he would pray with *der ershte minyan*—the earliest prayer group—and spend the day and much of the night in study. In the yeshiva system of *chavruta*, he studied with a partner, the pair explaining, exploring, debating the meaning of the talmudic text. Periodically, the partners would change. Hanan came to feel a foxhole intimacy with these students who shared with him an intellectual adventure. On Thursdays, they would study late into the night for the oral examination they would be subject to on Friday morning.

The spirituality of Sabbath in Mea Shearim was an experience that not even his reading of Agnon could have prepared Hanan for. With his new-found friends, he would attend the *tish*, or communal Sabbath repast, of *rebbes* in the quarter and join in the singing and dancing.

All the while, his ears were open to the political undercurrents in Mea Shearim. They did not, he discovered, run deep. "Nothing is secret there," he would say later. "There is no anonymity. Everybody knows about everybody." There was no underground and no serious conspiracy, he would report to his superiors. Just a few militants who were considered eccentric even within Mea Shearim. He had asked his friends to meet Reb Amram Blau, head of the Neturai Karta. It was not an unusual request since many wanted to meet the charismatic figure. Hanan found an elderly man with the face of a child that seemed to radiate light. It was, he would say years later, the face of "a real *tsadik* [righteous man]."

All in all, the inhabitants of Mea Shearim, he found, were innocents—not just of guilt but of guile. They lived in poverty, but not a poverty that deforms. Those who had a little more helped those who had a little less and there was much *matan beseter*—giving anonymously. He himself, when he moved into a room in the Mea Sharim compound after joining Tora V'yira, was helped with contributions of clothing, sheets, food, and other necessities by people who had little more than the bare necessities themselves.

In the social hierarchy, the pinnacle was reserved for the learned, rather than the wealthy. The ultimate authority, Hanan learned, were the *gdolai halacha*—the sages of Jewish law—from whose judgments there was no appeal.

In his conversations with his fellow yeshiva students in Mea Shearim, Hanan found that quite a few were afflicted with doubts about the basic "givens" of orthodoxy. An eye is kept on backsliders by a "Modesty Brigade," one of the many ad hoc organizations in Mea Shearim charged with one or another aspect of religious life in the community. If a yeshiva student is spotted, for instance, going into a cinema, his rabbi will be informed and the student will be summoned for a talk. If he is spotted again, the Modesty Brigade may take direct action. *"Kanaim pagu bo* [zealots beat him]," Hanan discovered, was a phrase that dissociated the Mea Shearim leadership from direct involvement.

During his undercover months, Hanan's situation was similar to that of an agent dropped behind enemy lines, except that the lines in this case were a fifteen-minute walk from his squad room. The knowledge that you could walk away anytime you chose increased the need for motivation to stick it out. In Hanan's case, the motivation was provided by the fascination of learning about a rich new world.

During a Sabbath demonstration in Sabbath Square, in which Hanan participated, he was seized in a police charge and hustled into custody along with a number of other Haredim. The arresting officers were friends from headquarters precinct but they did not distinguish this bearded, black-clad Haredi from the others identically clad and bearded. In the police lockup in the Russian Compound, he managed to surreptitiously get a message out to a senior police officer, one of the few who knew of his new identity. Shortly thereafter, the cell door was opened and the whole group told to go on home

Apart from this brief jailing, Hanan never left Mea Shearim during the four months after his entry and his communication with headquarters was via a "drop," where he left and received messages. He would believe that his reports had a moderating effect on the police command in their attitude towards the Haredi community.

Hanan's very success in playing his role would cut it short. As an eligible young man, he found himself under increasing pressure from his yeshiva mates and rabbis to take unto himself the bliss and obligations of marriage. A matchmaker was discreetly brought into the picture, and Hanan one day found himself being escorted to an apartment by a coterie of chaperones to meet a young woman and her family. Hannan wasted no time in contacting headquarters. It was time to get out.

The extrication was executed with the same adroitness as the insertion. Hanan informed his principal and his yeshiva collegues that he had received a message from his parents in New York that his grandfather was dying. He was to catch a plane the next day. His comrades insisted on accompanying him to the airport to see him off. After warm farewells, Hanan took the escalator to the departure lounge and headed immediately for a men's room where he changed into "civilian" clothing. His yeshiva comrades had long since departed when he descended from the other side of the building, himself once more. Reaching home, he looked at his bearded face in the mirror for a long moment before shaving away the last physical remnant of a life that already seemed like a dream. He then lay down to a long and deep sleep.

Promoted for his dazzling performance to a job in national police headquarters, Hanan would remain in Jerusalem for another decade but would have no dealings with Haredi questions nor would he enter Mea Shearim. In the mid-1980s, he left the police to go into law practice in Tel Aviv.

Hanan had felt no anthropological detachment from the people he had gone to observe, particularly the young men with whom he had spent most of his waking hours for months and who had shared with him not only their minds but their souls, including their doubts.

Years afterwards, he encountered one of his study partners while walking in downtown Jerusalem. The Haredi looked quizzically at Hanan's bareheaded, unbearded face, recognizing it as familiar but unable to place it. Hanan did not pass him by. Identifying himself, he explained that he had returned to the secular world and was now a lawyer. He had found he could not live a Haredi life, he said. "I decided it wasn't for me." The Haredi tried to persuade him to come back for a Shabbat to Mea Shearim—to meet his old friends, to attend a rebbe's tish—but Hanan demurred. Nevertheless, he resumed contact with several of his former friends. He would telephone before holidays to extend greetings and ask about their families. He would even meet sometimes with one particularly close friend—the meetings taking place in the secular part of the city. On one occasion, he returned to Mea Shearim to attend the wedding of the son of one of his friends to whom he had given his home telephone number. It was known in Mea Shearim that Hanan had returned to the secular world but this was not an unusual event. He did not tell any of his old friends there of his police connection but the story was leaked in 1986 to a reporter by a police official. Hanan assumed, correctly, that the ensuing article was called to the attention of those who knew him in Mea Shearim and he did not attempt to resume contact.

In telling his own children about the experience, Hanan attempted not to oversentimentalize life in Mea Shearim. "I don't want them to become penitents, and I point out that not all the light is there in Mea Shearim nor all the darkness here. I want them to have the values of

Judaism and that means first of all to be a mensch. It isn't only Judaism that has values. All religions do but part of our personal identity is that we're Jews." Although he was not tempted to become a penitent, the enthusiasm he developed for Talmud study was not feigned and he would in later years peruse a Talmud tractate in his home from time to time.

Less than a year after discarding his Mea Shearim uniform, Hanan had temporarily donned another uniform, fighting with his reserve unit through the harrowing battles on the Golan Heights in the Yom Kippur War. For some time after he returned home, he would recite kiddush at his Friday night meal.

He does not think he will ever see the sons of his Mea Shearim *chavruta* wearing a military uniform. "And it's a pity. They'd be good soldiers. They're idealists and they'd fight for what they believe. And the experience wouldn't harm them either."

His experience in Mea Shearim left Hanan convinced that, between the Haredi and secular worlds, there is more that binds than separates. "I see us as one people. We've got to talk to each other, not provoke each other. When you talk, you see that the other side doesn't have horns. You don't throw stones at someone you talk to. Divisiveness only brings troubles." The agent sent to spy upon the enemy had discovered that they were his brothers.

E I G H T

The Hassid Who Loved Nietzsche and Hated the State

GRAY-BEARDED AND GAUNT, he looks older than fifty-nine, but the yellowing newspaper clippings of thirty years before describe him accurately, if inadequately, as a twenty-nine-year-old zealot.

To reach his garret workshop, one climbs exterior wooden stairs so steep as to require the use of hands. In this aerie above the rooftops stretching toward Mea Shearim, Leib Weisfish looks out upon a world that encompasses more of heaven and earth than most men see in a lifetime. On a worktable are vises, strips of leather, and glue pots used in making tefillin, the phylacteries worn by Orthodox men on their arms and foreheads during morning prayers.

"Do you know Nietzsche?" asks Weisfish. It is the third sentence he has spoken beyond the proprieties, and it is soon evident that only great self-restraint prevented it from being the first.

He settles into a battered easy chair next to a small bookcase containing Nietzsche's works in Hebrew, German, and English. There is also a Hebrew version of Tolstoy's *Kreutzer Sonata*. A small photograph of a white-bearded Tolstoy is pinned up on the wall. "He looks like the head of a yeshiva," says Weisfish. Near it is a picture of the greatest of all cantors, Yossele Rosenblatt, whose scratchy records are still treasured among the cognoscenti, striking a singing pose as he stands on a skiff on the Jordan River—"He died the next day in Jerusalem," notes Weisfish. Above it is a placard containing quotations from Diogenes.

Once the most notorious man in Israel, Weisfish is virtually unknown today outside the Haredi community, and even there he is regarded with the tolerant amusement reserved for eccentrics.

Militant anti-Zionism won him the attentions of the state, including four months' imprisonment for crossing into Jordan in what was believed then to be an attempt to escape army service. Infatuation with Nietzsche, who wrote that God is dead, lost him his credentials in the militant ultra-Orthodox camp.

Fanatic seems an inappropriate term for a Mea Shearimite who quotes approvingly from Stevie Wonder and attacks his life's foe, political Zionism, with wit rather than abuse. "The national anthem," he says, "isn't hatikva [hope], it's" "The Whole World's Against Us,' [a satirical Israeli pop song].''

Weisfish is, or at least wants to be, a believer. His life, from the time he grew up in a Jerusalem orphanage, has been a search for a worldview that would incorporate both the God he would not forsake and the tragedy that would not forsake him.

The search has taken him where few others who retained the faith have dared to go—a reconnaissance of the soul that risked despair, madness, and agonizing loneliness but was pursued relentlessly.

Born into a family that had lived in Jerusalem for 150 years, Weisfish was one of seven children. The family was desperately poor. One of his brothers died of malnutrition during World War I before the British captured Jerusalem from the Turks in 1917. A benchmark in young Leibele's life—he is still called by that affectionate diminutive in Mea Shearim, but resents it—was the death of his father. His mother was unable to look after all the children, so six-year-old Leibele and a brother were placed in an orphanage.

The orphanage offered austerity and a barrackslike discipline, with which Leibele was able to cope during his ten-year stay there, but what afflicted him without end was the loss of his father. "I was very attached to him. He lived simply and with an internal restraint. He was forty-two when he came down with a cold and died of pneumonia a week later. I missed him very much." The expressive face turns inward. "I still do."

The beginning of political consciousness came at the age of fourteen with the murder in Jerusalem of Jacob de Haan by the Hagana, the incipient defense organization of the Zionist movement in Palestine. De Haan was another eccentric character whose restless mind had carried him from Jewish Orthodoxy to anarchism, Christianity, Zionism, and back to ultra-Orthodoxy as a leader of the then militantly anti-Zionist Agudat Yisrael, which plotted with Arab nationalist leaders against the Zionists who would create a secular Jewish state.

"I wanted to know how Jews could kill Jews in cold blood," says Weisfish. "I began to interest myself in the conflict between religion and Zionism. I felt helpless at this 'European' invasion of Jerusalem and the destruction of religion. I had an instinctive feeling that the modernizers [the Zionists] were not justified."

At seventeen, Weisfish was already a combatant in the ranks of Agudat Yisrael. The antireligious atmosphere was much more poisonous in those days than in contemporary Israel—in Jerusalem, the Jewish Workers' Council deliberately organized a festive meal on Yom Kippur.

Enrolling in a yeshiva in the Tel Aviv suburb of Petah Tikva, Weisfish encountered the Tnuat Musaar (Moral Movement), a tradition of the great yeshivas founded in Lithuania, which emphasized the study of ethics and morality. With its philosophic probing and its references to Plato, it was a radical departure from the closed world of the Jerusalem yeshivas he had known.

"I was electrified. I felt the need to search more into the chaos around me, to find the place of Judaism. Within my loneliness and yearnings for the past, I searched for substance."

He began to visit the libraries of Tel Aviv to read works by the wordly philosophers. Such excursions into the world of secular thought were sternly frowned upon in the yeshivas, and he led his rabbis to believe that he was doing research into Jewish thought.

In 1936 the Arabs of Palestine launched a guerrilla campaign aimed at stopping the inflow of Jews from Europe, which threatened to tilt the demographic balance in the country. As attacks on the Jewish community mounted, the majority of Aguda leaders began to cooperate with the Zionist camp. Young Weisfish was active among the anti-Zionist diehards who broke away to establish Neturai Karta as an independent anti-Zionist organization. He was forced to leave the yeshiva after right-wing elements in the Jewish underground had made inquiries about his whereabouts after discovering that he was the author of an anti-Zionist tract published anonymously in a nationalist Arab newspaper.

A terrible depression seized Weisfish as he saw "the street" steadily increasing its hold on the Jewish community. Between the two world wars, many of the ultra-Orthodox young in Palestine were lured from the fold by the glitter of the secular world and of Zionism which pledged to build Jerusalem in this world, rather than await the descent of the heavenly Jerusalem that the sages had promised with the coming of the Messiah.

Zionism, Weisfish argued, turned religion into a political tool. He again read Jeremiah and Isaiah, and it was as if he were reading a prophecy made about the coming destruction. Weisfish decided to seek his own Jerusalem in eastern Europe. There, he heard, was the bastion of real *yiddishkeit*. There were the great yeshivas, the great scholars, the great Hassidic courts. There were the Jewish masses still uncorrupted by false prophets. The only thing that prevented him from embarking on the trip to Lithuania, heart of the yeshiva world, was lack of money for a ticket. This time, poverty would prove Weisfish's friend, for in a year, war would come and the Jewish world of eastern Europe would be consumed forever.

Left to contemplate the horrendous riddle of the holocaust, Weisfish found himself turning more and more to the secular philosphers. "I wanted to know what Hitler thought. He wasn't a dog. He was a human being and he thought. I had to search."

In the Hebron Yeshiva in Jerusalem to which he had transferred, Weisfish found kindred souls who read and discussed Kant in secret. One day he entered a library on the fringe of the Mea Shearim Quarter and settled down to read Spinoza, the Dutch Jew excommunicated for heresy by the rabbis of his time. As the young yeshiva student sat reading in the silent library, he began to weep. "For the first time, I encountered a psychological analysis of man."

He was in his early twenties when he left the yeshiva world in order to establish himself economically. He found work in a small diamond plant in Netanya on the coast and there met a former yeshiva student, now nonreligious, who told him about the German philosopher whom Hitler had taken as his ideological fount. The friend lent him a copy of *Thus Spake Zarathustra*, the only book by Nietzsche translated into Hebrew at the time.

Weisfish saw immediately that Hitler's reading of Nietzsche "was a perversion—that the power that Nietzsche's 'superman' strove for was power over himself, not over others." Beyond this, however, Nietzsche's boldness of thought and insight left Weisfish mesmerized. In the subsequent decades, the ultra-Orthodox Jew would be transformed into a "Hassid" of the German Christian philosopher, convinced of Nietzsche's divine wisdom. Nietzsche's writings included anti-Semitic remarks as well as praise for the Jews, Weisfish would concede. He insisted, however, that the philosopher regarded the Jews more highly than he regarded his own Germans. "He admired the Jews more than the Jews do themselves. The Jews were the only people he admired."

While the Nazis had distorted Nietzsche, says Weisfish, the Zionists had distorted him a generation earlier. "Already at the First Zionist Congress in 1897, there was an argument between two distinguished delegates, Ahad Aham, who said that superman was a superman of the mind, and Berdychevski, who said it was a superman of power." Those who take Nietzsche's statement "God is Dead" literally, says Weisfish, are misintepreting a man who in the depth of his soul was the greatest of believers.

Weisfish returned to Jerusalem from Netanya and was soon active in the inner leadership circle of Neturai Karta. The establishment of the state in 1948 presented him with a major new crisis. There were secret meetings in Mea Shearim and the ultra-Orthodox town of Bnai Brak of small groups of militants who discussed the creation of an armed ultra-Orthodox underground that would rebel against the state. Of all those participating, Leib Weisfish was the only one who took the idea seriously enough to try to implement it.

Weisfish is one of those unsettling people who carry the logic of their conviction past the bounds of convention. Reading in the newspapers that the Arab League was holding an organizational meeting in Cairo, he decided to attempt to reach Cairo via Jordan.

"I wasn't trying to escape the draft," he says of his plan. "I crossed into Jordan to get weapons and money for an armed underground. Without arms you're nothing. We needed supplies and a hinterland. People asked, 'How can you kill Jews?' But what did the Hasmoneans do when they wanted to purify the temple?" The Arab League, he hoped, would provide the help the underground movement would need.

Aside from studying Arabic, reading the Koran, and informing Neturai Karta leader Amram Blau of his plan, he made no other preparations.

He slipped into Jordanian territory at Bait Safafa in southern Jerusalem in the early summer of 1950, carrying only his tefillin and a Berlitz book on English. The fence dividing the Arab village between

Israel and Jordan had been trampled down and Weisfish just walked across.

Dressed in a black coat and hat, he startled the Arab workers in an ice factory on the border when he suddenly appeared and asked them to bring their soldiers. Two Jordanian Legionnaires quickly arrived. They blindfolded him and led him to a police station. On the way, someone came up on horseback and struck him on the head, the only blow he was to receive during his seven months in Jordan.

After extended questioning at police headquarters by officials who seemed uncertain that they understood his halting English correctly, Weisfish was confronted by a short civilian with a round, genial face who addressed him in Hebrew. Who was he and why had he come, asked the man. Weisfish repeated his tale, this time at length. When he was done, his interrogator opened a bag and to Weisfish's astonishment produced a Bible in Hebrew. "Let us study a bit," said the interrogator. The man, Hamdi Nubani, was a Jordanian journalist who had undertaken Jewish studies at Hebrew University in the 1930s. He had been asked by the police to speak to the bearded intruder only in Hebrew to win his confidence and establish whether he really was what he said he was. A brief incursion into the Bible was sufficient to establish Weisfish's bonafides. Weisfish asked Nubani to tell the Jordanian officials that his object was to have the Jews of the country living under Muslim protection. "Islam protected the Jews for thirteen hundred years," he said.

Weisfish spent most of the next seven months in a Jordanian military prison camp across the Jordan River—part guest, part prisoner. He had been taken on a visit to the Western Wall, met the Jordanian foreign minister, and been permitted to study the Bible periodically with Nubani. But his one-man political initiative met no response. Jordan, he discovered, was at odds with Egypt, and there could be no passage to Cairo. The hoped-for Arab hinterland, it appeared, was a troubled political swamp. Offerd by Jordan to return to Israel through the Mandelbaum Gate or to go abroad, he opted to return. "I was lonely for my family."

The transfer of the bearded Weisfish through the crossing point under UN auspices was a major story in the Israeli press. Ensconced in prison, he disdained a lawyer and told his family to inform the authorities that he was mentally disturbed. When a psychiatrist was dispatched to talk to him, Weisfish confided that there was something wrong with his head. "If someone says he's crazy," said the doctor, "it's usually a sign that he's not." Seeing that this tack would get him nowhere, Weisfish said that he had been an orphan and that his nostalgia and yearning for the world of the past made if difficult to confront the reality of today.

This self-analysis struck close to the psychiatrist's own reading. He told the District Court Judge before whom Weisfish was tried that the defendant's tragedy was an overdeveloped sense of responsibility. The court sentenced Weisfish to six months' imprisonment. The lenient sentence was part of a deal worked out with the state under which Weisfish would leave the country upon release from jail.

Before going into exile in the United States, Weisfish enrolled in an English course and read the New Testament. He had indicated to his prosecutor, Attorney-General Haim Cohn, that he would not engage in anti-Israel activities abroad but he was soon passing out anti-Zionist pamphlets at the United Nations. He made such a nuisance of himself that after twenty months the Israeli government revoked his passport and had him repatriated to Israel.

Weisfish settled down to life in the Zionist state, establishing his own workshop for producing tefillin and fathering eleven children. He became known as the "foreign minister" of Neturai Karta, serving as liason with journalists, diplomats, and other messengers from the outside world, a task for which he was uniquely suited within the closed world of ultras.

The Neturai Karta leaders were uneasy at the enthusiasm with which Weisfish took up his task. "They used to ask me why I read *Haaretz* [Israel's leading newspaper]. When I asked if they were willing to, they said no. I said 'Then I will. Somebody must watch them.' To fight Zionism, I had to learn all kinds of idolatry."

Although he saw himself as spying out the enemy camp, the world outside Mea Shearim plainly intrigued Weisfish. Life itself intrigued him. He crossed the city to knock on the doors of Martin Buber, Hugo Bergmann, and other leading philosophers from Hebrew University and introduce himself. He would often go to their homes to borrow books and discuss philosophy. "I told Bergmann that Hitler had distorted Nietzsche and he said I was mistaken. He was the rector of Hebrew University and I thought, well what do I know. Then Thomas Mann came here and gave a talk in which he said that Nietzsche had been distorted by Hitler." After David Ben-Gurion, whose government he had wanted to topple by force, retired from the premiership and settled in Kibbutz Sde Boker, Weisfish traveled down to the Negev to see him. The two men argued for hours about Greek philosophy in the retired premier's hut at the edge of the desert until Ben-Gurion's wife came in to put a stop to it.

Israel Eldad, a former idealogue of the right-wing Lehi underground movement, met Weisfish shortly after the publication of the first volume of Eldad's translation of Nietzsche into Hebrew in 1969. Close to 10:00 P.M. one night there was a knock on the door. Eldad opened it to a bearded stranger who did not bother to introduce himself. "Do you think there's any significance to what you've done in your life?", began the stranger as he entered the room. "The politics, the writing, the translations? I've come to tell you you're wrong. You've acquired your place in the Hereafter with your translation of Nietzsche."

Weisfish began a dialogue whose first part ended only when Eldad shooed him out at midnight. They would maintain contact over the years in one of the strangest friendships in Jerusalem—between an ultranationalist and an ultra antinationalist who sought to bring down the state by force of arms.

A similar Nietzsche bond would years later bring Weisfish together with the attorney-general who had prosecuted him upon his return from Jordan, Haim Cohn. The latter had gone on to become one of Israel's most respected Supreme Court justices and leading civil libertarians. A mutual respect had existed from the time of the trial between the eccentric Weisfish and Cohn, long before they discovered each other's interest in the German philosopher. After Cohn's retirement from the Supreme Court bench, he agreed to Weisfish's request to appear with him in a public lecture on Nietzsche. The former judge introduced Weisfish but also took the occasion to expound his own learned views. The hall was packed with a population mix rarely seen in Jerusalem—black-clad ultra-Orthodox and secular men and women.

Weisfish regards himself as the world's leading authority on Nietzsche but has declined to write a book about him for fear that he still does not understand him sufficiently. His self-appraisal is not shared by other Israeli philosophers. "His thoughts are very confused and eccentric," says one, "Nietzsche was ambivalent about the Jews—he admired their will to live but not their historical role and the fact that they gave birth to Christianity. Weisfish has developed the positive side of Nietzsche's ambivalence. He sometimes speaks to the point but his thoughts aren't connected."

Weisfish attempts periodically to organize an international conference on Nietzsche in Jerusalem. From his desk he produces a letter from Professor Walter Kaufman of Princeton, one of the world's most prominent philosophers, written shortly before his death in reply to Weisfish's conference proposal.

Kaufman terms Weisfish's views "very interesting, the more so for being rather unusual. Most Nietzsche scholars see Nietzsche quite differently. Your suggestion that the only thing he admires was Judaism and the Jews strikes me as quite odd and I should think that few people will agree with you on that."

Kaufman's reservations do not disturb Weisfish. His principal goal is to create a Nietzsche House in Jerusalem to serve as a center for Nietzschean studies. He would also like to see Nietzsche's remains buried on Mount Zion. In the meantime, he would like to visit the philosopher's grave in East Germany.

Weisfish himself has a low opinion of modern philosophers. But he has a great respect for the late Buber, the foremost modern scholar of Jewish mysticism, whose secular mind spoke to him with greater relevance, Weisfish admits, than the great Jewish religious philosophers.

"You ask a religious Jew 'Do you believe in God?' and he'll say, 'Sure I believe in God. Don't bother me.' There are so many penitents today that the religious are saying, 'Maybe there really is a God' They don't ask questions—Why God? What God? I had to explore the metaphysical foundations of Judaism."

His exploration has taken him across the range of human experience. The secular religion of modern times, nationalism, has absorbed much of his attention. "Nationalism is outdated in today's world of technology. Everyone knows it except the politicians who are hanging on to their seats. Soon you'll be able to fly around the world in an hour. What is the meaning of borders? Stevie Wonder says music cuts across boundaries and languages. He's right. Barbara Streisand makes a record in America and they're singing it the next day in Hong Kong."

If nationhood is not an answer for Weisfish, neither are earthly utopias like the kibbutz. His cousin, Nahum Sarig of Kibbutz Bait Hashita, is a former commander of the elite Palmah strike force and one of the outstanding personalities of the kibbutz movement. Weisfish is on good terms with him and has stayed over at Bait Hashita as well as at other kibbutzim where he has been invited to talk about Nietzsche.

"The kibbutz is a childish illusion based on the destruction of the family," he says. "It is generating not individualism but invalidism.

There is no personal responsibility. A father in a slum area worries about where he will earn bread for his children tomorrow. Not in the kibbutz. It is a fatal spiritual anesthetic. The kibbutz today is only an economic monastery.''

Weisfish still remembers enough of the Arabic he learned before his crossing into Jordan to serve as a translator for Neturai Karta leaders seeking contacts in East Jerusalem. He accompanied one man who wished to invite a leading East Jerusalem dignitary to the wedding of his son in Mea Shearim. In the middle of the conversation in the Arab leader's salon, Weisfish pulled out a copy of Nietzsche and began quoting from it enthusiastically in broken Arabic. Displaying sublime eastern courtesy, the host heard him out politely and accepted the wedding invitation.

Aside from such occasional translation service, Weisfish has long since stopped playing an active role in Neturai Karta. There are some in Mea Shearim who believe that he thought it best to step out of the radical limelight in order not to taint his offspring with his notoriety as they reached marriageable age. Others say he was eased out because of his quasi-heretical devotion to the Christian philosopher. Two of Weisfish's beautiful daughters married the sons of foreign millionaires. One of the weddings was attended by Menahem Begin, then leader of the opposition, who knew the father of the groom. Weisfish was introduced to him by Israel Eldad.

"I understand that you read Nietzsche," said Begin.

"If you knew Nietzsche," said Weisfish, "you would be greater than Menahem Begin."

Weisfish knew that Begin hailed from Brisk (Brest-Litovsk, in Poland), which had been a stronghold of anti-Zionism.

"Are you a Brisker or a Zionist?" asked Weisfish.

"Both," said Begin.

"Neither," said Weisfish.

Begin wasn't a Brisker, he explained, because of his Zionist views. And he wasn't a Zionist either because, shifting to Yiddish, "*di kenst nisht* tsiyen *fuhn keshine*" ("you can't pull money out of your pocket"), a play on words—*tsiyen* (pull), *tsionist* (Zionist)—that alluded both to Begin's much-publicized difficulty at the time in raising money to pay off his party's debts and to Weisfish's dismissal of Zionism as a fund-raising enterprise.

Despite his remoteness from its everyday affairs, Leib Weisfish remains a self-appointed sentinel on the forbidding walls of the "old yishuv"—the remnants of the prestate, ultra-Orthodox community in Jerusalem, part of which never accepted Zionism. He ignores the community's ban on television and watches programs that interest him on an acquaintance's set. His dilemma is that he has far more in common intellectually with people outside the ghetto walls than with his fellow black-coats who piously go about their business within them.

"I used to be terribly depressed and pessimistic. Now I'm the happiest man in the world. Also the most alone. But not lonely." Nodding at the red-tile rooftops outside the window, he adds "I've learned to look at the world from up here."

After a few hours of following Weisfish's mind as it darts between metaphysics and historical footnotes, between scepticism and sublime faith, long psychedelic paths strewn with warm Jewish humor and mysteries that will not be spoken, the visitor's mind clogs and there is an urgent need to break away into the mindless world outside. The visitor suddenly picks up his tape recorder, utters his thanks, and heads for the door. He is not quick enough. Leib Weisfish is out the door first, snapping on a lock and climbing down the ladderlike steps ahead of his guest to make sure there is no escape.

"Have you read Spinoza's ethics?" he asks as they walk through the alleys of the Bait Yisrael Quarter. "Not that either? Tell me, you planned from the start to be a journalist? And for this you probably graduated [from] a few universities in California. That is to say, you don't need an education to be a journalist. Aiyai. That's why America is collapsing."

At the corner, Weisfish says, "Walk with me. I'll pay for your bus fare home."

Does his wife take an interest in philosophy? "She's an expert in mopology and cookology."

He has not had much sleep. Two nights ago he was at a kibbutz discussing Nietzsche until two in the morning with one of the kibbutz members, a former university teacher, who had invited him. He was so worked up afterwards that it was a couple of hours before he could fall asleep.

The next night he had met with a Hebrew University student doing his doctorate on Nietzsche and had had to walk home from the other end of town because the buses had stopped running at midnight.

"My nephew has asked me to write an article on faith for his school. I have to give a lecture next week in another high school to the graduating class. Millionaires come to see me. But I have no time for them. I have too much to do."

He pulls his overcoat around him. White threads show where the sleeve is about to wave farewell to the shoulder.

"A man should study when he's young. Why? Not just for knowledge or glory but so that the second half of life shouldn't be boring."

At the corner he says goodbye. "Did you tape the whole discussion? Not all? Good. Then I can deny." He slips into the crowd and is soon indistinguishable among the black-clad figures on Mea Shearim Street.

NINE

The Muslim Talmudist

PRESSING HIS EAR AGAINST THE IRON GATE in the courtyard in Jordanian Jerusalem, Hamdi Nubani heard a single word in the June dawn.

"Hitpazair."

"It was Hebrew," he told relatives and neighbors when he returned to the basement of his house. "Someone on the street said 'spread out.'"

The shouted command by an officer to paratroopers who had just broken through the Jordanian lines north of Mandelbaum Gate on the second day of the Six Day War was the first Hebrew word Nubani had heard "live" since reading the Bible with Leib Weisfish seventeen years before. But the language was as fresh to him as the previous day's newspapers. For more than a decade he had been monitoring the Hebrew press—copies were brought through the Mandelbaum Gate by UN officials every morning—as well as Israel Radio for the Jordanian newspaper *Ad-Difa*.

When the Israeli troops came to search his home later the next day, Nubani was upset that he and the other occupants were made to stand facing a wall but he noted that when a soldier took a soft drink from his refrigerator an officer ordered him to put it back. Nubani did not speak to them in Hebrew for fear of being suspected of being an

110

intelligence agent. Had the soldiers searched his study they would have been taken aback to discover a Hebrew library.

During the years of the city's division, Nubani had maintained a set of the Mishnah—the ancient compilation of Jewish oral law—in his study similar to the sets in the homes of the Mea Shearim quarter a few hundred meters away on the Israeli side of the city. Unlike the Mea Shearim libraries, however, which were devoted entirely to religious works, his also included the poems of the modern Hebrew poet, Bialik, some of which he had committed to memory. On his worktable was a copy of one of the six tractates of the Mishnah that he was in the process of translating into Arabic.

It had been a query from an Egyptian professor whom Nubani met during a visit to that country in 1964 that started him on the project. The professor, dean of oriental languages at Alexandria University, asked for a translation into Arabic of works by the medieval Jewish poet Yehuda Halevy as well as the original Hebrew version. The professor also asked Nubani about Judaism's attitude towards women. Nubani sent him quotes from the Mishnah's tractate on women. Deciding that Arab scholarship could profit from acquaintance with the Mishnah, he undertook to translate the entire tractate into ornate Koranic Arabic.

As Nubani saw it, the Mishnah was more evocative of contemporary rural Arab life than of the modern Jewish state. The method of pressing olives described in it was still practiced in the West Bank countryside with donkeys turning grinding stones. "I like the Mishnah because it is so vivid," Nubani would explain to Israelis who wanted to know why he was drawn to the ancient work. "I feel when I read it as if I were sitting in a circle on the floor around a sage who is reciting and I am writing what I hear. This is the way it was done in the time of the Mishnah, and it is still done this way in Islamic academies."

Nubani first came to the attention of Israelis shortly after the war when a Tel Aviv journalist wrote an article about him. The journalist had gone to interview one of East Jerusalem's leading political figures, Anwar Nusseibeh, and was astonished when Nubani, who was present, began speaking to him in literary Hebrew. His astonishment grew when Nubani mentioned that he was working on a translation into Arabic of the Mishnah.

It was not the injunction of Know Thy Enemy that had prompted Nubani to begin studying Hebrew in his youth but rather Know Thy

Neighbor. He had grown up in the Old City and would look back at that period as a golden age in Jerusalem. Arab and Jewish neighbors would visit each other to share in each other's family celebrations and in each other's sorrows.

The son of a qadi, a Muslim religious functionary who performed marriages in the Ramallah district north of Jerusalem, Nubani was selected by the British mandatory authorities for the Arab College, in which an intellectual Palestinian elite was trained for the civil service. Graduating in 1932, he began to work for the government education department under a well-known Jewish educator, Avinoam Yellin. The next year he enrolled at Hebrew University as its first Arab student. "I felt it would be important for Arabs to know Hebrew in the future," he would later say. The university's president, Dr. Judah Magnes, an early leader in the effort to win Arab-Jewish understanding, took a special interest in Nubani and invited him to his home on several occasions.

The golden age that Nubani remembers did not last long. The Arab uprising that began in 1936 took its toll all around him, the rebels killing many more Arabs than they did Jews. Avinoam Yellin, whom he greatly admired, was gunned down at the entrance to the education department's main offices on Mount Zion in 1936. The next year, Nubani's own father was abducted by unknown persons and not seen again. The family would never learn where he was buried. Nubani himself was advised in 1938 by Magnes to stop attending classes at the university for fear that he might become a target for terrorist attack. He worked as a clerk in the archives of the Rockefeller Museum for archaeology. After 1948, he was also sought after by Jordanian newspapers as a monitor of the Israeli radio and press.

During the ensuing years, Nubani was to feel almost part of the life going on across the border, a border which he could see from his window. The home of the eccentric Jew, Weisfish, with whom he had studied the Bible, was just a few hundred meters away, he knew. Through the years, Nubani closely followed the Israeli scene. He would listen to every speech by Ben-Gurion and Golda Meir and the other Israeli leaders that was broadcast, and read whatever was printed about them in the Hebrew press. He was particularly fond of Nahum Goldmann, president of the World Zionist Organization and a political dove. "He was lovable," Nubani would say. "Sometimes he spoke Yiddish and I was able to follow because I know German. The day after he would speak, Nahum is in the Jewish press and in the Arab press of Hamdi Nubani." After the 1967 war, Israelis who had monitored the Arab press visited Nubani and acknowledged their surprise at the accuracy and absence of embroidery in these reports—in sharp distinction to the distortions that marked similar monitoring in other Arab media.

"The secret is me," he told them. "Hamdi Nubani was in the picture."

He found the quality of the Hebrew language he monitored improving over the years. Where before it had borrowed mainly from Arabic, it now began to borrow from other languages as well. In addition, Nubani detected a return to the Mishnah. He was delighted one day to hear then prime minister Moshe Sharett during a speech in the Knesset note that the newly adopted Hebrew word for an airline hostess derived from a word in the Mishnah.

After the Six Day War, Nubani obtained a position as a translator in Jerusalem courts, including the Supreme Court. When he retired from that position, he devoted most of his time to the translation of the Mishnah. His translation of the tractate on women, the first time the Mishnah has ever been translated into Arabic, was published in 1987 with a grant from the Israeli Education Ministry. Shortly afterward, he was granted by the Jerusalem Municipality the title Honored Citizen—an award bestowed annually to distinguished residents—at a formal ceremony in City Hall at which Nubani delivered a moving speech dotted with talmudic quotations.

Nubani, who spent years monitoring life beyond the border separating Arab and Jew, has difficulty recognizing political borders in his own life. He is an admiring follower of King Hussein—"He's the man who can bring peace"—but he refers in passing to an Israeli ex-diplomat as the man "who was *our* ambassador" to Washington, and to "our Knesset." For that matter, he still refers with considerable pride to the years that "I devoted myself to the service of the British Empire." During his years as a Jordanian monitor, he translated into Arabic books and articles by writers on the Israeli left but also Menahem Begin's autobiographical work, *White Nights*. "I really liked his description of the sky in Siberia," Nubani would later say. "It was very poetic." When the right-wing leader subsequently learned that extracts from his book had been published in a Jordanian newspaper before the Six Day War, he invited Nubani to lunch at the Knesset.

When the Israeli soldiers came to his home in the Six Day War, Nubani would later say, he was not afraid. "I was still living in the dreams and shadows of the past when Jew and Arabs did not do any harm to each other." The dreams and shadows of the past temper for

Hamdi Nubani realities that have filled other men with bitterness or despair. He speaks with abhorence of terrorism, Jewish or Arab, and not even the murder of his father has altered the sweetness of his disposition.

When Hamdi Nubani says "I love the Arabs, they're very good" or "I really love the Jews, believe me,"these emerge not as meaningless banalities but as insights of a rare soul that has retained its childlike ability to reach out and touch even a stranger and see in him a kindred being.

A lifetime of living in the eye of the Arab-Israeli conflict prevents even Nubani from voicing easy optimism about the future but neither has he become a cynic. "A heavy curtain lies on the future. No one can foretell what it will bring. Let us pray that the future will be glittering and full of light and love."

For Hamdi Nubani, that vision is probably of a circle of people sitting on colorful carpets listening intently to a sage in the center.

TEN

The Arabs

A MONTH AFTER THE 1967 WAR, a well-dressed young man entered the office of the woman principal of the Bait Ha'am Hebrew language school in West Jerusalem and asked to register. The principal assumed the dark-complexioned applicant to be a Jewish immigrant from Morocco.

"Have you studied Hebrew before?" she asked.

"No, I'm from East Jerusalem," he said.

The notion that Arabs who a few weeks before might have been shooting at her would want to register in her school took the principal aback, but she enrolled the young man in a beginner's course. In the next few months, hundreds of East Jerusalemites were to follow.

As far as the Arabs knew, they were enrolling in an intensive five-month language course that would help them find work or get to know their enemy better, as the case might be. But in these state schools—known as *ulpans*—language is only part of a curriculum designed to turn immigrants from one hundred countries into Israelis. The students are taught Jewish history, religion, and customs. They learn about the covenant God made with Abraham to give the land to his offspring, about the early Zionist pioneers who had turned a waste into flourishing farmland, and about Israel's struggle with the Arabs who had attempted to annihilate the nation as it was being born. The appearance of Arab students in these classes in basic Zion-

115

ism was so bizarre that no one knew what to make of it—neither the teachers, the Jewish students, nor the Arabs themselves.

Thrown together against a common enemy—Hebrew grammar—something like friendship began to develop between Jewish and Arab students. Both sides were surprised that they laughed at the same things and an honest curiosity developed about each other's customs—"Do you mean you go into a synagogue with your shoes on?"; "How many wives do Arab men have?"

Some of the Jewish and Arab students invited each other to parties and the teachers, ebullient Sabras, had them to their homes. Once, when a teacher stayed after class to help an Arab student fill in a form he needed for employment, he turned to her and said: "Your kindness is confusing us." Both Jews and Arabs were unsettled by the human face of former enemies seen at close range. These sentiments, however, did not penetrate far beyond the classroom. In the real world outside, man was not just a social creature but a political animal.

The first terrorist bomb in Jerusalem exploded three months after the war in a small printing press opposite the Old City wall. The homemade device caused little damage. Two weeks later, in the crowded Zion Cinema in the center of Jerusalem, three persons rose in the middle of the film and walked out. A man sitting in the row behind them idly stretched his legs and felt an object below one of the vacated seats. He summoned an usher who saw in the narrow beam of his flashlight a device with wires attached to it. He picked it up and carried in to the lobby, where a policeman took it and raced to a parking lot outside police headquarters five hundred meters away. Moments after the policeman placed it beneath a tree, it exploded.

For the Arabs of Jerusalem and the West Bank, the shock of defeat had worn off. With increasing vehemence, they would now attempt to show that they had not reconciled themselves to the consequences of the war. Local Arab leaders met to formulate a policy of noncooperation with the Israeli authorities. Leaflets circulated in the alleys of the Old City calling upon Arabs to boycott everything Israeli and "not even to smile" at the conquerer. Women and youths marched through the streets to demonstrate against Israeli rule. And every few weeks, sometimes every few days, the bombs went off. On a Friday morning, when the stores are filled with customers shopping for the Sabbath, a bomb exploded in the biggest supermarket in the city, killing two Hebrew University students. The university itself was a target a week later, when a bomb exploded in the library cafeteria, wounding twenty-nine. The biggest explosion of all came at the end of 1968 in the city's main open-air market at Mahane Yehuda. Again the time was Friday morning. A car whose trunk was filled with one hundred pounds of explosives and bottles of benzine exploded, killing twelve and wounding fifty.

The Israeli authorities proved as capable of dealing with urban terrorism as with conventional warfare. There could be no fencing off of Arab Jerusalem the way the French had fenced off the casbah in Algiers. That would have been an admission that half of Jerusalem was conquered territory and not an integral part of the city. The measures used were tough but not draconian, and superb intelligence work enabled the Israelis to penetrate the guerrilla cells, generally before they had a chance to launch operations. Group after group fell or attempted to flee across the Jordan. By spring 1969, the back of the guerrilla movement was broken. Terrorist activity thereafter would be episodic and have little political impact.

Overt political opposition was likewise effectively supressed. Demonstration leaders were detained overnight for failure to obtain a permit. Outspoken leaders of the civil resistance movement were sent into cushy exile in Israeli resort cities, where they stayed at hotels for several months and were free to receive visitors. A few leaders who persisted in what the Israelis regarded as incitement were expelled to Jordan.

With terrorism and civil resistance contained, the Jewish and Arab residents of the city were left to work out their relationship with each other without the strain of violence and counterviolence affecting their daily lives.

To someone coming on the scene for the first time, it looked like the battle for Jerusalem being played out again, this time with the Arabs in the ascendent. Shortly after dawn, thousands of Arabs poured out of the gates of the Old City and advanced on Jewish Jerusalem. Instead of weapons, however, they carried tools and lunchboxes. Within a year after the war, Arabs constituted the bulk of the workforce in the booming construction industry and were employed throughout the West Jerusalem economy. In the initial years, civil defense personnel would be posted on the former border to search the lunchboxes for bombs but this was eventually stopped.

It was at the proletarian level that relations between the two populations were most direct. During the construction of Jerusalem's first high-rise office building, the Rassco Tower, Arab and Jewish workmen were organized in separate teams. Fights would break out periodically between the two groups when Arab workmen, listening to news broadcasts, applauded reports of Israeli casualties in border skirmishing or terrorist activity. The foreman solved the problem by forming mixed Arab-Jewish teams. Instead of taking their lunch breaks separately, the Arabs and Jews began to eat together of their own accord. If someone put on the news, each group kept its reaction to itself. Thousands of Arabs working in West Jerusalem joined the Israeli trade union federation, the Histadrut, in order to receive the same pay and benefits as Jewish workers. Some even were elected head of workers' committees.

The former Arab political leadership dwelt in a twilight world, lacking power but consulted frequently by foreign correspondants, foreign diplomats, and Israeli authorities—the latter sounding out reaction to various political ideas and using the Arab leaders to float ideas across the Jordan to the authorities in Amman.

One of the first sectors in which Arabs and Jews worked together on the basis of mutual trust and cooperation was the underworld. Burglars and pickpockets made contact in seedy cafes in East Jerusalem, where they eyed each other over cups of thick Turkish coffee. "They're professionals," commented Jerusalem's police chief. "They have no trouble recognizing each other." Integrated gangs were soon working both sides of the city. The Jewish thieves provided operational expertise and knowledge of police techniques. The Arabs fingered targets in East Jerusalem and provided fences in West Bank towns where stolen goods were not likely to be traced.

The police proved no less adaptive. Dozens of East Jerusalem Arabs, many of them veterans of the Jordanian police force, were recruited into the Israeli force, even though they chose to retain their Jordanan citizenship rather than adopt Israeli citizenship. The authorities preferred that Arab neighborhoods be policed by Arabs, but so well did the integration work that Arab policemen were also posted to traffic duties in West Jerusalem. Virtually unnoticed in the swirl of post-1967 Jerusalem was the sight of police patrols made up of Jews and Arabs jointly keeping the peace of the city.

In enterprises like restaurants and garages, half a dozen open partnerships between Jews and Arabs sprang up, but unofficial links were more common—a West Jerusalem businessman, for instance, channeling goods through an East Jerusalem outlet in order to take advantage of the lower taxes collected from Arab businesses.

Jewish taxi drivers, who had originally objected to East Jerusalem taxis picking up fares in West Jerusalem, rallied to the side of their Arab colleagues when an Arab taxi stand outside Jaffa Gate was declared a traffic hindrance and closed down. The association of Jewish taxi drivers accompanied a delegation of Arab drivers to a city council meeting and organized a convoy of Arab and Jewish taxis to cruise the city with signs spelling out their grievance. The city finally agreed to a slight shift in the taxi stand's location.

There was at least one contact at a more spiritual level. A group of ultra-Orthodox rabbis and Muslim qadis met one night in the Old City to formulate a common protest to the United Nations against immodest garb being worn by women in Jerusalem's holy places.

The municipality organized periodic meetings between Arab and Jewish youth clubs. After a soccer game to break the ice, the youths would repair to the host club's quarters, where the floor would be thrown open to questions about each other's way of life. "Is it true that people in a kibbutz marry when they're twelve years old?" "What are the traditions of Arab hospitality?" The only subject barred was politics.

All these contacts, however, were transient experiences liable to be wafted away by the first strong political wind. The Israelis attempted to forget that they ruled in Jerusalem by virtue of military conquest. The Arabs were determined not to let them forget. The relations between them were entirely pragmatic as far as most of the Arabs were concerned. For two decades, the Arab population saw its patriotic duty as simply hanging on and maintaining the Arab presence in Jerusalem. The Arabs were determined to live as peaceful and prosperous a life as possible while awaiting the hoped-for change in their political status.

The village of Issawiya clings to the eastern slope of Mount Scopus, sheltered from the strong west wind that sweeps across the ridge each afternoon. Where the village ends downslope, the Judean Desert begins. Its bare hills, falling away to the Dead Sea, lowest point on the face of the earth, can be seen fifteen miles to the east, from Issawiya's windows. The gaunt wilderness, pitted with caves, was a retreat for prophets and a haven for fugitives at least since David fled there from Saul's wrath. Issawiya's location gives it an air of timelessness—a village suspended between the desert and civilization.

In 1948 time caught up, when fighting between Israeli and Arab forces swirled around Mount Scopus. The fighting ended with Israel in possession of Hebrew University and Hadassah Hospital on the crest of the hill but cut off from Israeli Jerusalem by a mile of Arab-held territory. Under the armistice agreement, the Israeli enclave could be supplied by convoy every two weeks and its garrison rotated.

If the 120-man Israeli garrison on Scopus was besieged, however, so was Issawiya. Cut off by deep gulleys to the north and south and by the desert to the east, the villagers could reach the outer world only by crossing the Scopus ridge on a path controlled by the Israeli garrison. The Arabs were not permitted to use it until after 6:00 A.M. each day. The village's elderly milkman was said to have come to a special agreement permitting him to use the path each morning before it was officially opened. In order to get his supply of goat's milk to the Old City market in time, he had to leave Issawiya on his can-laden donkey by 4:00 A.M. Under the deal said to have been arrived at, the milkman would supply the garrison with fresh milk each morning in return for early passage.

The Six Day War ended Issawiya's isolation. The nighttime barriers came down and the village, which had been outside the municipal boundaries of Jordanian Jerusalem, found itself embraced by the expanded boundaries of Israeli Jerusalem. The village's way of life was revolutionized when electric cables were laid to it across the Scopus ridge for the first time. With refrigerators soon installed in every house, women no longer had to make daily trips to the market for fresh fruit and meat. The women's lot was eased further by washing machines. Piped water ended the colorful but arduous trip to wells by the women who carried water jugs atop their heads.

Before the war, villagers would come home from work by four and be in bed by eight. Now they would be up sometimes till after midnight. Television was the reason for some of this change in life style, but a broader nighttime social life was opened by the installation of street lights that permitted villagers to visit one another after nightfall. They had not ventured out before across the darkened slopes on casual visits.

Most of the village men found jobs in the booming construction industry in West Jerusalem and earned three times what they had made before the war. The village, which had been too poor to build a minaret on its small mosque, could finally afford one, a graceful structure designed and built by the village mukhtar.

Prosperity also meant that the village's young men could afford to marry earlier. Before the war, young men without means sometimes had to work into their early twenties before they could afford the bride price every groom must pay. Now practically any sixteen-year-old could raise the money. Some of the young men in the village even made inquiries about attending Hebrew University, which had loomed over them since childhood as an enemy bastion on Mount Scopus.

These dramatic improvements in Issawiya's condition did not assuage its sense of political grievance. When the wave of terror struck Jerusalem in the late 1960s, it was in Issawiya that the security forces found many of the perpetrators.

On a winter day in 1972, Israel Radio's Arabic station broadcast a special message to ex-Jerusalem Mayor Ruhi el-Khatib in Amman, informing him of his mother's death in Jerusalem and advising him that he would be permitted to attend her funeral the following day, Khatib, who had been mayor during the Six Day War, had been expelled from Israel four years before for incitement, and the invitation was a humane gesture across the void of hostility.

The body was carried the next day from the Temple Mount to the Muslim cemetery outside Lion's Gate. For two hours the mourners waited beside the open grave for Khatib to come. Escort officers stood by at the Jordan River bridges past closing time in order to rush Khatib to Jerusalem. But for him the void was too deep to cross and his mother was laid to rest in his absence.

Two Arabs wearing *kheffiyas* swooped down on Sara Kaminker's car as she backed into an alley in an Arab village in northern Jerusalem in order to make a turn. It was a long two minutes before she reappeared. "They knew I was from the municipality and wanted me to hear their problem," she explained to her assistants watching the scene from a distance.

For several years, Kaminker, a street-smart ex–New Yorker, had been prowling the alleys of East Jerusalem even in times of tension when sensible men kept clear. "I've been stoned by the best people in town," she would remark in passing. Kaminker was in charge of Team Five, a small group of municipal planners charged with responsibility for the rural areas that made up the bulk of East Jerusalem. It was a mandate that went beyond order and aesthetics, the normal concerns of planners, to touch on the deepest political and human instincts—fear, respect, feelings of family, and nation—that translate into houses and open space. Kaminker's guidelines were flexible and she relied heavily on her instincts as she moved through the gray

area where Israaeli sovereignty and Arab self-interest tried to accommodate each other.

The land annexed in 1967 had no zoning recognized by Israeli law.
Construction was therefore permitted only at the discretion of the
municipality until an official plan was drawn up, which would take
many years. Once a week, Kaminker went into the field to visit the
sites for which building requests had been filed and meet the appli-
cants. The two sides would make their points edgewise over cups of
coffee, sometimes over a game of backgammon, amidst chatter about
the family.

On this day, she had come to see a family in the old village nucleus of Shuafat which wanted to build a two-story house next to its
one-story dwelling. During their chat over coffee in the living room,
Kaminker established the number of children in the family, which of
them was studying abroad, and who was about to get married. There
was talk about water, employment opportunities, the expanding city
and, by the way, the application for the new building. When she
went out to see the site, Kaminker saw that it was less than two meters from the neighboring building which would lead her to reject the
application. "We want them to build decent housing, and it's rules
like this that help make decent housing," she would explain.

In the large village of Silwan, twenty-four mukhtars and heads of
clans were waiting to meet her to discuss a site for a new local school.
In the Jewish sector, the authorities would simply have selected the
most suitable site for a school and, if it belonged to private persons,
would have offered them equivalent land elsewhere. In Arab Jerusalem, however, Kaminker had learned, this procedure would not
do. "For them, their land means this one specific plot marked by
stones laid out by their great-grandfather. They don't want to build
on a comparable plot five hundred meters away."

There was far less communal orientation in the Arab sector than
in the Jewish and far more family orientation. The Israelies had been
astonished to discover in 1967 that car owners in Arab Jerusalem did
not have vehicle insurance, it being generally accepted that in the
event of emergency, the extended family would cover expenses.

In Silwan, Kaminker told the assembled notables that she would
leave it to them to assemble land for the school. To hasten the decision, she informed them that until they did, all other construction in
the area would be banned. By the time she would return for her next
visit, she knew, the plot would have been assembled.

North of the Old City, Kaminker visited a site on which the Greek

Orthodox church wanted to build apartments for its followers, all of them local Arabs. Under Israeli law, 40 percent of the plot must be deeded for roads and other public use when a building permit is granted, but the clerics who met Kaminker maintained that under church law they were forbidden from deeding away any of its property. In that case, said Kaminker, the church could undertake to build the kindergarten and clinic the municipality wanted the land for. After consultation with their superiors, the church officials would agree.

In another village, where land had to be expropriated for a kindergarten, Kaminker was careful to choose a site owned by a wealthy resident who had ample land elsewhere on which to build. At the poorest end of the village she and her party happened on a couple dragging out matresses to dry in the sun. "The damp," explained the woman. She and her husband insisted that the visitors come into the house for coffee. The furnishings were old and musty and in lieu of cups they served the coffee in glasses. Despite the poverty, the couple exuded an inner tranquility. "Life is a balance scale," said the Arab member of the team, nodding at the couple fussing over the coffee in the corner serving as a kitchen. "The more you have, the lower you go. The less you have, the higher."

Despite the tensions, the two peoples in Jerusalem lived side by side for twenty years—until the 1987 explosion—with a restraint that surprised Jerusalem's elders, who remembered the communal riots in the decades before the city's division. For Jerusalem's Arabs, it required the ability to bend to realities without sacrificing self-respect. This flexibility was illustrated by an East Jerusalem tour guide, duly licensed by the Israeli Tourism Ministry, who explained how his patter had changed since he escorted tourists to the holy places under the Jordanian regime. "We used to say the Jews killed Christ," he said. "Now we say it was the Romans."

E L E V E N

Bait Safafa
When the Barriers Came Down

THE CROWD SEEN IN THE SLIDE projected on the wall of the classroom looks like a typical wedding procession in any Arab village—a large column of relatives and friends walking along a rural road from the bride's home to the groom's, singing as they go. Looking closely, however, the students in the class see that the road is divided down its length by a high chain-link fence. Half the crowd is on the other side of the fence from the smiling bride and groom at the front of the procession.

The slide being shown to Arab students in the Bait Safafa high school in southern Jerusalem is intended to illustrate to the students the way life was lived in the village during the nineteen years it was divided by the border that divided Jerusalem. The man operating the slide projector, school principal Omar Othman, is the groom in the picture, which was taken less than a month before the Six Day War.

Bait Safafa is the one point in Jerusalem where the border divided not just a city but a community, one made up of extended clans whose members suddenly found themselves living in different countries from each other. Half of Bait Safafa, the larger half, was in Jordan. The remainder was part of Israel. It was the railroad linking Jerusalem with the coastal plain that had split the village. In the armistice negotiations following the War of Independence, Israel had insisted on retaining control of the rail line. Jordan had finally ceded the part of the village through which the tracks passed to the Israeli side.

Although the soldiers on both sides attempted to prevent any communication across the border fence dividing the village or the transfer of objects for fear of smuggling or espionage, the villagers managed to pass messsages and wedding presents across at night. The only occasions when the soldiers permitted the two sides to openly associate at the fence was when there was a funeral or a wedding. The families from the two sides would then walk along side by side to mourn or celebrate as if the fence were not separating them.

Sometimes, a marriage would be arranged between a young couple from opposite sides of the village. The bride would have to "emigrate" from her half of the village and her country via the crossing point between Jordan and Israel at Mandelbaum Gate in the northern part of Jerusalem. Tearful parents taking leave of their children would see them a few hours later across the fence, waving back from another world.

When the fence came down in 1967, the villagers rushed to embrace relatives and former neighbors whom they had seen over the years through the fence but who had been changed by two decades of different acculturation in ways that had not been apparent. The seven hundred villagers on the Israeli side spoke Hebrew, worked in the Jewish sector in the city, understood the workings of Israeli bureaucracy, and had been educated—the younger generation—in the Israeli school system. The two thousand villagers across the line held Jordanian passports and had remained rural—they had been too far from Jordanian Jerusalem to be in daily contact. Hundreds of the Jordanian Bait Safafans worked in the Arab oil countries and sent home remittances that were put into the construction of handsome homes. They were wealthier than their brethren on the Israeli side but the Israeli Bait Safafans were more sophisticated.

The differences would be perpetuated, albeit less sharply, after unification. Almost all those on the former Jordanian side chose to retain Jordanian citizenship rather than accept Israeli citizenship. All the village children went to the same local elementary and high schools now but in two entirely separate educational streams. The Israeli children studied according to the Israeli Arab curriculum taught in the Arab sector all over the country. Down the hall, children from the former Jordanian part of the village studied according to the curriculum being offered in Jordan—although anti-Israel references would be excised from the textbooks imported from Jordan. The Jordanian matriculation exams that the "Jordanian" students took would permit them to go on to universities in the Arab world or the West Bank. The school administrators were troubled by the fact that the Jordanian curriculum hardly changed over the years while the Israeli curriculum was constantly being upgraded.

In the school courtyard, two decades after unification, youths in the schoolyard during recess would still cluster according to "Israeli" or "Jordanian" groupings. In part, this no doubt stemmed from the fact that they studied in separate classrooms, but the apartness seemed to go beyond that. "The children from the 'Jordanian' side regard those from the 'Israeli' side of the village as snobs," said one school official. But there was also a different political orientation. Those from the Israeli side regarded themselves as Palestinians in the Israel-Arab dispute but they recognized that they were part of Israel. The "Jordanian" villagers found it more difficult to see themselves within an Israeli framework.

Although the "Jordanian" children were keen to meet Israeli Jewish peers in get-togethers arranged by the municipality, only those from the Israeli side of Bait Safafa would agree to join with Israeli Jewish schoolchildren in youth exchange excursions to Europe organized by the municipality. "Jordanian" parents agreed to send their children to a "computer camp" in Cairo during summer holidays, but while the children from the Israeli side of Bait Safafa simply took a direct bus from Jerusalem to Cairo, the "Jordanian" children traveled first to Amman in Jordan, from where they flew to Cairo, thus avoiding any Israeli stamp in their Jordanian passports.

To the seemingly endless permutations by which Jerusalem's groupings subdivide themselves, another had been added.

Although Bait Safafa was reunited by the Six Day War, a dozen other Arab villages around the periphery of the city were administratively divided by the annexation. Parts of these villages were incorporated inside the expanded bounds of the Israeli capital while parts were left on the West Bank. The villagers would learn to make the best of both worlds.

Residents of A-Tur atop the Mount of Olives enjoy in their daily comings and goings a breathtaking view. To the west, the Old City lies at their feet and beyond sprawls the modern city. To the east, the Judean Desert falls away to the Dead Sea and the distant Mountains of Moab in Jordan, which turn purple in the afternoon mist. In these two contrary directions lie the villagers' political fortunes.

Most of the residents live atop the ridge, which lies within the bounds of Jerusalem, but the bulk of their reserve lands lie across a wadi at the foot of the eastern slope—a wadi that divides the municipality, and the state of Israel, from the West Bank. In the prosperity that followed the Six Day War, new homes began to be built on the eastern slope. At first the municipality did not intercede, even though building there was illegal in the absence of an approved master plan. When the tempo of construction increased, however, warnings were issued and then building inspectors started knocking on doors to inform the owners that they owed the municipality sizeable fines for having built without a permit. Under Jordanian administration, land owners had had virtually free rein to do what they wished on their own land. As residents of Israel, the villagers discovered, they were subject to building codes which severely limited construction. These codes, however, did not apply on the West Bank across the wadi, where Jordanian law continued to prevail since Israel had not annexed it. By the 1980s, hundreds of homes had been built there, mainly for young couples.

To provide infrastructure for their now scattered village, the three mukhtars—a grocer, a shopkeeper, and a clerk—appealed both to the Jerusalem municipality and the Jordanian government. The mukhtars would prove more adept at international financing than many an accredited finance minister. The Jordanians, who regularly channeled funds to the West Bank in order to maintain their links, agreed to pay for four kilometers of road that would connect the new neighborhood east of the wadi with the rest of the village. The municipality, which the mukhtars had asked for a sewer line on the slope within its jurisdiction, was loath to make the required investment for a scattering of single family homes, but it provided the sewer pipes and planning while the villagers undertook the installation. The mukhtars would find it easier to obtain funding from two sources, each for half a village, than to have one pay for the needs of an entire village.

Living between two sets of rules, the villagers would demonstrate their ability over the years to exploit both to their own needs. The Israelis, too, would learn, in their dealings with East Jerusalem's Arabs, to sometimes temper the evenhanded but blank-faced approach of Western bureaucracy.

Among the first Arabs and Jews to seek each other out when the barriers came down in 1967 were men who had worked together in the power plant on Bethlehem Road, which had furnished Mandatory Jerusalem its first electricity. The plant had fallen on the Israeli side of the line in 1948, and five of the Arab workers had even chosen to remain behind, moving to the Israeli side of Bait Safafa and continuing to work alongside their Jewish colleagues. Most of those who had crossed to the Jordanian side of the city had found employment in the power plant that was later set up there.

Even after unification, politics and the shadow of an enterprising Greek named Euripedes Mavrommatis would continue to keep the city supplied by both "Arab electricity" and "Jewish electricity".

Mavrommatis, whose name would become familiar to students of international law, was living in Turkey in 1914 when he acquired a concession from Ankara to generate and distribute electrical energy in Jerusalem, then under Turkish rule and still illuminated palely by kerosene lamps. The concession area was fixed at a twenty-kilometer radius from the point chosen by medieval cartographers as the center of the world—the dome of the Church of the Holy Sepulcher, traditional site of Jesus' crucifixion and resurrection.

However, World War I intervened and Jerusalem continued to be without electricity for well over a decade. Mavrommatis, who had sagely moved to London by this time, demanded in the courts that Britain, which had driven the Turks out of Palestine, recognize the concession the Turks had granted him before the war. He won his battle, and in 1926 the British government restored to him the concession. Mavrommatis promptly sold his rights to a British firm, Balfour-Beatty, which proceeded to build the power plant on Bethlehem Road next to the railway station, where it could easily be supplied by fuel.

The division of Jerusalem in 1948 plunged the Old City and the rest of Arab Jerusalem back into biblical darkness for two years except for street lights fed by a small generator. Balfour-Beatty continued to operate the plant on the Israeli side, and in 1950 it set up a generator in Jordanian Jerusalem.

Balfour-Beatty was thus running plants on the two sides of the city, and both the Israelis and the Arabs soon developed the same dissatisfaction over its services. For the company, supplying Jerusalem with electricity was a commercial exercise, not a religious calling, and it was not interested in modernizing its system unless assured of profit. In Israeli Jerusalem, the voltage was so low that elderly Jews studying the Talmud at night would supplement their light bulb with candles. In East Jerusalem, most of the neighborhoods had no electricity at all.

In October 1954, the largely government-owned Israel Electricity Corporation purchased Balfour-Beatty's shares in the Bethlehem Road plant and linked the Israeli half of the city to the national grid. This meant that Jerusalem's electric supply was as adequate now as

Tel Aviv's. The Jordanians emulated the Israeli move in 1956, when six municipalities, including neighboring Bethlehem, together with private shareholders, formed the Jordan-Jerusalem Electricity Company (JJEC) and acquired Balfour-Beatty's holdings there. A new plant was built and the number of consumers increased twentyfold in the next decade.

The Six Day War resulted in an anomalous situation in which two utilities were supplying electricity in the same city. The original Mavrommatis concession had been measured from the center of the world. But that world had been divided and each half had developed separately. How were they now to be reunited?

At the beginning, the question remained academic, both companies continuing to provide electricity on their side of the former "green line." When banks of lights were set up at the Western Wall, the Arab-owned company furnished the electricity since the Old City was within its concession area. The firm also supplied the adjacent Jewish Quarter, the restored Hebrew University complex on Mount Scopus, and even Israeli army bases on the West Bank.

The crunch came with the beginning of large-scale Jewish housing developments across the former border. The residents objected to being tied to the Arab grid, since the rates of the JJEC, which had no state subsidy, were considerably higher and breakdowns frequent. There were objections too on security grounds, various terrorist scenarios involving a deliberate blackout being put forward. Some objected to paying rates to a company owned mostly by shareholders living in enemy Arab countries. After deliberation, however, the government decided to honor the Mavrommatis concession to which the JJEC was half an heir, requiring it only to equalize its rates with the Israeli utility. To shut down the company, which was the largest Arab employer in Jerusalem and the West Bank and a source of Arab pride, would have been considered a political act, not simply an efficiency move.

The massive influx of Jewish residents into East Jerusalem and the West Bank, which the company also served, was a boon for the lagging fortunes of the JJEC, which now had to begin printing its bills and notices in Hebrew as well as Arabic. The Jews, with their numerous appliances, used far more electricity than Arabs and the company soon had to buy electricity in bulk from the Israeli utility to supplement its own output. The tie-in between the two systems was made in former no-man's-land near Ammunition Hill. Often during winter storms, one side of the city would be blacked out by downed power lines while the other side continued to glitter. When the failure was on the Jewish side, the residents grumbled against nature or alleged inefficiency on the part of the company. When it happened in the JJEC area, many of the Israeli clients would see in it some Arab nationalistic ploy. The equipment in the Arab grid was much older and breakdowns much more common. Frequently, residents of blacked-out neighborhoods would form late-night convoys that would drive to Mayor Kollek's house in the quiet Rehavia Quarter and sound their horns in protest.

With the termination of the Mavrommatis concession in 1987, the Israeli government decided to permit the Arab-owned company to continue serving its Arab clients but to shift the Jewish neighborhoods to the Israel Electric Corporation. There were some Israelis who would regret the abandonment of this one instance in Jerusalem where Arabs were the suppliers of an important public service and Jews the clients. It was, they felt, loss of an important psychological equalizer that would in the long run have made coexistence a much more meaningful notion. But for the authorities who saw the JJEC link to Jewish homes a source of ongoing friction, the solution was alternating currents.

TWELVE

A Vision of the Ark

THE UNIVERSITY PROFESSOR who has dropped out of his tour group and donned a white robe to announce his resurrection on a Jerusalem street corner is gently led away by a police officer and escorted to a sanatorium on the outskirts of the city. There, he is given sedatives and talks with his family in New York over the telephone. After a few days he returns to himself and is put on a plane home.

Each year since 1967, about a dozen tourists with no history of mental illness have suffered breakdowns on their first encounter with Jerusalem, experiencing delusions of being the Messiah or a character in the Bible. These victims of the "Jerusalem syndrome" are mostly American Protestants. Psychologists see this syndrome as being specific to the city, triggered probably by the difference between the visitor's imagined Jerusalem and the earthly reality. Unlike former mental patients such as Dennis Rohan, these victims are able to resume their life routines without a relapse and with a sense of having had a good experience.

Even usually rational people are sometimes drawn to Jerusalem by a mystical pull stronger than their sense of logic.

Frida Schlain and her dream caught up with me one day at my desk at *The Jerusalem Post*.

131

"This woman would like to talk to a reporter," said the reception-ist who brought her.

As soon as the visitor began talking in her Argentine-accented En-glish about the dream she had had, I understood the import of the receptionist's wink. Glancing at the clock, I waited for the first oppor-tune moment to thank the visitor for sharing her dream with me, and then to escort her to the door.

As she continued, however, I began to find myself listening. Until she had had the dream a few months before, she had lived an unre-markable life. Married to a doctor and a mother of two children, she resided in a wealthy district of Buenos Aires; she was a middle-aged Jew almost totally assimilated into Argentine culture.

She had experienced what she thought was an extrasensory vision a few months before. She believed this to be a one-time episode with no significance beyond her own life. She had been driving back alone from the farm she owned one thousand kilometers upcountry to Bue-nos Aires. At one point, sleepiness overtook her, and she came within a hair's breadth of crashing. As she swerved to safety, she thought she heard a voice say: "You're not supposed to die yet." Almost matter of factly, she answered aloud, "You're right."

There was still something unfinished in her life. She had not yet made a future for her eighteen-year-old mongoloid daughter, the cen-tral concern of her and her husband. For a long time, she and other parents of mongoloid children had been in contact about the creation of a home for the retarded in the Buenos Aires area. Sensitized by her brush with death to the urgency of finding a solution while she was still alive and healthy, she took the initiative in searching for an appropriate building and within a few weeks had located one. Money was raised and work begun on the building's renovation under Fri-da's chairmanship. Heavy rains delayed the project, and concern about having the building finished by the scheduled date had been weighing heavily on Frida's mind when she went to sleep the night of the dream.

First she saw events from her real life in which through accident or sickness she had come close to death. Then she heard a voice, the same authoritative voice she had heard in the car. "This has all been conditioning for now, so that you will be ready to listen and to do what we ask."

Then she saw herself flying high over a strange landscape. On one side was a large body of water; on the other, a lake. Near the lake, a flat mountaintop. In the center of the mountaintop was a circular wall of small stones surrounding a hole. Soldiers were digging in the hole as she alighted near them. They were pulling a box from the hole, a large box covered with dirt. From one end, the dirt fell away, revealing a golden metal. "This is *el arca della alianza* [the Holy Ark]," says the voice. "This is energy." Frida must go to the mountain and dig up the box, says the voice. The metal glows so powerfully that it knocks Frida back, waking her up.

Two nights later, she and her husband were visiting friends and she recounted to them the vivid dream. Taking a piece of paper lying on the coffee table, she drew the diamond-shaped mountaintop and the lake beside it. As she completed it, almost simultaneously she and her host, a well-known Argentine journalist, said the same word—Masada. She had never been to Israel and was unaware of ever having heard the name before, but the word had seemingly forced itself out of her mouth. Her host, a Christian, had just returned from a visit to Israel. He took down a book from his shelves and showed it to her. There on the cover was the diamond-shaped mountain of Masada on which the last Hebrew defenders had made their stand against the Romans in A.D. 73, before finally taking their own lives. Next to the mountain was the lake of her dream, the landlocked Dead Sea.

The identification was electrifying. There was now not only a disembodied voice but an earthly address and an earthly assignment. The thought that she might be the agent of some supernatural power was at once absurd, frightening, and impelling. She consulted a psychiatrist whose professional distance seemed to melt as she told her story. "We're entering a no-man's-land here," he said. In the end, the psychiatrist told her to follow her dream. So did her husband. Frida hesitated. Was it all ridiculous? Was it real?

The answer came at a party she and her husband gave two months later. Their twenty-one-year-old son, a heretofore stable youth, suddenly went berserk. In the middle of the sedate party, he began shouting, ripping off his clothing, and leaping about. When he was quieted down, he could not explain what happened. Frida took the incident as a signal. She immediately began to wrap up her affairs and to find someone to run the home for retarded children.

On the day of the party, she would later learn, an Israeli freighter named Masada sailed from the port of Ashdod in Israel. A few days later, it disappeared in the Bermuda Triangle.

Frida had had premonitions before. She had had a premonition that she would have a mongoloid child. She had had a premonition that she would be in a traffic accident that would severely cut her face shortly before she was actually in such an accident. But these premonitions had never been of a religious nature. She was not a religious woman and had never felt any particular kinship to things Jewish. She had in fact been educated mostly in Protestant and Catholic schools.

It was just turning spring when Frida arrived in Israel in 1981. Immediately after leaving her bags with friends, she joined a bus tour to Masada, a two-and-a-half hour drive from Tel Aviv. This time, she alighted on the mountaintop from a cable car. The scene looked familiar but in the brief time her group remained there, she could not locate the circle of stones. A few days later, she returned on her own on a regularly scheduled bus rather than with a tour, in order to have the time to wander freely. This time she found the circle. It was located in the center of the mountain alongside a restored archaeological site labeled the Western Palace.

In the next few weeks, she would make half a dozen trips to Masada. On one of these occasions, she had slept over on the mountaintop three consecutive nights with the consent of National Parks Authority personnel who supervised the site. So taken were they by her story, that despite the rules against anyone staying on the mountain after visiting hours, they let her stay in a dust-filled storage shed. A mattress on a stretcher in one corner served as her bed. Frida discovered on the first night that she was sharing the shed with a rat. She rolled half a tranquilizer pill toward it, hoping it would go to sleep and let her do likewise, but the rat ignored it. Frida's half of the pill proved more effective.

Her only human company was soldiers in a military post. They invited her to share their supper and then wished her goodnight when she returned to her shed. There was enough moonlight to allow her to see her way and keep her from falling off the mountain. In the moonlight as in the sun, she spent hours in the circle of stones thinking about what might lay below. She had done considerable reading since discovering the Masada connection at her friend's house and had come to the conclusion that the metallic box she had seen in her dream was the Holy Ark, which contained the two stone tablets inscribed with the Ten Commandments that Moses brought down from Mount Sinai.

The ark had been carried by the Israelites in their wanderings and was finally brought to Jerusalem by King David. In the temple built by his son, Solomon, the ark occupied the Holy of Holies, the inner sanctum entered only by the high priest on Yom Kippur. The Babylonians destroyed the temple four hundred years later, but scholars believe the ark was hidden before they reached the sanctuary. In the long biblical inventory of temple vessels carried into exile, there is no mention of the Holy Ark or the tablets. There is a talmudic tradition that the ark was hidden below ground on the Temple Mount. According to a legend in the apocryphal 2 Maccabees, Jeremiah hid it on Mount Nebo across the Jordan. One of the Dead Sea Scrolls—the Copper Scroll—contains a detailed list of instructions of the nature of "thirty paces from the bent tree" for finding a hidden treasure that some believe to be the temple treasures, perhaps including the Holy Ark.

Masada was developed as a fortified retreat by King Herod more than five centuries after the fall of the First Temple, but the existence of this remote and natural fortress was known to the authorities in Jerusalem long before Herod and could have been used as a retreat during the Babylonian invasion. After spending days and nights surveying the circle of stones, Frida came to her own conclusion about why the last defenders of Masada had killed themselves: not to avoid going into Roman captivity but to preserve a secret.

What Frida wanted was for archaeologists to excavate the stone circle. The National Parks Authority was charged with supervising Masada, which had become one of Israel's major national monuments since its excavation in the early 1950s by Professor Yigael Yadin of Hebrew University. The authority's personnel on the mountain told her that only Professor Yadin could authorize such a dig, since it was accepted practice never to conduct an archaeological dig at a site without permission from the man who had previously excavated there, if he were still alive. When she wrote Yadin, he replied that she must make formal application to the head of the Government Antiquities Department. "To be honest," he wrote, "if I shall be asked, my advice will be in the negative." Undeterred, she had contacted other archaeologists and prominent personalities whom she thought might be able to pressure Yadin or find some way of getting around his veto. But to no avail. When all else failed, she had come to the press in the hope that pressure could be brought this way.

After tuning into her remarkable story shortly after she had started speaking, I had listened carefully for the sound of dissonance—the loose thread that would betray a mode of thinking beyond mundane rationality. But I could detect none. When she had finished, I looked at Frida again. A handsome woman of about fifty with no makeup visible—not on her face or on the image she was projecting. She knew that what she way saying was fantastic but she didn't seem to give a hoot whether I believed her or not. She just wanted the story printed. She was saying, in effect, "Take it or leave it, but this is the truth and I need your help." I told her I would think about it and let her know.

My initial instinct was that there could be no newspaper article. One did not write about people's visions in a serious newspaper. If one did, where would it end, especially in a place like Jerusalem where visions often crowd out the real world? But the story, and the hard edge of Frida herself, stopped me from dismissing it out of hand. If she were legitimate and not just a Convincing Crazy, a breed in no short supply, then there might be a valid story in a wealthy Argentinan woman who, because of an obsession, sleeps atop Masada and wages a campaign for an excavation that the authorities refuse to carry out.

The National Parks people on Masada had told Frida that they thought the circle of stones had already been excavated in Yadin's dig, but she remained convinced that it had not. I called an archaeologist I knew who had dug on Masada with Yadin. When I described the circle's location, he knew what I was talking about. "No, we never did dig there," he said. I called several people who had been in contact with Frida, and they spoke enthusiastically about her as an honest, rational, and intelligent woman, albeit driven.

I invited Frida back and on the grounds that I had not made notes the first time, I had her go through her story again from the beginning. I listened closely for deviations from her first telling. There were two minor changes, but when I brought them up at the end of her hour-long account she had a reasonable explanation for both.

The story was run on an inside page on a midweek day under a modest two-column headline. Despite the poor play, the reaction to it was greater than to any other story I had ever written—not only in scale, but in intensity. Many callers wanted to know how to contact her. Knowing she would approve, I passed on her telephone number.

One of those was a prominent businessman, one of the wealthiest men in the country, who had both mystical and nationalist inclinations. Another was an American woman immigrant who described herself as a psychic. She questioned me closely about Frida and about whether I thought she was sincere. She wanted to invite Frida to a meeting the following night of a group of psychics who met regularly in Jerusalem. I told her that Frida would probably welcome the invitation. A physicist said that the part of the dream in which the ark emits a power need not be an otherwordly vision. The Bible tells us that the ark was made of wood sheathed in metal—gold. In certain circumstances, he said, this kind of construction could emit static electricity.

When I spoke to Frida a week later, she told me that she had traveled with the group of psychics to Masada by bus. When they reached the circle of stones, she said, the leader of the group—the woman who had called me—stepped inside. The woman was wearing a hat that with a broad floppy brim which suddenly flapped upward as if a strong breeze were blowing. "But there was no breeze," said Frida. The woman's face, she said, turned deep red.

The article drew a bemused reaction from most Israeli archaeologists who read it, but one of them said he would be willing to carry out the excavation if permission were given by the Antiquities Department for the dig. The head of the department declared, however, that sponsorship by a scientific organization was a prerequisite for any excavation in the country. "There's no paragraph in the law covering heavenly voices."

By chance, I had scheduled an interview with Yadin himself a few days later on an unrelated archaeological story. The meeting was in his house in the Rehavia quarter, the same house in which his father, Professor Eliezer Sukenik, had in 1947 excitedly brought the first Dead Sea Scrolls after their acquisition from Bedouins. At a suitably relaxed moment in the interview, I mentioned Frida and her campaign. Yadin smiled wearily. Years before, he said, his late wife Carmela had begun keeping what he called "a nut file." It contained letters from people offering to locate the lost treasure of the temple and other wonders. Once, Yadin had succumbed to the entreaties of a wealthy American businessman, a fundamentalist Christian, who begged for permission to dig in a specific cave in the Judean Desert that he had first seen in a vision. The businessman promised to bring an American archaeologist who would conduct the dig on a scientific basis and, of course, the businessman would pay all expenses. In a moment of weakness, Yadin gave his assent, reasoning that nothing would be lost by the excavation and, who knows, maybe something would be found. The dig produced nothing and Yadin vowed never to succumb again. Archaeologists, like others, could be guided occasionally by inspiration but not by dreams. It was clear that there would be no gesture to Frida.

When I informed her, she asked for another article to step up the pressure. I told her that there could be no more articles unless there were a development to warrant it, such as a decision to dig.

In the time since her first visit, Frida had become weary and homesick. On her first visit she had showed me a neatly written letter from her daughter expressing longing. "It's very easy to love a mongoloid child," she said. Despite her feelings, she radiated determination to go on to the end, whatever the end was. "I sometimes think that if I can't get permision to dig, I'll just get some people, Bedouin or whatever, and just go up there some night and dig up the ark and hold it hostage until I'm compensated for my troubles." If an excavation were carried out and nothing found, she said, she would feel a bit ridiculous "but that doesn't matter." Much more frightening—in its mysteriousness and in its confirmation of her supernatural mission—was the prospect of sinking a shovel three meters down and striking something. "I don't want to think about it." She had moved up to Jerusalem, staying first with the head of the psychic group, then on Mount Zion with a woman from South America who was the widow of Israel's best-known sculptor.

Frida would call from time to time and I found her growing increasingly mystic. She respected my skepticism and my wish to keep professional distance from her and her obsession, but one day she called to invite me and my daughters to Mount Zion for coffee. I accepted and we fixed the visit for Thursday, three days later. Several hours before the appointed time, I received a call at home from a nurse at a local hospital. Mrs. Schlain had had an accident, she said, and asked that I be notified that the meeting could not take place as scheduled. When I asked what happened, the nurse sounded evasive. I called Frida's hostess on Mount Zion, but there was no answer. When I finally reached her, she sounded in a panic. She had been to the hospital but declined to tell me on the phone what had happened. I must come over immediately, she said.

When I arrived, she said that Frida had that morning gone to town to buy a cake for my visit. The hostess had told Frida that she should not bother, that she would bake a cake herself. But Frida had insisted. As she was waiting to cross Ben-Yehuda Street in the center of town, she had suddenly fallen. An ambulance was summoned and she was taken to Shaarei Zedek Hospital for treatment of what was presumed to be a leg broken by a fall. But she had not tripped. The doctors discovered that a hip bone had given way because of an advanced case of cancer.

Frida said she had not known about the cancer, but the doctor with whom her hostess had spoken had been skeptical about that. Furthermore, it had emerged that Frida was not the wife of a wealthy doctor in Buenos Aires or of anyone. She was a divorced woman, and she had so little money that she had not even bought health insurance before leaving for Israel. The hospital bill was about $200 a day, and hospital administrators were pressing for Frida's immediate departure unless someone agreed to pay for her hospitalization, said her hostess. She was willing to continue putting her up but this was no permanent solution. Would I, she asked, call the wealthy businessman who had made contact with Frida through me and ask whether he would foot the bill.

I went to the hospital feeling both stricken for Frida and betrayed by her. If her story about her husband was false, then it was all false. Instead of a dream and eerie coincidences, there was only the obsession of a women with cancer, and perhaps with a mongoloid child, determined to give some meaning to her life.

There was no nurse at the reception desk on the floor of Frida's ward to tell me what room she was in. The only person visible was a women patient lying on a stretcher next to the desk, talking on the telephone. Her back was to me and when she half-turned to replace the receiver, I casually glanced at her and was struck by her beauty. It was a moment before I recognized her as Frida. Someone who had known her had told me she had been a candidate for Miss Argentina as a young woman but I had found it hard to believe. Now I was able to see it. She was radiant.

Without waiting for me to say anything, she started telling me about her husband as if she realized that I must know and that it had undermined my trust in her. She had indeed been married to a doctor with whom she had two children, she said. The birth of their daughter had thrown a shadow over their lives. Her husband had been present at the delivery and taken the baby in his hands. He recognized immediately from the configuration of the baby's palm that it was retarded and for an instant hesitated in whether or not he would let it live. "I decided to let it live and instead condemned a family to death," he would tell Frida despairingly in later years. Although she continued to love him—*because* she continued to love him and felt his pain, said Frida—she decided to divorce him and free him from his familial bonds. She married a man who had been their close friend and then divorced him as well. They had all remained friends and often on Sundays both ex-husbands would come to visit at the same time. The men would play cards with each other in the salon while she prepared lunch. She had told me she was married to the doctor, she said, because in her mind she still considered herself to be married to him.

Frida was flown home on a stretcher a few days later. She subsequently wrote that the paralysis that had afflicted her for the previous four months had passed and that she was able to stand and even to get out of a bathtub unaided. "The doctors, with my husband at the head of the list, do not accept this recovery as a reality. They say it is a mind suggestion." She indicated that she had been receiving only psychic assistance, refusing to accept medical treatment. She was determined to return to Israel to finish her task, she said. In a subsequent letter, she wrote of pain in her arm and said the Jerusalem group had sent her a "parapsychic." She had no objection to my writing in the newspaper about her illness. She also enclosed for forwarding a letter to an archaeologist who had indicated readiness to carry out the dig if Yadin's approval could be obtained.

A few months later she wrote that she was confined again to bed. She appeared to be accepting medical treatment. For the first time, she sounded despairing.

It was the last letter I received from her. Several months later, a mutual acquaintance I ran into in downtown Jerusalem mentioned in passing that Frida had died.

T H I R T E E N

The Professor in Search of the Temple

DR. ASHER KAUFMAN SAT IN HIS LIVING ROOM in Jerusalem's Bait Hak-erem Quarter in the winter of 1974 reading aloud to his wife, Joseph-ine, from the Bible. Since the death of their nineteen-year-old daugh-ter, Rachel, three years before, it had been their custom to read a portion of the Bible daily, as Rachel had done. This time, the Hebrew University physicist read aloud from Ezekiel. As he reached chapter 8, verse 16, he straightened up.

"And He brought me into the inner court of the Lord's house, and, behold, at the door of the Temple of the Lord, between the porch and the altar, were about five and twenty men, with their backs toward the Temple of the Lord and their faces toward the east; and they worshipped the sun toward the east."

The band of renegade sun-worshippers had signaled to Kaufman across the ages a possible answer to the problem he had been strug-gling with for years.

Since the Six Day War, when the Temple Mount had become acces-sible, Kaufman had been wondering about the precise location of the ancient temple. The assumption universally accepted by scholars and laymen was that the temple site had been covered since the seventh century by the most prominent landmark in Jerusalem—the golden-domed Islamic shrine, the Dome of the Rock. The fifty-four-year-old scientist felt that this concept was incorrect, although he could not say why.

With the Temple Mount for all practical purposes an extraterritorial entity run by the Supreme Muslim Council, an archaeological probe for any remains of the Hebrew temple was out of the question. In addition, the rabbinical authorities forbade Jews from treading on the mount for fear of unknowingly entering the temple's holy precincts from which all but ritually pure priests had been banned. Most Orthodox Jews complied with this ban, although Ashkenazi chief rabbi Shlomo Goren maintained it permissible to enter the southern part of the mount, which clearly had not been part of the sanctified area.

In 1970 it occurred to Kaufman that, despite these restrictions, science might offer a clue to the temple's location. For a millennium, animals and birds had been sacrificed at the temple's altar, which was, in effect, an abattoir. So clean, however, was the site, according to the Talmud, that not a fly was ever to be seen. What kept it clean was constant rinsing, the water coming from aqueducts leading from King Solomon's pools near Bethlehem to the south and from the Hebron Hills beyond.

The Mishnah describes the altar as having two holes through which the blood flowed "and mingled in the sewer and ran out into Wadi Kidron." Kaufman conjectured that a millennium of this kind of blood irrigation might have left a trace in the soil of the Kidron Valley. By employing chemistry, physics, and other sciences, he felt, it might be possible to trace the point at which the sewer from the altar breached the western city wall above the Kidron Valley. This could give a rough idea of where the altar—and the temple—was located.

Kaufman spelled out his theory to another Bait Hakerem resident, archaeologist Michael Avi-Yonah, who had designed a large scale model of Jerusalem during the Second Temple period, the best-known representation of the ancient city. Professor Avi-Yonah encouraged Kaufman to put his theory to the test. Dedicating his sabbatical year to the project, Professor Kaufman soon discovered that implementation of his fairly simple idea involved tremendous problems, including determination of the ancient course of the Kidron. As the months of his sabbatical year passed, he began seeking alternative avenues of exploration.

He focused increasingly on the Talmudic tractate *Middot* compiled in the late Temple period and shortly afterward—apparently by Rabbi Eliezer Ben-Ya'akov, whom Kaufman was soon referring to as "my great pal." *Middot* offered a more detailed description of the temple and its practices than any source. Although there were many gaps in its description, some scholars felt it had been compiled as a guide for the temple's reconstruction. Kaufman spent months trying to put himself in Rabbi Eliezer's place, that is, surrounded by terrible destruction and trying to understand how he would impart to posterity information about a temple that no longer existed.

Although *Middot* supplied details as precise as the height of temple steps, it did not specifically mention where the temple itself stood on the massive Temple Mount platform. Kaufman believed there may have been a written manual that enabled the historian Josephus and the compilers of *Middot* to make such accurate descriptions years after the temple's destruction. In the absence of maps, Kaufman believed the compilers of *Middot* may have offered some written indication of the temple's location. If there was one, it seemed to have been connected with the ceremony of the red heifer.

The only way to purify persons who had been in contact with the dead so that they might enter the temple was to sprinkle them with water containing ashes of the heifer. From time to time, heifers would be led out from the eastern gate of Jerusalem to the Mount of Olives across the narrow Kidron Valley. There, the high priest would slaughter the young cow, which would be burned on a pyre and its ashes gathered. The Bible (Numbers 19:4) describes the priest sprinkling the blood of the heifer "opposite the front of the tent of meeting [the temple] seven times." This passage seemed to mean that the priest standing on the Mount of Olives was facing the main entrance to the temple sanctuary.

This notion was reinforced by *Middot* in its description of the temple compound's walls. "All the walls were high except the eastern wall so that the priest who burnt the red heifer might, while standing on the Mount of Olives, by directing his gaze carefully, see the entrance of the sanctuary at the time of the sprinkling of the blood."

Kaufman had been mulling over this detail when he read the passage from Ezekiel that Friday night. He had read it before, but now, its meaning suddenly electrified him. The sun-worshippers turning their backs on the temple to face the rising sun indicated that the Temple was on an east-west axis—that it had been built facing away from the sun in a renunciation of sun worship. To Kaufman, the fact that the passage from Ezekiel was read during Sukkoth also had significance, because that was the period of the autumn equinox, when the rising sun was closest to due east.

As soon as the Sabbath was over he took out a map of Jerusalem and began tracing east-west lines of sight from the top of the Mount of Olives to the Temple Mount about eight hundred meters distant. Kaufman presumed that the ceremony was conducted near the crest in order to permit the priest to look over the eastern temple compound wall. (Although this wall was lower than the rest, it could not be too low because the temple compound also served as a walled fortress.)

The flat crest of the Mount of Olives was for the most part too northerly to permit an east-west line of sight to the Temple Mount. From the crest's southernmost end, however, Kaufman drew an east-west line that reached the Golden Gate near the northern end of the Temple Mount, about ninety-five meters from the center of the Dome of the Rock. There could be no east-west line of sight to the Dome of the Rock itself from the ridge. It was for Kaufman the first solid clue as to the temple's location. But it was not evidence.

For this he had to look at the Temple Mount itself. He began with aerial photos, which showed numerous small rock protuberances—the remains of ancient structures—in the northern part of the mount. Over the years—particularly since 1967—the Muslim authorities had made many changes on the mount—covering some areas with plantings and paths and excavating other areas in order to install water pipes and electric cables.

With the assistance of the Hebrew University geography department, Kaufman obtained numerous old aerial photos of the Temple Mount, including excellent military reconnaissance photos by German aircraft in 1918, shortly after the city fell to the British. Fresh aerial photos were made for him by a private mapping firm and by the government survey department.

The aerial photos revealed "plant lines" of stunted vegetation that suggested underground structures, including a two-meter thick line that Kaufman considered to be the outline of the northern wall of the Court of Women, one of the spaces in the temple compound.

To make a proper investigation, however, the Orthodox Jewish scientist had to find a way around the rabbinical ban on setting foot on the Temple Mount. He found it in a passage in *Tosefet* that says it is a mitzvah to enter the temple to build, repair, or clean it—even for a nonpriest. In researching the temple, he decided, he was working on its rebuilding, albeit theoretically, and therefore was eligible to tread on the hallowed ground.

In scanning the Temple Mount from where he thought the high

priest might have stood on the Mount of Olives, he had taken an east-west sighting on the Golden Gate in the Old City wall and on a small cupola in the same line more than two hundred meters beyond it on the Temple Mount. Kaufman had a lot to think about on his way home; foremost was the apparent central position of the cupola in the area he presumed was the temple site. In a reference work in his study, he found the cupola to be an Islamic structure called the Dome of the Spirits. When he read that it stood over a circle of bedrock, he literally jumped in his chair.

If the Dome of the Rock was not the temple site, then the large stone around which it was built was not the Foundation Stone which had been in the Holy of Holies, the temple's innermost sanctum. The bedrock beneath the Dome of the Spirits, at first glance was a possible alternative. As his research progressed, this possibility became an absolute certainty for Kaufman.

One of the first outcroppings Kaufman sought out on the Temple Mount was a stepped ensemble of hewn rock—subsequently earthed over by the Muslim Council—which had caught his attention in the aerial photos. Bedrock cut in this fashion, he had learned, could be an indication that a gate had been built there. Kaufman would subsequently identify this as part of the northwestern corner wall of the temple's inner court.

In all, Kaufman would identify some twenty objects—rock cuttings, wall remains, and cisterns—as part of the Second Temple complex. There were two things that most of them had in common. They were either 43.7 centimeters in length, multiples of that length, or half that length. And many were oriented either nine degrees south of west or nine degrees north of west.

The common unit of measurement linking these finds, Kaufman deduced, was the cubit, so often mentioned in *Middot*. This cubit measurement was smaller than most scholars thought, but this, Kaufman was convinced, was plainly the cubit dimension peculiar to the Second Temple.

The different orientations also fit a pattern if the temple axis was exactly east-west. The cut rocks on the northern side of this axis were inclined south of west, and those paralleling on the southern side were inclined north of west. This clearly indicated to Kaufman opposite walls of a single tapering structure.

Taken together with the descriptions in *Middot*, Josephus, the Bible, *Tosefet*, and other sources, these finds in the field permitted Kaufman to construct a painstakingly detailed plan of the Second Temple.

The 170-meter-long temple compound he depicted was roughly rectangular except for the tapering walls at the western end. Most of the eastern end was taken up by the large Court of Women. Men were permitted to pass from here through a gate into the temple's inner court. Israelites could pass no farther than a narrow strip just inside this court.

Most of the inner court was the province of the priests, who performed sacrifices at the open altar. Dominating the court, and the temple complex as a whole, was the sanctuary, the equivalent in height of a modern fifteen-story building. Its beauty was legendary. "He who has not seen the temple has not seen a beautiful building," says the Talmud. An inner room of the sanctuary was the Holy Place (Kodesh) accessible only to select priests. Beyond it, and set off by a double curtain, was the Holy of Holies, which could be entered only by the high priest and only on Yom Kippur.

In the First Temple, the Holy of Holies contained the two Tablets of the Law that Moses received on Mount Sinai and the Foundation Stone whose appearance and whose function, if it had any, are unknown. In the Second Temple, the room was empty except for the Foundation Stone—no mention being made in the sources of the tablets after the destruction by the Babylonians in 586 B.C. of the First Temple. The Ark of the Covenant, which had carried the tablets from the Sinai Desert into the Promised Land, was saved with its sacred contents, according to one Mishnah text, by being buried next to the Court of the Women. Kaufman thought he knew where it still might be.

The soft Scottish brogue and shy smile of the physicist who began to expound these incredible notions publicly in the early 1980s disarmed those braced for a religious zealot. Israeli archaeologists who came to know him did not accept his theory—at most, some would leave the question open—but treated his arguments with respect.

In the Second World War, the University of Edinburgh–trained physicist had helped develop an RAF gunsight for the bright skies of the Pacific. He subsequently did fundamental research on nuclear fusion, and in 1959 emigrated with his family to Israel.

When Kaufman began publishing his findings in Israeli cultural journals, the dry details were incomprehensible to most readers. The outlandishness of his theory—and the notion that everyone but he was wrong about the site of the Temple—did not win him any following. This would change somewhat after he came across a report that an archaeologist had, in 1970, seen an ancient wall in a pit dug on the Temple Mount by the Supreme Muslim Council. Archaeologist Zeev Yeiven had been summoned to the mount by a telephone call from an acquaintance who had seen the wall in a pit being dug for a reservoir one hundred meters north of the Dome of the Rock. Following the al-Aksa fire the previous year, the municipality had urged the Muslim Council to dig reservoirs for additional water supply in future emergencies.

The wall that Yeiven saw was two meters thick, five meters long, and several courses high. It could have been from the Roman or Byzantine periods but there was something about its massiveness that led him to speculate in the report he wrote for the antiquities department that it might be a Herodian structure from the period of the Second Temple. He did not suggest that it might be part of the temple itself because, like everyone else, he had no doubt that the temple had occupied the site of the Dome of the Rock one hundred meters to the south. But it could have been part of some other Herodian structure, he wrote in his report. When Yeivin returned a week later with two senior archaeologists, he found that the wall had been destroyed in order to build the reservoir. At the suggestion of his superiors, Yeivin did not publicize his report because of the political sensitivity involved in attributing a possible Jewish character to remains uncovered on the Temple Mount—Jewish nationalists might raise a furor, passions would be unleashed among the Muslims, and international repercussions would not be far behind. In the wake of the al-Aksa fire, the last thing the Israeli authorities wanted was another outburst of protest on the Temple Mount issue.

Few Israeli archaeologists were to hear of the wall. When one of those who did happened to mention it almost a decade later to Kaufman, the latter promptly contacted Yeiven. The archaeologist agreed to show him a copy of his report.

"Is there anything interesting in it?" Yeiven asked when Kaufman had finished reading.

"You have no idea how interesting," answered Kaufman.

Pulling out his own plan of the Temple, he showed that the uncovered wall was almost precisely where the eastern wall of the Temple should have been.

A major question asked of Kaufman by archaeologists is why the builders of the temple would not have followed common practice by constructing it on the highest available point—the site of the Dome of the Rock—instead of the secondary peak Kaufman has suggested. In reply, the physicist pointed to Samuel 11 (24:18) describing how

King David came to buy the site for fifty shekels of silver in order to build an altar. "And God came that day to David and said to him, 'Go up, bear an altar unto the Lord in the threshing floor of Araunah the Jebusite.'" The location then of the threshing floor fixed the site of the altar, says Kaufman, and therefore of the temple that King Solomon would subsequently construct on the site. Herod's Temple would make use of the same altar. "As a threshing floor, this makes sense," says Kaufman. "It's lower than the ground to the west and therefore has some protection from the wind which is prevalent from that direction."

In formulating his theory, Kaufman made use of some twenty disciplines, including mathematics, civil engineering, ancient Jewish art, ancient netrology (fixing standards of measurement), aerial photographic interpretation, and comparative architecture, backed, of course, by extensive reading in Jewish and secular sources.

Kaufman admits to adjusting his theory a number of times when he found himself in error. But he dismisses these as "second-order corrections", borrowing a term from physics. Despite widespread skepticism, he is convinced with a calm certainty that the temple plan he has drawn up is accurate to within ten centimeters.

"The jigsaw fits beautifully. It's impossible that this is anything but the temple. Those who say it isn't have to find an alternative explanation for what I've found." So far, no one has.

F O U R T E E N

Religious Seekers

IF THE BUSINESS OF AMERICA IS BUSINESS, the business of Jerusalem is prayer. Even in the depths of a winter night, the Western Wall is almost never deserted. At least one petitioner, meek or zealous, will be standing before the ancient stones thanking God for the miracle of life or asking for some lesser miracle: a son to return safely from the army, health, a husband for an older daughter. The crevices between the stones fill each day with written requests—special delivery messages to heaven—that are regularly gathered by the rabbinical authorities in charge of the wall and buried, as is done with holy script that is discarded. A curious university lecturer, serving a stint of reserve army duty in the vicinity, plucked a note from the wall one night and found it to contain a lottery number left by a Chicago tourist who also included his home address to ensure that God would know where to send the winnings.

The Holy Sepulcher Church, traditional site of Jesus' crucifixion, likewise continues to function as a channel between man and his Maker long after the lights have gone out in the government offices, at the university, and in homes around the city. The massive doors are shut to the public at night, but clergymen from different denominations who sleep inside the huge building take turns saying Mass until dawn.

The most impressive public prayers each week are held on the

149

Temple Mount on Fridays where thousands of Muslims kneel together and touch their foreheads to the ground as the voice of the imam inside al-Aksa Mosque is projected over loudspeakers. At both the Western Wall and Holy Sepulcher, prayers are offered by a host of different congregations, but on the Temple Mount worshippers form a single, massed assembly responding impressively in unison. Among the keenest auditors of the Friday sermon delivered in al-Aksa are members of the Israeli security services. The imam's words, dealing often with current affairs, are an important insight into the political mood in the Arab community and can themselves stir their hearers into rioting in times of tension.

There is more to piety, of course, than prayers. In Jerusalem and the desert to the east, men have long come to their own private terms with the eternal mysteries.

At night, says Father Photius, looking straight up from the bottom of the canyon at the sliver of blue sky, one sees an array of stars that people living in civilization never imagine. The Austrian-born monk has been looking up and wondering at that spectacle for more than a decade. He is sixty-six now and the sole occupant of the monastery in the upper part of Wadi Kelt less than ten kilometers east of Jerusalem.

The monastery is almost as old as Christianity. Shortly after it was built, more than 1,600 years ago, colonies of hermits took up residence in the caves dotting the walls of the wadi. Encouraged by the Byzantine rulers anxious to build up a Christian presence in the desert to counter increasing Arab pressure from the east, some 7,000 hermits lived in the Judean Desert. Food was provided by the desert monasteries. Today there are no more hermits in the caves and Father Photius is himself considered a hermit. In the absence of any support system, however, he must return to civilization periodically to stock up on food. Every two or three weeks, the elderly monk walks up the steep track leading from the canyon floor to the Jerusalem road, where he catches a bus to the Old City.

A modern-day hermit like Father Photius has a post-office box in town. In it, he finds mail from home and Austrian newspapers. He scans the newspapers in town but does not take them back to the monastery, where they would divert the mind from contemplation. A convivial man, the monk enjoys the human contacts on these trips. Attending an Easter reception once at the "White Russian" headquarters in the Old City, he had met a *landsman*—a fellow Austrian,

Teddy Kollek. The two were soon conversing in Viennese dialect. When Father Photius mentioned in passing that his cisterns had run dry—the ancient channels that had brought rain runoff had long since broken—the mayor dispatched a municipal team that dragged a generator across the wadi slopes to pump water into the cisterns from the springs on the wadi floor.

Photius divides his days between prayer, contemplation, writing a history of the monastery—the oldest in the country—and physical work, such as gardening and repairs. "Without a strict daily discipline, you couldn't make it," he says. He has been writing the history by hand since Bedouin youth stole his two typewriters while he was making a trip to Jerusalem.

"This life has brought me inner tranquility. It has permitted me to learn sufficiently about myself to advise others." Some time before, a priest who had decided to leave his order had come to the monastery to discuss it with Photius. For two days they talked and at the end the priest decided "to stay where God put him," relates Photius.

The monk knows that he cannot live this life much longer. He does not feel loneliness, but for him the climb up from the canyon that he must make periodically has become exhausting now that he is older. Once he fell and lay unconscious for three hours. He plans to retire eventually to his home in the Tyrol with an Austrian government pension. There is a picture of the house with its peaked roof on the wall of his room. But he does not want to leave before a replacement can be found. It will not be easy, he knows, finding one, and he fears that the monastery will be closed down when he leaves. When he does go, he will bear with him the memory of the Wadi Kelt cliffside changing color with the shifting sun and of the carpet of stars at night.

"Here," he says, "you feel the almightiness of God."

The elderly woman at the dinner table is talking about her grandfather, Reb Duvid, one of the founders of the ultra-Orthodox quarter of Mea Shearim. She still recalls the astonishment with which she had tugged at her mother's dress the first time she heard her grandfather recite the kiddush prayer over wine on a Friday night. They were the first words she had ever heard him speak, and they would be the only words she would ever hear him speak. Years before, after his first two children had died of disease, Reb Duvid decided that he was to blame, that he had sinned by speaking *lashon hara*, intemperately. He made a vow that he would not speak again so that his wife might bear healthy children. He would keep that vow until his death twenty-five years later and his wife would bear him several children. Reb Duvid would say his daily prayers silently and the only words that would pass his lips were those of the kiddush on Friday nights. He communicated with his children and his grandchildren, whom he dearly loved, with grunts and sign language in the knowledge that it was his silence that had permitted them life. One of those grandchildren is today a nuclear physicist at the Weizmann Institute near Tel Aviv.

Each Christian sect in Jerusalem makes its own terms with God. The Greek Orthodox monks in the Holy Sepulcher Church sleep on the simplest of beds in sparsely furnished cells without running water or heat and sometimes punish their bodies by dressing lightly against the winter cold. They are not to be distracted from their holy duties by reading newspapers or similar incursions into the modern world. Those who break church rules may be sent for a time to one of the desert monasteries or, worse, deprived of communion for a period. The monks in the Armenian Quarter a few hundred meters away not only read newspapers every day but have television sets in their rooms that they purchase out of their salaries. Trained to work in Armenian communities around the world, the young monks study sociology, psychology, and other worldly subjects. The only self-punishment they are expected to endure is two days a week without meat.

Few of the Christian clergy in Jerusalem were born in the city or even in the country. They come from the corners of the Western world, usually within the framework of a highly organized church. Sometimes, however, will come the solitary seeker.

FIFTEEN

Sister Abraham and the Ethiopian Church

SISTER ABRAHAM WAS AT HER DESK in the Ethiopian archbishop's residence in Jerusalem's Old City one day in 1971 when she was summoned to the salon. She found the room already filled with monks and nuns, dressed in their holiday finery, gathered about a stranger of distinguished bearing seated in the center. The senior clergyman present spoke to him in English, a language that few of the others in the room understood.

Sister Abraham, whose acceptance into the Ethiopian church had never been enthusiastic, was not introduced to the stranger but she listened closely to the conversation. It concerned the small Deir es-Sultan Monastery adjacent to the Holy Sepulcher Church. The monastery had been the subject of a bitter dispute between the Ethiopian and Coptic churches for centuries. The Copts had had the upper hand, but in the latest turn the year before, the Ethiopians had changed the locks on two chapel doors while the Copts were at Easter prayers and had taken possession. The move had had international repercussions—with Egypt championing the cause of its native Copts. The Israeli police had declined to intervene, terming the situation a political issue, and the Ethiopians were still in possession.

The elegantly dressed caller was plainly familiar with the dispute and seemed annoyed at the way the Ethiopians were handling it. He spoke with surprising frankness. "If your diplomats took more inter-

153

est in research and less in cocktail parties, you would be able to find
out more about your rights.''

The stranger was the only white person in the room—except for
Sister Abraham. It was not, however, racial identity that made her
receptive to his words but the thrust of his remark about the need to
base the Ethiopians' claim on hard research. The university-educated
nun had long had a deep desire to probe the story of the Ethiopians
in Jerusalem. ''I have what is needed,'' she thought to herself. ''Why
don't I do it?'' That same day she began.

The research carried out in the subsequent years by the Danish-
born nun, apparently the only white nun ever to join the Ethiopian
Orthodox church, resulted in a scholarly yet highly readable work,
The History of the Ethiopian Community in the Holy Land, published a
decade later. The book illuminated a little known corner of Jerusalem's vibrant church world, a world where politics and personalities
play no less a role than theology.

Beyond scholarship, Sister Abraham would demonstrate the
ability of a determined and talented woman—in this case, one who
had mastered fifteen languages, modern and ancient—to find her
own way, even in a nun's garb, even in a clerical world where the
keys of the kingdom are still held by men.

Born Kirsten Pedersen in Denmark in 1932, she grew up as a Lu-
theran but decided at age thirteen to become a Catholic after reading
a book on the saints. Ten days after finishing her matriculation examinations at age nineteen, she entered a closed convent. She would
not emerge for eleven years, except for once-a-year visits to a nearby
monastery during her last five years. With a bent for scholarship and
a ready grasp of languages, she was assigned as a teacher, or nun's
mistress, to young nuns entering the convent. A crisis in the order
impelled her to give up this life of surety. The dispute was between
those who favored ''Italianization'' of the order and those, including
herself, who wished to nurture a Scandanavian approach to piety,
which included a desire to offer a broad education to nuns. The sides
could not be reconciled and the order was dissolved.

Remaining a nun, although no longer connected with an order,
Sister Abraham enrolled in the University of Copenhagen, where she
majored in Semitic philology for three years. In the summer of the
second year, she and another nun who had left the convent with her
traveled to Israel to work as volunteers at a kibbutz. This first contact
with the Holy Land was sufficient for her to determine that she would
return the following year to spend the rest of her life there.

In the well-organized structure of the Catholic church, nuns are normally no more free to pick permanent overseas postings than are diplomats. As a nun living outside the regular church framework, however, Sister Abraham could do so as long as she could support herself. Intent on continuing her studies at Hebrew University, she arrived in the summer of 1964 with enough money to pay for two years' tuition. She had learned Hebrew at fifteen and could read medieval Hebrew poets as well as the Talmud. She enrolled in a course in modern Hebrew and in the fall began her university studies. Focusing on Scriptures and Hebrew literature, she took thirty-five hours of courses a week instead of the normal twenty-two so as to be able to squeeze three years of work into two. To earn food and board, she worked as a cleaning woman in a convent.

It was at the university that she first came into contact with Ethiopians—Christian students whom she helped by translating work from English to Hebrew. Through these students she met clerics in the local Ethiopian church as well as a niece of the former Ethiopian emperor, Haile Selassie, living in Jerusalem. Searching for a way to stay in the country, Sister Abraham had already considered joining one of the Eastern churches. She loved their liturgy and poetry and felt that they were closer to the spirituality of the early desert fathers than the Western church. The contact with the Ethiopians seemed to offer a heaven-sent opportunity. Soon Sister Abraham embarked on a study of Amharic, the main Ethiopian spoken language, and Geez, the language used in Ethiopian liturgy. Impressed by her scholarship, the Ethiopian archbishop asked her to undertake translation work and teaching. Sister Abraham took up residence in the Ethiopian church headquarters in the Old City.

She adopted the Ethiopian custom of tatooing a small cross near her thumbs and performed considerable service for the community as a contact with the outside world. It was she, for instance, who would look after passport matters. Nevertheless, many of the monks and nuns did not accept her. Apart from her being white, there was a perception of her among the Ethiopians as a threat—a dynamic, intellectual force unleashed in a passive, nonintellectual society.

With the arrival of a new bishop in 1972, Mattewos, Sister Abraham's services were put to extensive use. Mattewos was an innovator who placed great emphasis on education. The Ethiopian monks were generally ignorant of other languages. He wished to oblige them to learn at least English, Hebrew, and Arabic, and he expanded the curriculum to include other languages in addition to mathematics, basic biology, and physics. Sister Abraham was extensively employed in teaching the monks, although, to her disappointment, only one nun chose to avail herself of the educational opportunities. Mattewos himself engaged in historical research and permitted scholars ready access to the extensive, centuries-old documentation in the Ethiopian monastery. Sister Abraham used this opportunity fully during his five-year tenure. After Mattewos's departure, access to the archives of the monastery was closed to her by his successors, less broad-minded than he. But she had already gained sufficient material for her book.

In it Sister Abraham traces the Ethiopian community in Jerusalem from the fourth century A.D. until 1974, when a military uprising overthrew the regime in Addis Ababa. The small Ethiopian commu-nity in Jerusalem was a window to the outside world for governments in remote Ethiopia during much of this period and a door into Africa for European countries, including Russia and England, which offered their protection to the Jerusalem Ethiopian community.

The neglect and lassitude that had enveloped Jerusalem during centuries of Turkish rule began to give way following the opening of the British consulate in 1838, the first consulate in the city. It was soon followed by consulates of other powers who played out their rivalries in the holy city. The Crimean War that erupted in 1854 was ostensibly fought because of differences over the holy places in Jeru-salem. The establishment of a Protestant see in Jerusalem in 1841, and of the Latin (Roman Catholic) patriarch seven years later, created a three-way competition with the older Orthodox churches, particu-larly the Greek. In this sea of rivalries, small churches like the Ethio-pians would themselves be in need of strong protectors.

During the nineteenth century, the British government had played that role, attempting to secure the Ethiopians' tenuous hold on holy places that were being challenged by the Copts and other churches. The Russians later became the Ethiopians' protector. Following devel-opment of the Russian Compound outside the walls of the Old City in the late nineteenth century, the Ethiopians built their own church compound nearby. According to Ethiopian sources, this project was financed by three boxes of gold captured by the Ethiopians from the Turks at the battle of Gur'a. Numerous houses were built near the church in the ensuing decades by members of the Ethiopian aristo-cracy and royalty.

Under an agreement formulated in 1910 at the initiative of the Ethi-opian government, monks and nuns in the Jerusalem monastery were forbidden from spending their time in idleness and were advised to take up agriculture, probably because most of the monks were of peasant origin. However, an official sent from Addis Ababa in 1966 to examine the state of the church in Jerusalem described the monks and nuns as idle and declared that they hated work.

More than a third of the year for the Ethiopian clergy consists of fast days in which no food or drink is consumed before early afternoon. The monks and nuns, numbering about fifty in Jerusalem, are obliged to come to church for prayer services between 4:00 and 6:00 A.M. and 4:00 and 5:00 P.M. each day. Every month each member receives a small sum of money for his or her personal use, and once a year money is distributed for the purchase of clothes.

Although some members of the Ethiopian aristocracy came to live as nuns in Jerusalem, the Jerusalem monastery did not become an institution for aristocratic ascetics, as was the case with some European monasteries during the Middle Ages. Almost all the monks are from priestly or peasant families; in Ethiopia, as throughout the Orthodox world, village priests are mostly married farmers. Some of the nuns are priests' widows. Others came to the country as servants of noble ladies and became nuns later.

The Italian invasion of Ethiopia in 1935 had a powerful impact on the Jerusalem community. Emperor Haile Selassie was forced into exile the following year with his family, spending a few weeks living in Jerusalem's fashionable Rehavia Quarter before moving on to England. In 1939, after the League of Nations formally recognized the Italian takeover of Ethiopia, the Italian government attempted to gain control of the Ethiopian property in Jerusalem, beginning with the house of Empress Zawditu on Prophets' Street. "At this point in the story," noted Sister Abraham in her book, "the Ethiopians found a learned, clever, and dedicated helper in the Jerusalem lawyer, Mr. Nathan Marein."

The Jewish lawyer lived on Ethiopia Street, directly across from the church, and was personally acquainted with its leaders. He had reportedly studied together with Haile Selassie in Heidelberg. British Mandatory officials suggested that the Ethiopians hand over the building to the Italians to save themselves court expenses, but Marein fought the case through the courts and won. Italy's entry into the war on the side of Germany in 1940, effectively canceled its claims against other Ethiopian property in Jerusalem.

Coming across Marein's name in the documents in the Ethiopian monastery, Sister Abraham became convinced that he was the distin-

guished gentleman whose remarks had inspired her to undertake the
history. However, Ethiopian church officials whom she asked denied
it and said that Marein was long dead. It was only six years after that
1971 encounter that an abbot confirmed that the visitor had indeed
been Marein but repeated that he had died. Convinced, however,
that he must still be alive, Sister Abraham succeeded in tracking him
down to an address in Boston. Marein responded with enthusiasm
to her letters and made available to her his records that were de-
posited with his niece who lived south of Tel Aviv.

Sister Abraham learned that Marein was from a Danish Jewish
family. His father, a fur merchant, was caught in Jerusalem when the
First World War broke out. The elder Marein could not leave the
country but managed to have his family transported to Palestine. Nathan went on to study law at Heidelberg. His defence of the Ethiopian
interests in Jerusalem brought virulent condemnation from Italy and
Germany. Marein later told relatives that there had been an attempt
to murder him but he did not give details.

When Selassie returned to Ethiopia after the Italians had been
ousted, he invited Marein to join him in order to formulate a modern
legal system for the country. A book written by Marein in the 1950s,
The Judicial System and Laws of Ethiopia, identifies him as advocate-
general and advisor to the imperial Ethiopian government. He and
his wife were childless, but every year Marein would visit his extensive family in Israel.

In 1975, a year after the Ethiopian revolution, Marein left the country for good after twenty-five years as one of the Emperor's most
influential advisors, and settled in Boston, where he taught international law at Harvard. His American-born wife was from the well-
known Sachar family.

When Marein fell mortally ill late in 1982 a few years after his wife's
death, he came back to Israel to be near his family. One of his first
requests was to see Sister Abraham. His niece telephoned the request
to the Ethiopian monastery several times but it was never passed on.
When Sister Abraham subsequently learned of it, she was deeply upset at this lost opportunity to meet a man she had greatly admired
and to whom she owed so much. She would often visit his grave,
and established close ties with his Israeli family.

The nun, who could often be seen traveling around Jerusalem on
her bicycle, left the Ethiopian monastery after several years and
found quarters in a convent on the Mount of Olives. She enrolled in
the Hebrew University School of African Studies, where she com-

pleted a doctorate based on analysis of Ethiopian critical interpretations of the psalms.

Sister Abraham remains an independent nun, unaffiliated with any order. She earns her living by painting icons and teaching languages and history in monasteries. It is a life of material poverty but, she notes, monks are accustomed to living in great poverty.

In the conclusion of her book, Sister Abraham urged the Ethiopian community in Jerusalem to seek a synthesis between eastern spirituality and the openness of the West. "Jerusalem more than any other place in the world offers a possibility of realizing such a synthesis," she wrote.

There would be no better example in Jerusalem of this synthesis than Sister Abraham herself, who successfully merged West and East while remaining true to her faith and her intellect.

S I X T E E N

The Whites and the Reds

IN THE EVENING, after vespers, the nuns are reluctant to make their way up the slope to their stone cottages, where they will rest in the arms of the Lord till dawn.

The tranquillity of the Russian convent in the Ein Kerem Quarter has been breached by murder, and the silence reverberates still with the unheard screams of Sister Barbara and her daughter, Sister Veronika.

For the past two weeks at dusk, when the last light slips down the valley, the nuns have been putting on their coats against the evening chill and gathering in the refectory, where the long table with the high-backed chair at one end is already laid for next morning's meal.

They sit there, talking out their fears, until Sister Feodosia, the elderly nun acting as mother superior, reassures them that the danger is past and that God will preserve them. Eventually they make their way to their rooms and shut fast the doors.

In truth, Sister Feodosia herself is terrified. "Since the murder, even the trees seem dejected," she says. The trees mask the century-old convent from the outside world, except for gaps revealing terraced and wooded slopes across the valley, which looks as distant and unobtrusive as a biblical picture-book. The hush is so deep that the chirping of a bird on a branch overhead can be startling.

The cottage occupied by sisters Barbara, 68, and Veronika, 43, is reached by a narrow path winding upward through terraces thick with greenery. Some of the steps are cut into the rock. A stone-built lower floor containing the kitchen supports an upper story faced with tin and reached by an outside staircase that has been partially enclosed. It was in the upstairs quarters that the killer found them.

A police officer said the fully clothed bodies lay sprawled on the floor but the nuns say they had been laid out side by side, their heads propped on a suitcase. "As if they were sleeping," said Feodosia. The small living-room in which the bodies were found gives way to an even smaller bedroom where two beds form an L-shape, their heads touching.

Barbara had taken to a convent in the Soviet Union with her infant daughter after her husband was killed early in World War II. They had been in the Holy Land twenty years. Veronika had grown from childhood to middle age in convents, alongside her mother. The outside world was sifted through that double veil of protectiveness. Veronika was a sweet, active person who led the choral singing in the chapel, said the nuns. For some time, age had prevented Barbara from participating in the strenuous maintenance work the nuns are obliged to do, and she was assigned on the convent's duty roster largely to prayer in the chapel.

Despite its ramshackle exterior, the apartment was not a gloomy cell but a bright, even cheerful place with trees and flowers visible from every window. A writer could find no more congenial retreat, nor, presumably, could a nun.

There was disorder but no signs of violence. A stack of letters from the Soviet Union lay on one table. Officials of the Russian church mission had said the mother and daughter wrote letters only to persons in monasteries in the Soviet Union and were presumed to have no close relatives.

On a table in the bedroom was an attractive cosmetics bottle labeled "Skin Dew Herbal Lotion." It was an unexpected sight in a nineteenth century convent, where water is still drawn from a cistern filled by the winter rains and where no radio, newspaper, or other wordly intrusion is permitted.

The convent is called Gorney—"mount" in Russian—and it houses most of the forty-five nuns maintained by the Russian Orthodox church mission in Israel. The other serve in Jaffa, Tiberias, and Haifa, where there are also Russian churches. Their principal task is prayer, and this is carried out according to timetable rosters drawn up by the senior nuns. They are also expected to do most of the maintenance work, even roof repairs.

The nuns venture out of the convent walls periodically to mission headquarters in downtown Jerusalem, where they are responsible for maintenance and where they can read newspapers from the Soviet Union. Another regular outing is to the colorful open-air Mahane Yehuda market. Here they mix unobtrusively with the residents of the city.

The nuns rise at 4:00 A.M. and begin praying in the chapel an hour later. Breakfast is the only meal they take together. They come to the refectory kitchen to cook their lunch but take it back to their cottages to eat. There is no dinner at all.

"We're forbidden to eat fattening foods," says Feodosia. "It interferes with the life of the spirit." They eat no meat and three times a week—"fast days"—refrain from fish, milk, and eggs as well.

It was the absence of Sister Veronika and her mother from breakfast and morning prayer that led a nun to seek them out in their stone cottage. No screams had been heard, but the nun who lived closest to them, about twenty meters distant, is deaf.

Only one male resides in the Ein Karem convent, Archimandrite Vartolomi. Three other priests live at mission headquarters in the Russian compound downtown, from which they regularly visit the other church properties around the country to hold prayers with the resident nuns. It is commonly assumed in Jerusalem that there is a KGB presence in the mission. Since the Soviet Union severed its relationship with Israel in 1967, the church mission is the only official Soviet representation in the country.

But the mission is not the only Russian clerical presence. Across town, nuns gather each evening in the Russian convent on the Mount of Olives for vespers. Some are elderly women who last saw Mother Russia when they were young girls. Most are young nuns who have never seen it at all. Although they bear names like Larissa, speak perfect Russian, and pour tea for the mother superior from an ornate samovar, the young nuns are in fact Palestinians brought to the convent as girls. In the absence of clerical reinforcements from Russia itself, the Arab nuns have become the mainstay of the church-in-exile in the Holy Land.

The White church, established by émigrés after the Russian Revolution and headquartered in New York, had been given possession of all Russian church properties in Palestine by the British mandatory authorities after World War I. Following the establishment of the state of Israel in 1948, the government of David Ben-Gurion permitted the Red church to displace the Whites from Russian church property as a quid pro quo for Moscow's early recognition of the new state. Whatever restrictions the Soviets place on religion within their own boundaries, they recognize its usefulness abroad in reinforcing the Russian presence. The Whites continued to control the church properties in East Jerusalem under Jordanian rule.

Since the Six Day War removed the barrier between them, the two churches have acknowledged each other's presence only in the courts, where the Whites initiated litigation to recover their properties in Israel from the Reds. The nuns from the two sides meet often in the Holy Sepulcher Church on Sundays and exchange traditional greetings like "pray for us." The priests, however, maintain their distance. Father Anthony, head of the White church in East Jerusalem, refers to the Red mission as "the eyes of Moscow." The Reds accuse the Whites of having abandoned their spiritual flock by having cut their ties through self-imposed exile from the Soviet Union.

A few days after the murder, two White priests rang the bell of the Red mission to offer condolences from Father Anthony. The latter would subsequently tell journalists, however, that he was not authorized to recognize the Red church by any formal contact and had merely asked two Greek Orthodox priests to act as intermediaries in passing on "to the believers—the sisters" in the Red mission that special prayers would be said for the murdered nuns by the White nuns. The first direct contact between the Reds and Whites since the Bolshevik Revolution had not occurred.

In the Gorney Convent, rarely visited by outsiders, a journalist accompanied by his own interpreter is permitted entry by the Red mission chief interested in applying pressure on the Israeli authorities to find the killer. Sister Feodosia is made available to answer questions, but a young nun, Sister Feodora, is at her side. Father Vartolomi explains that the interpreter might have difficulty understanding the senior nun's Ukrainian. Feodosia, it turned out, spoke a pure Russian and Feodora made few interjections.

The young nun had a pleasant, intelligent face with an expression that seemed to hover between amusement and reverence. She had been working as a lay librarian in the religious center of Zagorsk, forty miles from Moscow, and had taken her vows just before being sent to Ein Karem. She had arrived three years ago and had already been home on a visit. Would she like to spend the rest of her life in the Holy Land? "As God wills," she said.

Sister Feodosia arrived in 1956 and has visited home three times. Although nuns come out with the avowed intention of remaining forever, longing for Mother Russia and family often prove stronger than youthful intentions. In the past three years, fifteen of Feodosia's oldest friends in the convent had gone back. They have been replaced by thirty young nuns.

It soon becomes apparent that the nuns are haunted not only by the thought of a murderer still at large but by the suspicion that he might have been politically motivated. Feodora makes a point of noting that Sister Veronika had been "very much in favor of Israel." It seems an incongruous remark until Father Vartolomi, in the midst of a discussion of the murders, notes how much Israel owes the Soviet Union for its assistance in creating the state. The clear implication is that someone perhaps acting on behalf of Israel against a currently unfriendly Soviet government had disregarded an old political debt and in the process killed someone who was a friend of Israel.

The priest was not certain that agents of the state were involved— he left open the possibility that Jewish religious fanatics might have been responsible—but he declared that the killings could be understood as meaning that someone wanted the sisterhood to leave. He hoped the police were working hard on the case. "If they really want to find the murderer, they will."

Such attitudes about political motivations and all-powerful police stem from other climes, where terror was long a jealously guarded state monopoly. But the fear felt by the women at Gorney as the sun went down had nothing to do with political dialectics. To mitigate it, the authorities had taken the unusual step of installing a direct emergency link from the convent to police headquarters.

The two policemen posted at the convent gate since the murder peer inside cars of those entering and leaving and the beat of horse's hoofs could be heard as a mounted patrolman circled the perimeter of the convent. But Gorney's stout walls suddenly seemed frail protection against the world outside.

Two months later, police arrested a twenty-nine-year-old American Christian living in Ein Karem and charged him with the murder. A dabbler in the occult, he spoke to friends often of black magic and had been sent to a mental hospital for observation after an altercation with guests in the hostel in which he worked. He had been released a month before the murders. A woman friend would testify that he had told her that he had killed the nuns because they had been sent by the KGB to kill the year-old King of Israel whom he had seen at Jerusalem's central bus station with his parents.

The nuns at Gorney breathed easier after the arrest but their continued sense of vulnerability would be reflected by the doubling in height of the surrounding walls that turned the convent into a Kremlin-like fortification.

S E V E N T E E N

Jews in the Muslim Quarter

NOWHERE ARE JERUSALEM'S ETHNIC COMMUNITIES more clearly apart than where they are closest together—the Old City. Within its kilometer-square walls, the population has for centuries been divided among four distinct quarters—Armenian, Christian, Jewish, and Muslim. Although Jews and Muslims had lived in each other's quarters in the past, this ended almost completely in the 1930s when intercommunal tensions erupted in Arab riots. When the decision was made in 1967 to restore the Jewish Quarter, Kollek supported the relocation of all 5,500 Arabs living there, most of them refugees—on the grounds that coexistence in Jerusalem could endure only if there were some space between Arabs and Jews.

On the same grounds, he fought requests by Jews to return to Jewish-owned property in the Muslim Quarter. For more than a decade after the Six Day War, Kollek and like-minded government officials succeeded in this goal. It would be an amiable innocent who would finally succeed in circumventing them, and thereby insert a fuse in the powder keg.

It had begun as an offhand joke voiced one day on the Golan Heights to Menahem Hacohen by one of his friends in the yeshiva, where they were dividing time between army service and Talmud study in a special program. They had been studying tractates discussing priestly practices during the period of the temple two thousand years before. Alluding to the fact that Hacohen, like all persons bearing the name Cohen or derivatives thereof, was descended from the priestly caste, the friend said that Menahem should relate to the session not as an academic discourse but as vocational training.

Hacohen had smiled but afterwards the remark would not leave him. The twenty-three-year-old soldier-student, whose parents had immigrated from Germany and helped establish a religious kibbutz, was not a Messianic visionary contemplating the imminent restoration of the temple. But, he was indeed a *cohen*, or priest, and the coming of the Messiah was something that he and all religious Jews prayed for every day as part of the regular prayer service. If the Messiah did come, then, would it not be incumbent upon him and others of the priestly caste to perform the temple service?

In the yeshiva library, Hacohen found a work written at the turn of the century by the renowned Chafetz Haim, in which the sage laid down procedures for priestly duties in the rebuilt temple with the immediacy of a work roster being drawn up for any about-to-be-opened institution.

Hacohen wrote to Rabbi Zvi Yehuda Kook, in whose Jerusalem yeshiva he had studied for a year to ask whether it made sense for him to pursue the subject. The elderly rabbi replied by suggesting that he devote part of his time to temple studies. Hacohen understood that the rabbi was telling him not to lose his sense of proportion about the matter, but to go ahead.

Encouraged, the young yeshiva student then wrote to another former mentor to suggest that a symposium on the subject of the temple be organized. The rabbi replied that it was a good idea and referred him to two prominent rabbis in Jerusalem. Hacohen made the long trip from the Golan Heights to find that the rabbis were prepared to participate in such a symposium but were unwilling to organize it.

Hacohen was both discouraged enough and emboldened enough to attempt the organization of the symposium himself. There were, he had discovered, enough scholars prepared to take part. All he needed was a place, a date, and an audience. He printed brochures announcing a two-day symposium on the temple to be held in Jerusalem the following Passover, the venue to be announced at a later date. The brochures were posted on the bulletin boards of a number of yeshivot. To his astonishment, he received three hundred replies.

Less than two weeks before Passover, he traveled again to Jerusalem to search for a hall. The Jewish Quarter, from which the Temple

Mount could be seen, was the logical site but no hall was available. It was a woman to whom Hacohen had gone to arrange catering for the event who suggested that he look at a building in the adjacent Muslim Quarter. The former Torat Hayim Yeshiva was one of a number of Jewish-owned buildings that had existed in that quarter before 1948, she said, and was now used for Sabbath services by a congregation made up of former Jerusalem underground fighters from prestate days. The rest of the week it was unused.

Hacohen was not enthusiastic about premises in an all-Arab neighborhood but in view of the imminence of the symposium and the lack of alternative space he decided to look at it. He was immediately won over. The yeshiva on Haggai Street had been preserved intact with all its books and furniture by its Arab watchman, who had continued to guard the building after the Jews left in 1948. When they returned in 1967, he handed back the keys to the Israeli authorities. In the library bookcases, two thousand religious tomes were still neatly stacked.

The symposium was a rousing success, and it had produced so many unanswered questions, despite the learned lectures, that another was scheduled for the fall. One of the participants, congratulating Hacohen on his initiative, said he believed that a special yeshiva should be set up to pursue studies in this specific field. It was a conclusion Hacohen was in the process of drawing himself. "The [Messianic] redemption is approaching." said one of the participants. "You have to be blind not to see it."

A Jewish-owned building around the corner was rented for the purpose. It was not Hacohen's intention to shove a Jewish presence down the throat of the neighboring Muslims. The building was simply available, and it was also physically closer to the Temple Mount than the Jewish Quarter, a nice symbolic touch. That Hanukkah, 1978, Hacohen and seven other young men "of the priestly caste" moved in to become the first Jews to resume residence in the Muslim Quarter since riots in 1936 had driven the last ones out. By the following Passover, a yeshiva named Ateret Cohanim, the Priestly Crown, was functioning in the building. The fifty students studied the priestly routine, including methods of animal sacrifice on the temple altar, and even practiced weaving priestly garments.

In the nineteenth century, thousands of Jews had lived in the Muslim Quarter, mostly in rented premises, and many Arabs had lived in the Jewish Quarter. With the tensions following the First World War induced by the upsurge of the Zionist movement and ensuing Arab riots, Jews began to leave the Muslim Quarter.

After the Old City fell to Jordan in 1948, Jewish-owned property was taken over by the Jordanian Custodian of Enemy Property, who sold or rented it to the local Arabs. The same process in reverse was happening in Israeli Jerusalem. When Israel took the Old City in 1967, the custodian's records showed thirty Jewish properties listed in the Muslim Quarter. Kollek and Meron Benvenisti quietly worked with government officials to block the return of these properties on the grounds that ownership had not been established clearly enough to permit transfer. Their real motive was to avoid exacerbating intercommunal tensions by inserting Jews into an Arab neighborhood. However, pressure by the owners on the government and court action resulted in the return of thirteen of the Jewish properties over the years, including the building housing Ateret Hacohanim. In none of the other buildings had Jews taken up residence. Where their Arab residents could show that they had legally leased it from the Jordanian custodian—the vast majority of cases—they were regarded by the Israeli authorities as protected tenants who could not be removed even if the Jewish owner wished to move in.

The Ateret Cohanim students made it a point to establish friendly relations with their Arab neighbors, and Hacohen picked up fair colloquial Arabic. When he married in 1981, twenty of his Arab neighbors came to the wedding in West Jerusalem. One day, an Arab living in a former yeshiva across the street offered to sell him his apartment. A private donor put up the money and Hacohen was able to acquire the apartment for his yeshiva. Most of the other protected tenants in that building followed suit, happy to be able to give up their primitive dwellings for handsome sums that enabled them to purchase modern housing outside the walled city.

The idyll exploded when students from a new yeshiva called Birkat Avraham (Abraham's Blessing) began moving into some of the rooms vacated by the Arab families. The newly religious student body of this "penitent yeshiva" was a strange mix of violent ex-prisoners and wide-eyed innocents searching for themselves through religion. The way offered them by Birkat Avraham was through the obscure teachings of Reb Nahman of Bratslav, a nineteenth-century Hassidic mystic whose followers regularly go into the countryside to commune with God by crying out their innermost feelings at the top of their voices. Rabbinical scholars had ruled that only the emotionally stable should undertake to study Reb Nahman's words, and even then it was strongly recommended that they also study Reb Nahman's opponents for balance.

Birkat Avraham's students, regarded as aberrant even by the main-line Bratslav Hassidim in Mea Shearim, were anything but stable. They forced out Hacohen and his students from the rooms they had occupied in the building by methods that Hacohen would subsequently decline to describe. However, the Arab residents remaining in the building had no hesitation about talking about the methods used by the Birkat Avraham students, methods that allegedly included beatings and exposing themselves.

Even when they were inside their premises, the Birkat Avrahan students would force themselves upon their surroundings by shouting prayers late into the night. Residents in the Jewish Quarter one hundred meters distant frequently would call police to complain of being disturbed. For the Arabs living in their proximity, it was a nightmare. The yeshiva sponsors eventually gained title to the building, and it became impossible to evict them although they would in time become somewhat more domesticated.

In time, a third yeshiva opened nearby, dedicated like Ateret Cohanim to study of priestly law. In all, some 200 Jews—almost all married students and their families—would take up residence in the Muslim Quarter within a small area adjacent to the Jewish Quarter. In demographic terms, it was a miniscule number compared to the 14,000 Arabs living in the quarter. Politically, however, they constituted a menace to Jerusalem's continued tranquility.

"Their presence enhances the Arabs' deeply-rooted sense of insecurity," said Meron Benvenisti. "All minorities cluster. It gives a sense of security, a place where you can drop your shield. This is where they could come back to in the evening and curse the Jews." Now the Jews are there among them.

Hacohen himself and the colleagues in his yeshiva were the opposite of provocateurs. They indeed constituted models of how Jews and Arabs could live in neighborliness with mutual respect. Walking with Hacohen one day, a reporter was struck by the friendliness of the local Arabs, all of whom seemed to know the bearded young Jew. A middle-aged Arab woman wearing a kerchief smilingly gripped his hand at a street corner. "Kif Yousef?—[How is Joseph?]," he asked in Arabic, inquiring about her husband who had been ill. She assured him all was well. "And how's your baby?" she asked about his year-old son. "Getting big," he said.

Down the street, a young Arab man came up to Hacohen and shook his hand. "I've been up to see the new families on Serraya and wish them luck," said the Arab. He was referring to new Jewish families from the yeshiva that had just taken up residence on Serraya Street. Hacohen and four other Jewish families lived in a complex that had been built a century before with money sent by a rabbi in Galicia, and its synagogue was still intact. "When we moved in," said one of Hacohen's Jewish neighbors, "the Arab families downstairs supplied us with water and electricity."

At a meeting with Mayor Kollek over the violence at Birkat Avraham Yeshiva, Arab residents had pleaded that the troublesome yeshiva be removed and suggested that a new one "like Ateret Cohanim" take its place.

"We haven't come here to create tensions," Hacohen told a visitor one day. "I don't know if such good neighborliness exists among Jews in their own quarters as exist between us and the Arabs here. If irresponsible elements try to settle here it won't be the Arabs who refuse to absorb them, it will be us."

But he had set in motion a process that had become too complex for him or anyone else to control. Birkat Avraham (its name would later be changed to Shuvu Banim) had forced its way in despite his opposition.

Said a government official dealing closely with Jerusalem: "Everything in Jerusalem is volatile and dangerous. Teddy's greatness has been in keeping the fuse from the powder keg. Jewish settlement in the densely inhabited Muslim Quarter means inserting the fuse. A single explosion could touch off others. There would be a dynamic that would be beyond anyone's control." The official, himself a kippa-wearing Orthodox Jew, remarked sardonically on the Messianism of the post–Six Day War period that had led to the creation of yeshivas for temple priests. "The Messiah is the strongest force in the country now. Except of course for the Finance Minister."

For the Jews in the Muslim Quarter, it would be the Messiah who would call the tune. But in Jerusalem as a whole, a remarkably delicate balance would be preserved among the religious claimants jostling for position at the gates of heaven.

EIGHTEEN

The Rabbi and the Mukhtar

THE MUKHTAR AND THE RABBI had passed many times in the Kidron Valley just below the walls of the Old City without recognizing each other as leader of the opposing camp. Abed Abu Diab was one of the mukhtars, or headmen, of the Arab village of Silwan, and he spoke for its fifteen thousand residents. Rabbi David Shmidl's constituents numbered many more but most were dead. The dispute between the two men was over which had primacy—the sanctity of the dead or the needs of the living.

The biblical valley, one of the most picturesque corners of Jerusalem, threads its way between the Old City and the Mount of Olives, whose slopes are lined with ancient graveyards and olive trees. On Judgment Day, according to Jewish tradition, the dead will rise from these cemeteries and make their way across the valley to the Temple Mount.

Several hundred meters down the valley lies Silwan, largest of the Arab villages incorporated into Jerusalem when the city's new boundaries were drawn in 1967. Until Israel's War of Independence in 1948, villagers could make their way up the valley to the main Old City gates a mile to the north on foot or on donkey along a dirt track between the Jewish cemeteries. Road access, for those few villagers with cars, was via a roundabout route to the west skirting the Jewish part of the city. The division of Jerusalem in 1948 closed off the vehicular route. It would be six years before the Jordanians built a new road to the village, following the line of the dirt path but expanding it to accommodate vehicles. In the process, the road was paved over hundreds of graves.

Destruction of graves occurred on a much larger scale elsewhere on the Mount of Olives. While much of it was carried out in the course of building new roads or parking lots, there was widespread desecration for its own sake. Hebrew headstones were uprooted for use in paving walkways or as flooring in Jordanian army latrines.

Following the Six Day War, the authorities rejected demands by Orthodox Jews to close interurban road links built by the Jordanians through the cemeteries. Although the Israeli authorities plainly would never have built roads through a Jewish cemetery, they were as reluctant as any other government to close down public thoroughfares. Acting on behalf of the ultra-Orthodox was a voluntary organization known as Atra Kadisha (Holy Sites), headed by Rabbi Shmidl. In 1973 Shmidl decided on direct action. His workmen began digging alongside the dual-carriageway road to Jericho, girding the Mount of Olives, and uncovered numerous graves. It was clear that they were Jewish graves because the feet of the dead were aligned toward the Temple Mount to the west, the direction it is believed that the risen dead will walk on Judgment Day. Muslim graves in the city are aligned toward the southeast, the direction of Mecca. According to local Muslim tradition the risen dead are to assemble north of the Old City, creating the prospect of a traffic jam of ghostly pedestrians as newly risen Jews and Muslims attempt to cross each other's paths in the narrow valley on Judgment Day.

In the process of clearing the roadside gravesites, Atra Kadisha undermined one of the carriageways, beneath which, it claimed, were many more graves. Infuriated at this severing of half a major traffic artery, Mayor Teddy Kollek rushed to the site and sought to have the roadway reopened. His obligation, he said, was to his living constituents, Arabs as well as Jews, rather than to the dead, even if they were his own ancestors. Public opinion had generally supported Kollek in his refusal to shut down the road in order to search for graves. However, even most nonreligious Jews would not accept the repaving of the roadway over graves once unearthed. This would not be living with someone else's act of desecration but a desecration itself. The carriageway would remain permanently closed, two-way traffic squeezing past each other on the single remaining carriageway on this stretch of the Jericho road.

The following year, Rabbi Shmidl ordered his Arab workmen to begin digging alongside the road to Silwan about fifty meters down-slope from the Jericho road. He rejected his colleagues' urgings to simply undermine the roadway at night or to hold mass demonstrations, even though he was convinced that it would be impossible for the authorities to stand up to a slogan like "Don't drive over our grandfathers' graves." Certain of the justice of his cause and its ultimate triumph, he kept the authorities well informed of the areas where he intended to dig. Unhappy as they were about it, they could not object to digging for desecrated graves on public land.

The workers soon uncovered scores of graves buried under four yards of debris. Within a few weeks, the Silwan roadway began to sag because of the nearby excavations, and traffic on it was totally halted.

Again the authorities found themselves outraged and outmaneuvered by Rabbi Shmidl. Nevertheless, he won their grudging respect for fighting his battle openly.

The slightly built, bespectacled rabbi, who introduced himself to strangers simply as "Shmidl," seemed an unlikely figure to be heading such a campaign. The father of nine children, he normally spent his days studying in a yeshiva in Bnai Brak near Tel Aviv, the family being supported by his wife, a teacher. However, his integrity and his intelligence won him the leadership of Atra Kadisha, a nonsalaried post. Despite his years of retreat in the scholarly yeshiva world, he displayed a strong executive talent for coping with earthly problems in his new position. In a major coup, he acquired aerial photos of the Kidron Valley taken for Israeli military intelligence in the early 1950s, just before the road was built, and with the aid of a magnifying glass was able to locate the site of graves along the future road alignment. To prepare himself for court action by the Silwan villagers, he scoured the National Library for maps and written references alluding to Jewish graves in the valley, particularly in the memoirs of Jewish and Christian pilgrims, and researched the archives of the former Jordanian municipality for references to the road's construction. He also interviewed old Jerusalemites who could remember where cemeteries had been located in the area.

One day, an army engineering unit arrived to construct a Bailey bridge over the graves at the request of the municipality. This plan was soon dropped, after the ultra-Orthodox complained that it was far too short to bridge the sanctified area and environmentalists insisted it was far too long to fit into the biblical landscape.

The closure of the road to vehicular traffic meant that Silwan villagers traveling by bus to the center of East Jerusalem had to take a seven-kilometer roundabout route instead of the one-kilometer route straight up the valley. The old footpath was still open to donkeys but more villagers had cars now than donkeys. Instead of a ten-minute trip to work or school, the bus trip could now be as much as half to three quarters of an hour during rush hour.

"We respect the memory of the dead," said Muhktar Abu Diab, "but we must also not forget the living. In every country in the world, the authorities open roads for people, not close them. Silwan is part of Jerusalem yet the main road serving 15,000 people has been closed."

Shmidl was not without sympathy for the villagers. The Kidron road had been cut through the cemetery, he acknowledged, not out of spite but because of perceived need. The villagers had been visibly embarrassed about the desecration of the graves after the Jews returned in 1967 and were relieved, he said, that the Israelis were not seeking vengeance or compensation. "I want to live in good neighborliness with the Arabs. It's best if we can find a solution satisfactory to both sides. But one thing is certain—there can't be a road running over graves." When a reporter interviewing Shmidl in the valley one day introduced the rabbi to the mukhtar who happened to be passing by, Shmidl said he had been looking forward to the encounter for some time and arranged for a meeting between the two sides. A few days later half a dozen bearded members of Atra Kadisha, in the black garb of the ultra-Orthodox Jew, and half a dozen village leaders, some in traditional Arab headdress, met to discuss the problem.

The villagers suggested that the graves simply be transferred to another site. But Jewish law is not as flexible as Islamic law in this regard. There are three clear circumstances, Shmidl explained, in which Jewish law permits graves to be moved: in order to move a person's remains closer to those of his ancestors, when a grave is endangered by an eroding slope or similar natural circumstances, or when burial is conditional from the start as in a military funeral. Jewish law also recognized a fourth reason—the concept of "the public good." If a grave is dug in the middle of an existing road, according to an example given in Jewish law, then there is an argument for moving it. But, argued Shmidl, he had searched the law closely and found no precedent for moving graves in order to make way for a new road.

Upon such talmudic calculations would depend the hour that Abu

Diab and his fellow villagers rose in the morning to get to work or school. In the end, this would turn out to be only about ten minutes earlier than before. The municipality provided a relatively short alternate route by improving a steep existing road, hitherto considered impassable for buses, up the City of David ridge on which Jerusalem had been founded five thousand years before. The honor of the dead was thus preserved without any serious inconvenience to the living.

It was inevitable in post–Six Day War Jerusalem that there would be religious friction between Jews and Muslims; the line between politics and religion is even finer in Jerusalem than elsewhere. Some residents of the Jewish Quarter were convinced that the mosque loudspeakers calling the faithful to prayer before dawn were tuned up expressly to annoy them, while Muslim officials complained that Israeli women visiting Islamic holy sites were dressed immodestly. The Temple Mount itself remained the ultimate powder keg.

Intense religious acrimony was also evident outside the parameters of the Arab-Israeli dispute. The Christians were the smallest of the three major religious communities in Jerusalem but, with dozens of denominations represented in the holy city, the most diverse. In planting their standards in Jerusalem, they often planted them on each other's toes. Or worse. Priests had clubbed each other to death with candelabras in the Holy Sepulcher Church as they waged battles for proprietary rights around the tomb of Jesus. Under a status quo arrangement worked out by the Turkish rulers more than a century before, every square inch of the church and every artifact in it is the property of a specific denomination, each of which guards its turf jealously against trespass by neighboring clerics. Any attempt by a priest to clean an oil lamp or a door sill not clearly in his denomination's domain will inevitably lead to an unholy row, because cleaning implies ownership. It had taken more than a decade of negotiations under the Jordanians before agreement could be reached among the churches represented in the Holy Sepulcher for much-needed repairs to the ancient building.

So hopelessly torn by dissension are the denominations contending for position in the Holy Sepulcher that the keys to this holiest site in Christendom have since medieval times been entrusted to a Muslim family whose reresentative opens the great doors each morning.

Three years after the Six Day War, Ethiopian clerics, who had long been consigned to African-style huts on the roof of the Holy Sepulcher, staged a major coup by changing the locks on a passageway leading to two chapels that they had long been seeking to wrest from the Coptic church of Egypt. They did this while the Copts were absent, conducting Easter services inside the Holy Sepulcher. The Israeli government dealt with the problem by appointing a ministerial committee which, when last heard from more than a decade later, was still looking into the matter.

Such rivalries between denominations were matched by internal dissensions within many of the churches. In elections for a successor to the deceased leader of an important church in Jerusalem—elections involving elaborate campaigning by several candidates among voting clergy—one of the contenders did not hesitate to tell a reporter who among his fellow clergymen in the other camps slept with women and who with boys. Police investigating a burglary in the home of a ranking cleric of another church were astonished to learn that he had a million dollars worth of jewelry in his private safe as well as a number of automatic weapons. At least one senior churchman made a fortune by illegally smuggling Dead Sea Scrolls out of the country. Cars of senior church leaders were permitted to cross the border from the Arab world without being searched. One was later found to be loaded with weapons intended for terrorists, and others were subsequently found to have carried gold and drugs.

Nevertheless, the bulk of clergymen in Jerusalem were pious men for whom service in the holy city was an exquisite religious experience. But even among churches farthest from the taint of corruption, like the Latins (as Roman Catholics are called), religious passions in Jerusalem periodically spilled over into worldly confrontations.

The courtroom was filled with Catholic clergymen, including senior prelates listening in fascination to a debate on church law being waged by two Jewish lawyers. Both Israelis had studied canon law and were experienced in representing churches before the courts, but neither they nor the clergymen had ever before encountered a case like this, in which the Vatican was bringing one of its own monastic orders to trial in a secular court.

The case involved the five hundred-room Notre Dame hospice just outside the Old City walls. Built by the Assumptionist Order in 1887 to serve Catholic prilgrims, Notre Dame had been on the front line, during Israel's War of Independence in 1948. Below its walls the Arab Legion was stopped in its drive towards the Jewish part of the city, an event marked by a gaping wound in the building's facade. In the ensuing nineteen years, the Israeli army maintained possession of the

wing overlooking the Old City fifty yards away and turned that part
of the hospice into a fortified military position. The Assumptionists
kept rooms for rent in the main part of the building, but with the
major holy sites now on the Jordanian side of the border there were
few pilgrims.

In the opening hours of the Six Day War, the hospice again was
engulfed in gunfire, as positions in the military wing engaged the
Jordanian army positions on the ramparts of the Old City wall. Following the war, the military returned the keys to the wing in a formal
ceremony, with expressions of hope that Notre Dame would once
more become a thriving hostelry for pilgrims in the united city. But
modern pilgrims, it quickly became clear, preferred comfortable hotels to the cell-like rooms of the old hospice. Government compensation for war damage was only a fraction of what was needed to restore the building to what it had been, let alone to modernize it. With
fewer than ten monks in Notre Dame and with no financial resources,
the Assumptionists regarded the return of the military wing as a very
mixed blessing. It was, in fact, a massive white elephant. Like all
Catholic orders, the Assumptionist Monks were financially self-sus-
taining and had to balance their own books. When they received an
offer from Hebrew University to purchase the building for use as a
dormitory, they could not resist the temptation. The order sold the
building for $600,000, intending to use the money for its activities
elsewhere in the Holy Land.

The Vatican reacted with pontifical rage. In a city where the Christian denominations were in constant contention for status and for
proximity to the holy places, Notre Dame was not merely a pilgrim
facility but a major assertion of the Latin presence in Jerusalem located just a few hundred yards from the site of Jesus' crucifixion and
resurrection. Moreover, its sale to a Zionist institution could endan-
ger the position of the Catholic church in Arab countries. When discreet messages to the Assumptionists failed to persuade them to
undo the deal, the Holy See took the highly unusual step of appeal-
ing to an Israeli court against one of its own orders, a move made
even more exceptional by the fact that the Vatican had never granted
Israel diplomatic recognition and maintained an attitude toward it
ranging between correct and frosty.

The Vatican contended in Jerusalem District Court that church law
forbade any monastic order from selling its property without first
consulting the Holy See. A rare press statement released by the
Pope's representative in Jerusalem declared that "The Holy See

strongly deplores the sale of this church property made without its consent.''

It was apparent that the Assumptionists had not asked permission because they knew it would not be forthcoming. In theory, the heads of the order risked excommunication. Were it not for the liberal spirit prevailing in the Roman Catholic church since Pope John's ascendancy, such a display of independent spirit by an order would have been unthinkable.

The Jewish attorney representing the Holy See and the Jewish attorney representing the Assumptionists debated the finer points of canon law in Hebrew with talmudic relish, the priests, monks, and nuns in the courtroom occasionally nodding at a telling point. The black-clad priests, associated with the Latin patriarchate in Jerusalem, were mostly Italian. The Assumptionist monks were French.

Simultaneous with the trial, the Vatican had put out quiet feelers to Israel for an out-of-court settlement. Mayor Kollek urged the government to acquiesce to the Vatican's request before the case was decided and persuade Hebrew University to voluntarily relinquish the building. It would be a gesture that would convince the church fathers, he argued, that Israel respected the Christian status in the city and that Israeli sovereignty did not mean the Judaization of Jerusalem, which was a secret fear of the Vatican. Accepting his argument, the government brought pressure on the university, which reluctantly agreed as the trial neared its conclusion to sell the building to the Vatican at cost.

The building would be renovated with a sizeable investment by the Holy See as a modern hotel for pilgrims and would include one of the better restaurants in the city. Israeli observers believed they could subsequently detect significant moderation in the Holy See's attitude toward Israeli rule in Jerusalem.

"The churches don't just want to have holy places here," said Kollek afterwards in explaining the importance of conceding the hospice to the Holy See. "They want to keep a community. They are also looking for fields to work in. Not necessarily missionary work. The Anglicans and Catholics are too sophisticated nowadays to believe in conversions. They will not easily find use for their services among the Jews—not as nurses or as teachers. So for them the Moslem population affords an opportunity to be active in the Holy Land, while the small Arab Christian community keeps the churches from becoming empty monuments. As they have come to appreciate that we are not pushing out either the Christians or the Moslems, relations have improved. The Catholic church is no longer the church militant. It's the serving church.''

The monks on Mount Zion rose as usual before dawn, but instead of making their way to the chapel they gathered in the chill darkness of the alley outside. At soft-spoken directions, they deployed on the approaches to the building and took positions behind stone walls. They did not have long to wait. Footsteps on the cobblestones at 5:00 A.M. heralded the return of the intruder. The monks could hear him halt below the monastery. As he reared back to throw his first missile, the monks leaped from their hiding places.

Seized with a stone in his hand by the Benedictine monks from the Dominition Abbey was a born-again orthodox Jew from the neighboring Diaspora Yeshiva. He admitted to police that in a similar dawn attack a few days earlier he had used stones to break all the windows in the Dormition's new administrative wing. The ambush was staked out by the Benedictines the morning after new windows had been installed.

The closest equivalent to a church militant in post-1967 Jerusalem was Rabbi Mordecai Goldstein's Diaspora Yeshiva. The New York-born rabbi had turned his institute into a haven for American Jewish dropouts who drifted to Israel in the wake of the war. Although the yeshiva gained a reputation in Jerusalem as a gathering place for ''hippies and weirdos''—police periodically staged drug raids on the premises—Goldstein was often successful in keeping his young charges from dropping out again. The ethnic scene in Jerusalem was rendered even more colorful by the Diaspora students' garb, which reflected self-images in the process of shifting, stage by stage, from San Francisco's Haight Street to Jerusalem's Mea Shearim.

Before the Six Day War, Mount Zion—in reality, a modest hill—had been the holiest site in Jewish hands, but it had been a holiness deriving largely from being the closest Israeli territory to the Western Wall. It had assumed an ersatz holiness in its own right because of a mistake in address made in medieval tradition, which placed King David's tomb on the hill. Modern scholars are agreed that King David was buried on the next ridge to the east, the site of the city in biblical times. But with the closing of access to the Western Wall in 1948, Mount Zion and ''David's Tomb'' became the focus of popular Jewish pilgrimage, even though the hill lay on the border with Jordan—with Israeli bunkers facing Jordanian bunkers on the eastern slope at a distance of some thirty yards.

After the Six Day War, this religious focus shifted to the Western Wall. The vacuum on Mount Zion was filled by Rabbi Goldstein, who began taking over empty buildings and empty rooms in the complex of buildings scattered over the hill and nailing up large, blue Diaspora Yeshiva signs over their entrances. The problem was that many of these properties belonged to other institutions, both Jewish and Christian, and the yeshiva was soon involved in a running series of legal battles—often involving physical scuffles as well.

Christianity had better historical reasons than Judaism for attributing holiness to sites on the hill. Scholars are generally agreed that the house of the high priest, Caiphus, to which Jesus was brought for trial was on Mount Zion, as was probably the house in which the Last Supper was held.

Although the hill's population was sparse—much of its slopes were occupied by cemeteries—it seethed with religious rivalries. The Armenians and the Latins had each built their own churches on sites—several hundred meters apart—they contended was the location where Peter thrice denied Jesus before the cock crowed. The Armenians also made plans after the Six Day War for a new church whose principal feature was that it would be higher than the neighboring Dormition Church, the tallest structure on the hill.

The Greek Orthodox, who had a theological seminary on Mount Zion, built a wall across a large field in order to prevent its being used for parking by an adjacent American Protestant school. According to municipal officials, the Greeks were concerned not only about property rights but the impact on the young seminarians of attractive girl students on three-week study programs at the American institute.

The oldest rivalry on the hill surrounded the building reputed to be the site of the Last Supper and David's Tomb. These traditions were not altered by the fact that the building dated from the Crusader period and had thus been built more than one thousand years and two thousand years, respectively, after Jesus and David. Jews venerated "David's Tomb" on the first floor, while Christians venerated "the room of the Last Supper" on the upper floor. The Muslims built mosques on both floors and limited access to both Christians and Jews until 1948 when this part of the hill became Israeli territory.

In making repairs on the upper floor in the 1980s, the Israeli renovation team found two broken windows. Repairing the windows was a minor custodial chore but posed a major political problem. The stained windows had been installed by the Muslims when they displaced the Christian occupants and converted the room to a mosque.

To replace the broken windows with plain glass would have been regarded by the Muslims as altering the status quo. To restore the stained windows with their Muslim motif would have been regarded by the Christians as endorsing the Muslim takeover. The solution was to leave the broken windows as they were and to add two simple windows behind them to keep out the elements.

The weird dress and behavior often visible on the mount in the years after the Six Day War are little in evidence today. Says Rabbi Goldstein: ''There just aren't so many hippies around anymore.''

Eccentricity, however, is not altogether dead. The prior of the Dormition Abbey, Father Immanuel, who had laid the ambush of the yeshiva stone thrower, was surprised some weeks later to see the yeshiva student entering the church. He wished to make amends, said the youth. He asked the monks to supply him with wood so that he could build a hut inside the church. He had been so directed by a heavenly voice, he explained. ''My father was a carpenter.'' The monks gently guided him back to the yeshiva next door.

Despite Jesus' urgings to his disciples, Jerusalem has never been a place for turning the other cheek. Jews, Christians, and Muslims have long jostled each other for position in the holy city and when they have not been in dispute with one another they have engaged in lively, sometimes even deadly, controversies among themselves. The miracle of Jerusalem has been that somehow, despite the fiercely competing claims upon it by so many diverse religious constituencies, the center has held.

NINETEEN

Rebuilding Jerusalem

A FEW MONTHS AFTER THE SIX DAY WAR, a helicopter fluttered low over the approaches to Ammunition Hill in northern Jerusalem, where the fiercest battle of the war had been fought. From the surveying equipment projecting from the open door, the craft seemed to be carrying army engineers engaged in mapping the thick minefields as a prelude to clearing this, the most formidably defended stretch of former no-man's-land.

The men in the helicopter, however, were not a cleanup party dealing with the litter of past wars, but scouts of the future. Too impatient to wait for the mines to be cleared, government authorities had sent the surveyors aloft to map the topography for the first new neighborhood to be built across the ''green line,'' the colored line on the 1949 armistice map that had split Jerusalem in two.

The hovering helicopter marked the beginning of the most massive development enterprise ever undertaken in Jerusalem, modern or ancient. In the next two decades the two halves of the city would be cemented together in concrete and stone, changing its face, its scale, and its social fiber.

Not since King Herod rebuilt the temple and much of the city two thousand years before had there been anything approaching this scale of activity. In the first five years after the war, construction was begun on 24,000 apartments, half as many as had existed in all of Israeli Jerusalem on the eve of the war. The top of Mount Scopus, the highest ridge in the city, was lowered by eight meters in order to accommodate a massive new Hebrew University campus that would not project above the previous skyline.

Guiding this activity was an extraordinary planning concept that had gone out of fashion with the passing of the Middle Ages: the city as fortress.

A century before, the Jews of Jerusalem had emerged from the protective walls of the Old City to establish a new city on the open hills to the west.

Now they began walling themselves in again by building massive housing developments on the high ground along the outer edges of the city. These developments, although not contiguous, were identical in purpose to the battlements of the Old City—staking out the limits of the city and serving, if necessary, as fighting positions.

The concept of city as fortress had been effectively demolished in Europe with the development of artillery. It had, however, been revived in Jerusalem after the War of Independence in 1948. The battle for the city had raged from neighborhood to neighborhood and the absence of contiguity of Jewish areas had cost Israel the Jewish Quarter of the Old City and the Western Wall and left Mount Scopus isolated.

Following the armistice, the two sides of Jerusalem found themselves facing each other with no natural barriers between them. On the Israeli side, much of the border was undeveloped and open to infiltrators. The response was to build not a conventional defense line of trenches and bunkers or a Berlin wall but a living wall of housing to serve as a physical barrier and a trip wire. To close off the particularly vulnerable southern border, which was empty of housing, the government threw up the Katamon Quarter at the edge of no-man's-land the way kibbutzim plowed their last furrow right up against the border. At the army's request, the houses were limited to two stories so that machine guns posted on high ground to their rear had a clear field of fire over them toward the Jordanian lines beyond.

Elsewhere along the "city line," as the border was called, the two sides were separated at points only by the width of a narrow street. Although the Jordanians heavily fortified their side, Israel did not pull civilians back from the border. Instead, new apartment blocks were built to fill in gaps in housing.

Spaced along the border were buildings that had been converted to military blockhouses but even in some of these, civilians continued to live on lower floors. The newer apartment buildings were integrated into the defense system by their very design. They were laid out so that one long block facing directly onto the Jordanian positions shielded the buildings behind it from direct fire. The front building was provided with walls three time the normal thickness to withstand shell blast, and its windows were kept small to reduce the danger from sniping. Housewives were even provided with metal shields to place in the windows in the event of firing. On the roofs were concrete bunkers with firing slits for machine guns overlooking the Jordanian lines in the event of war.

To populate the vulnerable border, the government brought immigrants, mostly poor and often illiterate newcomers from Morocco and Iraq, straight from Haifa port or from transit camps—the poorest stratum of society, who were to serve a national purpose simply by staying where they had been placed. Over the years, the residents learned to live with the periodic eruptions of gun-fire along the border and with occasional casualties the way villagers on the slopes of Vesuvius had learned to live with the consequences of natural disaster.

The Knesset itself had to come to terms with its location in a frontline city. The army overrode the architects, who designed the new parliamentary building with its entrance facing south toward the lovely panorama of the Hebron Hills. Instead, the building was turned around by the architects because Jordanian machine gunners just two kilometers away could have easily cut down the country's leaders on its approaches.

The fortress concept was put to the test in the Six Day War when the frontline apartment buildings were taken over by troops of the Jerusalem Brigade as military positions. As the residents took shelter in the basements, the soldiers upstairs exchanged fire with Jordanian positions sometimes less than thirty meters away. The reinforced walls of the Shmuel Hanavi development opposite Ammunition Hill bore up to heavy pounding from shellfire. It was from behind its front buildings that the Israeli paratroopers launched their decisive attack across no-man's-land while machine gunners firing from the buildings provided covering fire.

Having thus proven itself, the concept was adhered to in fixing the new boundaries of the city drawn up after the war. Twice in less than twenty years—in 1948 and 1967—there had been fierce war in the streets of the city and the authorities had to assume that it could happen again. The boundaries were fixed by a team of military and civilian planners along clear tactical lines, incorporating the high ground dominating all major approaches to the city. Wherever possible, Arab-inhabited areas were left outside the city boundaries on the West Bank to limit Arab demographic weight within Jerusalem.

The thrust of the postwar building program was thus a response to past traumas rather than reflections of sweeping visions of the future city. The most immediate perceived danger was that Mount Scopus, with its supreme cultural symbolism, could be cut off once again from the rest of the capital, this time not by war but by international pressure on Israel to pull pack to its prewar lines. The founding of Hebrew University atop Scopus in 1925 had been a major landmark in the revival of the Jewish homeland. The armistice agreement in 1949 had left it an enclave behind the Jordanian lines, derelict and abandoned except for its 120-man garrison.

To permanently remove Scopus from its isolation in the Arab part of the city, the government decided to connect it to the nearest neighborhood in West Jerusalem with a new, mile-long neighborhood to be built through a wadi between Ammunition Hill and Mivtar Hill. Because the Jordanians before 1967 had feared an Israeli military attempt to reach Scopus through this wadi—the most direct route— they had heavily fortified the two hills and planted 12,000 mines between them. The Israelis had outflanked the minefields during the war, but they found them a formidable obstacle now. When Prime Minister Levi Eshkol visited the site a year after the war, he was astonished to see that construction of the neighborhood (one which would eventually bear his name) was being held up because not all the mines had yet been cleared. "How long does it take clear a minefield?" he asked. When a Housing Ministry official attempted to explain the difficulties, the normally amiable prime minister cut him short with "Don't tell me *boobemaises* (grandmother's tales)."

Still vivid in Eshkol's mind was the pullback from Sinai imposed upon Israel by President Eisenhower after the 1956 Sinai campaign against Egypt, despite then-prime-minister David Ben-Gurion's public assertions that Israel would never give up Sinai. Eshkol saw it as urgent to speedily create facts on the ground that could neutralize any international pressure—particularly American pressure—aimed at staying Israel's hand in East Jerusalem.

As the neighborhood to Scopus neared completion, the government began to think in broader terms of nailing down the new municipal boundaries with a permanent civilian presence as the pre–1967 boundaries had been nailed down. Plans were drawn up for a string of massive housing developments, some of them containing as many as 10,000 apartments, to be built on the periphery of the city. For this purpose, the government expropriated more than 5,000 of the 18,000 acres that had been annexed by Israel in East Jerusalem. Almost all the annexed land was hilly, nonarable land and almost all Arab houses within these tracts were left as enclaves. Large-scale construction was launched simultaneously on half a dozen developments on the fringes of the city, each larger than most towns in the country.

At the heart of Jerusalem, a totally different vision was being shaped—not by bulldozers but by chisels. The link to Mount Scopus was the second priority in Jerusalem and the creation of a defendable periphery the third. First was the return to the Old City. There lay the nation's roots. One of the most important planning decisions made in post–Six Day War Jerusalem was the one made in Mayor Kollek's apartment three days after the Old City's capture: the intimate alley at the foot of the Western Wall, where several hundred persons at most could pray at one time, would be transformed into a plaza capable of holding 250,000. It was to be done in time for the pending Shavuot holiday, in which Israelis would be able to visit the wall for the first time since its liberation. To do this, an Arab neighborhood containing 135 families as well as a mosque and the grave of a sheikh were destroyed overnight, the families given an hour's notice to leave.

Inhibitions about such action were overcome by a sense of Manifest Destiny, a feeling that Jewish history was charging this generation with a mission that transcended conventional restrictions. The same sense of mission guided Kollek and government planners in deciding to expropriate the Jewish Quarter on the heights facing the wall. The thirty acres they designated for restoration was roughly the size the quarter had been at the beginning of the century, when its population was 15,000, but twice its size on the eve of the War of Independence, when the Jewish population within the walls had shrunk to only 2,000.

Some 5,500 Arabs were living in the expropriated quarter, most of them refugees who had fled in 1948 from the western part of the city. Only about 20 percent of the Jewish Quarter had been owned by Jews. Most houses had been owned by Arab families, who had rented them to Jews since the latter began returning to Jerusalem following the defeat of the Crusaders in the twelfth century. The Israeli authorities offered the Arabs compensation, which was accepted by the refugees living in the quarter as tenants but not by the owners, who refused to accept the legality of the expropriation.

The Jordanians had systematically removed almost all signs of the Jewish presence, including buildings housing fifty-seven synagogues and institutions. Left intact were the Sephardi synagogues, a complex of four structures dating from the sixteenth century that had been the focus of life in the quarter. The complex had been built mostly below street level because of a Muslim edict against building synagogues higher than nearby mosques. This subterranean siting provided shelter from shelling during the fighting in 1948, and it was here that the civilians and wounded were gathered before the quarter fell.

The Arabs had apparently spared the synagogues because one of them, the Eliyahu, was also revered by Muslims. Arab women had traditionally been granted permission by the local Jewish community to offer a prayer against sterility to the Prophet Elijah in the synagogue and to light an oil lamp there. Revered or not, the abandoned synagogues had been used as stables.

The problem facing the planners was whether to try to restore the quarter the way it had been or to rebuild it in a modern idiom as every age had done. Defense Minister Dayan suggested cutting new streets through the quarter, rather than restoring the line of tortuous alleys. Israel's Founding Father, David Ben-Gurion, proposed knocking down the walls surrounding the Old City to lessen the prospect of the city ever again being divided.

Of the two hundred buildings in the quarter—most of them only a century old but all in a bad state of disrepair—the planners decided that half could be restored. The remainder would be demolished and replaced by new buildings, which would avoid deliberate stylistic quaintnesses, such as cupolas or arches—"no Disneyland," as one architect put it—but echo the scale and ambience of the older architecture. After more than a decade of painstaking labor during which old and new were wedded with minute attention to detail, the restoration of the Jewish Quarter would be regarded as one of the gems of post-1967 Jerusalem.

When the State Department expressed reservations at the end of 1969 about Israel's steps to physically alter the city and assume sovereignty over East Jerusalem, the building momentum was stepped up—partly as an act of defiance, partly in order to complete as much as possible in case the Americans really did crack down. On French Hill, where four-story apartment buildings were planned, the heights of most buildings were deliberately raised to seven or eight stories.

Reservations, however, were also being voiced with increasing concern by Israelis, though not on political grounds but on aesthetic ones. The Jerusalem public, normally quiescent on planning issues, began to stir for the first time, as high-rise buildings rose into the skyline and the government announced intentions of large-scale development.

At a public symposium, writer Yehuda Haezrachi told an overflow crowd that the government intended to create a massive Jewish presence across the green line in Jerusalem at a grievous cost to the city's beauty. It was objectionable even on narrow political grounds, he said, for the Israeli government, which sought world acceptance of its proprietorship of Jerusalem, to ignore the aesthetics of the city, which the British had gone to such lengths to preserve.

Particular objection was taken to the plans for Ramot, opposite the main entrance to Jerusalem. The city's master plan called for a small-scale, low-rise suburb on the site that would spare the sculpted beauty of the terraced hills. The Housing Ministry proposed instead a dense, 10,000-unit development. At a stormy press conference, Housing Minister Zeev Sharef made clear the government's motivation in imposing Ramot on the city. Pointing at the development plans hanging on the wall behind him, he said defiantly, "This is a Zionist exhibition." The object, he said, was to reinforce the Jewish character of the city.

Ramot violated one of the cardinal principles of the master plan, which envisioned Jerusalem as a compact city with a hard edge—reminiscent in its modern form of the walled Old City. The visually incoherent sprawl of Ramot would blur that edge at its most visible point—the city's gateway.

Displeasure with the Ramot plan voiced by State Department spokesman Robert McCloskey broke the last official resistance to it in Jerusalem, providing a convenient way out for politicians torn between the aesthetic and political arguments. Rallying around the flag, the city council, including Kollek, voted to support the proposal despite the serious reservations members had previously expressed. The Labor faction imposed party discipline in the vote, but Meron Benvenisti, now a Labor city councilman, declined to raise his hand to support the motion. He sat staring at the opposite wall with his hand on his mouth. Someone called out: "For history, Meron," but the wall held his attention. Wags soon began referring to Ramot as McCloskey Heights.

The Arab neighborhoods of Jerusalem were cut off by this building activity from the surrounding Arab hinterland on the West Bank, except for routes dominated by the new Jewish neighborhoods. Before the Six Day War, the term Jerusalem Corridor had meant the tapering strip of Israeli territory that linked the coastal plain with the capital atop the Jordanian-dominated Judean Hills. After the war a new corridor was created on the opposite side of the watershed, reaching up from the Arab territories to the east through a sweeping arc of Jewish settlements.

Spiritually, these corridors had their respective origins not in the foothills below Jerusalem but beyond the western sea and the eastern desert. Both reached out for the stone walls of the Holy City on the crest of the hills like outstretched hands groping for a crown.

The reception in the courtyard of the old Turkish inn opposite the walls of the Old City in the summer of 1969 bore the anticipatory air that used to mark the first night at sea aboard an ocean liner, when the passengers assembled in the salon for their first good look at one another.

The guests were almost all strangers to each other except by reputation but they would be living together for the next four days.

In one corner, wearing a "Nehru" jacket, sat a dark, inward-looking man with luminous eyes. "Tagore," someone whispered, nephew of the great Indian poet. Eagle-eyed and dapper, Carlos Garcia—ex-president of the Phillipines and former guerrilla leader—moved towards the buffet table, followed at a discreet distance by two aides, one of them carrying a dispatch case.

An Anglican priest from Australia stood nearby, his elegant robes whipping in the breeze like a cavalier's cape. The near-Caucasian features of Isamu Noguchi, the Japanese-American sculptor, surprised those who had never seen a picture of him before. There were African churchmen, European scholars, American architects and engineers, including the renowned Louis Kahn and Buckminster Fuller, an eighty-one-year-old Frenchman who for two decades had been curator of Islamic monuments in Cairo, a Brazilian sculptor with long sideburns who looked like a student revolutionary, and the handsome chairwoman of Barnard College's religion department. In the center of the courtyard, stood an urbane architect from Ceylon with a drink in his hand looking about him with an expression of amusement and interest.

The twenty-seven-person group, drawn from every continent, had assembled at the invitation of Mayor Kollek for the first conference of the Jerusalem Committee. In an act of high statesmanship, Kollek had conceived of a prestigious advisory committee as a means of heading off demands by the Vatican or UN for the internationalization of Jerusalem. Much of the Christian world was less than enthusiastic about Jewish sovereignty over the Christian holy places. Through the committee, Kollek felt, Israel would acknowledge that Jerusalem was a spiritual center for much of the world and be perceived as sharing with the international community decisions about the city's fate. The Foreign Ministry, fearful that such a body might diminish Israel's sovereign role in Jerusalem, declined to participate.

That first meeting would sound the majestic themes inspired by Jerusalem and discordant notes that heralded the eruption to come.

"The past is all around us," said Hebrew University President Avraham Harman in an address to the committee. "The desert is all around us. Evidence that the preservation of human civilization is by no means inevitable—this evidence is piled up all around us. It stirs eternal questions."

Two camps swiftly emerged: the modernizers and the preservers. "You offend the past if you copy it," declared Professor Bruno Zevi of Rome in urging a halt to the restoration of the Jewish Quarter. "They're rebuilding lousy buildings that were lousy when they were built." Harmony should be achieved, he said, not by copying the old but by setting off the old by the modern. Willem Sandberg, former director of Amsterdam's Municipal Museum, agreed. "Jerusalem was destroyed many times and was always rebuilt in the style of its own time."

An eloquent dissent came from Enrique Fabregat, a Uruguayan history professor who had served on the UN Commission for Palestine, which decided in 1947 on partition of the country into Arab and Jewish states. "Everything that comes from the past, from the human heart, comes from Jerusalem. I don't want to destroy the real image of Jerusalem. It doesn't come from empty space. It comes from the stones of Jerusalem. It is in the dreams of the people. They come to see that town, not a new town." Supporting the preservationists, the Reverend W. Brandful of Ghana said that to his rural parishioners, Jerusalem meant spirituality." Some would be surprised if told that Jerusalem was situated on earth."

So vibrant was the meeting, albeit inconclusive, that Kollek decided to hold another one the following year, this time of the committee's architects and town planners, reinforced by some of their leading world colleagues. They would be presented the new Jerusalem master plan, six years in the making, and asked for down-to-earth suggestions.

The suggestions at the meeting would prove far more down to earth than Kollek had bargained for. In an emotional outpouring, speaker after speaker rose to denounce the master plan in terms sometimes tinged with rage. "This plan is something awful," said Professor Zevi, his face white and his voice shaking with anger. "If my words insult, we are insulted by the plan."

Louis Kahn spoke in his usual gentle and poetic tones but his message was no less searing. "I'm completely puzzled by the plan because I don't sense the principles behind it. The solution for things like roads and parks comes out of what you're trying to do. Jerusalem deserves the aura of the unmeasurable." American architect Richard Meier called for the plan to be totally scrapped. The highly respected urbanologist Lewis Mumford could not attend the meeting because of age but sent a written analysis of the master plan, which he had studied. Jerusalem's planners, he wrote, had overlooked the lessons of Los Angeles and Rome in giving preference to the motor car over the pedestrian. He urged that a population limit of 500,000 be set for the city.

Tension filled the packed hall where Israeli planners and officials listened with a mixture of unease and anger to the scathing criticism. When San Francisco architect Larry Halpern paused in the middle of his remarks and said, "I forgot what I was going to say," an Israeli planner sitting behind him said, "Then don't say it." Halpern sat down and had to be prevailed upon to continue.

In the stunned silence that followed the last speaker, there was a sense of catharsis and of deep embarrassment. So total and unforgiving was the criticism of the distinguished foreigners that when Mayor Kollek rose it seemed an eminent act of courage. "All of us," he said, "even the planners, had some doubts about the plan. Your criticism was more devastating than we expected. Anyone who says he likes criticism is a hypocrite."

It was one of his finest hours. The mayor did not succumb to the moment and bow to the clear verdict of the committee that the plan be thrown out. The plan would be reviewed, he said, under the guidance of a well-known foreign planner yet to be chosen.

As emotions subsided, it became clear that while the committee's criticisms had been pointed, they were pointed in totally conflicting directions. While Zevi warned against turning the Old City into a stage setting, a Canadian planner urged that it be preserved by every architectural trick necessary. One planner argued eloquently for a mosaic of separate neighborhoods but this dispersal pattern con-

flicted directly with the concentration urged by other planners in order to permit efficient public transportation and reduce the use of
private cars. One participant said the plan was too detailed, another
that it was very incomplete. The bylaw requiring all Jerusalem buildings to be faced in stone was praised by some as a unifying factor and
condemned by others as architecturally restricting. Some committee
members were not opposed to skyscrapers. Others were.

It was Kollek who put the stormy Jerusalem meeting in perspective
a few days later when he addressed the World Congress of Engineers
and Architects in Tel Aviv attended by many of the Jerusalem Committee members. "You are fighting here battles you lost in your cities.
You would like to ride in Cadillacs and see us riding on donkeys. I
have a suspicion that you are asking us to do much more than you
have done in your own cities without telling us how."

His view was supported by architecture professor Harry Mayerovitch of Montreal, who had participated in the Jerusalem meeting.

"We are on a desperate quest," Mayerovitch told the conference.
"We are coming from cities decaying, from cities which destroy us,
where our best efforts have failed, hoping for our wounds to be
bound, hoping Jerusalem won't make the same serious mistakes."

One Jerusalem Committee member with a positive projection was
Philip Johnson, one of America's best-known architects. Addressing
the engineers' congress, he urged Kollek to undertake restructuring
of modern Jerusalem on the same sweeping scale that Pope Sixtus V
had cut new roads through the medieval mess that was Rome in the
sixteenth century. "Jerusalem is perhaps the only city in the world
where it's not too late," said Johnson. He proposed that a new city
center be developed in the kilometer-square area north of the Old
City. Hotels, offices, and dense dwellings would be shoehorned into
this part of East Jerusalem. "We build inner cities because we love
being together," he said. A "ceremonial way" would be built from
Mount Herzl at the western edge of the city through the heart of Jerusalem to Mount Scopus, five miles to the east, linking historical sites
and offering sweeping views. "These points will hang like jewels on
a charm strung between the two mountains. This could be greater
than any other Way in the world."

To shape the image of modern Jerusalem, said Johnson, would require a political leader like the builder-pope. "I think Teddy Kollek
will be our Sixtus. I've seen him handling people with a mastery I've
never seen anywhere else. Cities are people, not buildings. I hope
Teddy has the architects to do it but he'll have to do most of it him-

self. City planning is too important to leave to architects. They make monuments to themselves, design out of scale with the surroundings, make buildings twice as expensive as they need be, and take up twice as much room."

Jews had not had much chance to build cities since antiquity, noted Johnson, but they had not had much military experience either until Israel created its army. "Action is imperative in Jerusalem before American sprawl starts dribbling the city out into the hills. It's your last chance. The landgrabbers are near. Jerusalem is great. Everything is favorable. Start now."

It was stirring rhetoric but the Jerusalem that Johnson and the other world-wise architects envisioned was more akin to heavenly Jerusalem than to an earthly city shaped by stark political realities. The urban center of Israel's capital would not be shifted to the Arab neighborhoods north of the Old City—neither the Jews nor the Arabs would tolerate that. Not even a mayor of Kollek's stature had the power or financial resources to cut a "way" though the heart of the built-up city.

Despite its sometimes contradictory advice and idyllic tones, and despite the political reasons for its creation, the Jerusalem Committee would have significant impact on the development of the city. It forcefully condemned the master plan's ambitious road system, including a broad highway that would have cut through the picturesque Hinnom Valley underneath the walls of the Old City, and others that would have gutted some of its most picturesque neighborhoods. The Committee's criticism would be a major reason halting the proliferation of high-rise buildings. At its suggestion, a strong municipal planning arm was created. Its staff of young urban planners would take on the government's planners, sometimes by guerrilla methods, in the new battle for Jerusalem.

TWENTY

The Spoiler
Preserving Jerusalem

ART KUTCHER DRIFTED INTO JERUSALEM after the Six Day War with the dust of Europe on his feet and a kitbag over his shoulder. From the hilltops, he looked out at the city and began to sketch. Those careful line drawings by an unknown architect would have a greater impact on the face of Jerusalem than the work of any other architect in the frenzied decade of development after the war.

The intense young American from Sioux City, Iowa, made his mark not by anything he designed—he designed little more ambitious than a parking lot on Mount Zion—but by what he prevented from being built. His sketches were largely responsible for preventing a ring of massive hotels and apartment towers from encircling Jerusalem's Old City. Before being fired from the municipal planning staff as a troublemaker, he had helped create a new attitude toward planning in Jerusalem.

Kutcher, who had come to Jerusalem after a leisurely grand tour of Europe, was one of a dozen architects and planners—most from English-speaking countries—who were hired when the municipality decided in 1971, at the urging of the Jerusalem Committee, to acquire its own planning muscle with which to challenge the government's attempt to impose its development plans on the city.

It was a fight over the proposed development of an open field five hundred yards west of the Old City walls that first brought Kutcher to public attention. Eight apartment towers and two 500-room hotels were

195

planned for the site—known as the Omariya plot. Its development had been proposed before the Six Day War as part of the government's policy of filling in open space along the border of the divided city. The high-rises would radically alter the skyline as viewed from the Old City, but the authorities had little concern about how the skyline appeared from enemy territory. High-rise buildings, in fact, would have meant a better chance to see over the walls of the Old City. Now there was one city and one skyline but the change in thinking that this demanded was slow to penetrate official circles.

The first of the Omariya towers, a sixteen-story apartment building, went up in 1970 with the backing of the Housing Ministry and municipality but without a public hearing and without a building permit. Kollek dismissed these omissions as "technicalities." So unorganized was public opinion that the building was completed—a sore thumb jabbing into the Jerusalem skyline—before there was any reaction. An Arab taxi driver summed up the instinctive feeling of most Jerusalemites when he squinted up at the newly completed building and said to his passenger "too big."

In a dynamic society beset by massive security problems and driven by the desire to build a modern country, there had never been much time for concern about public opinion and aesthetics. But simmering anger over the Omariya issue exploded in a mass protest that succeeded, for one of the first times in Israel's history, in blocking development plans because of an environmental issue. In this explosion, Art Kutcher would be the detonator.

He was present in Kollek's office during a meeting between the mayor and Housing Ministry officials who were pushing for execution of the Omariya proposal. Kollek's initial support of the project had given way to doubts after the first building went up. He asked the municipality's new planning unit to draw up an alternative plan calling for reduced density but the ministry showed little inclination to budge from its position. It was in the business of providing housing, and Jerusalem needed housing. One could leave aesthetics until basic national needs had been met.

Kutcher was dismayed at the ministry's power to impose its will on the municipality, a heritage of the centralized colonial-style structure of the British Mandate. Returning to his office, he advised his colleagues that the planning unit wash its hands of the affair rather than compromise. "We're up against the heavies," he said.

However, Meron Benvenisti, who now held the planning portfolio on the city council, had another idea. Kutcher had executed striking panoramas of the downtown area in connection with plans being drawn up for the central business district, showing what the skyline would look like if various planning alternatives were implemented. Benvenisti now asked Kutcher to show what the Omariya plot would look like if the Housing Ministry's plan were implemented. With such a sketch, they would have something concrete in hand in arguing against the project. Kutcher grabbed at the idea. "I'll go with it to the press," he said.

He first showed his sketch at a public symposium organized by the Jerusalem branch of the Council for a Beautiful Israel headed by Yehuda Haezrachi, a poet who combined trenchant wit with a capacity for indignation. Haezrachi had written books about Jerusalem, and he would privately admit that his obsession with the city, past and present, sometimes struck him as a malady.

Although Kutcher's Hebrew was limited, he did not hesitate to use it in addressing the large audience that included much of Jerusalem's architectural community. With a slide projector, he showed two sketches of the West Jerusalem skyline as seen from Mount Zion opposite the Omariya. The first showed the existing situation with one tower. The second showed the skyline as it would look if the plan for eight apartment towers and two large hotels were realized. The sketch also showed a twenty-two-story annex planned for the nearby King David Hotel and a new eighteen-story hotel that had been approved alongside.

The view of the massed towers breaking the soft skyline drew an audible gasp. Some members of the audience got to their feet to demand an immediate campaign of harassment of the responsible officials, including late-night telephone calls. Some proposed court action. Others started collecting signatures for action committees. A fiery student leader from Hebrew University vowed to fight the plan "by all necessary means."

The municipality ordered Kutcher not to talk to the press or release the sketches. However, a bootleg version of the sketches reached the press. Reaction to their publication was dramatic. Within a few days, the owner of the King David Hotel announced that he was dropping plans for the proposed annex. "I wouldn't rest quietly in my grave if people said I ruined Jerusalem," he declared.

A thousand Jerusalemites led by university students poured onto the Omariya site to plant hundreds of saplings—"a people's forest," the demonstration leaders called it—in protest against the building plans. Among the protesters was Professor David Flusser, one of the world's leading authorities on the Dead Sea Scrolls, who lived in the adjacent Talbiya Quarter. "The older generation has not proved sensitive to the questions of environment," he told a reporter. "I'm happy to see the youngsters fighting for a more humane future."

The Housing Ministry, too, had been shaken by the sketches and by the outburst of public feeling. For the first time, ministry officials began to grasp the impact of the proposed buildings on their surroundings. In a move few would have anticipated, the ministry ordered architects to draw up a new plan for the Omariya, in which environmental considerations and not floor space would be the principal criteria.

The original plan calling for 120,000 square meters of floor space was eventually cut by three quarters. Where towers were to have risen, the Liberty Bell Park was created, one of the city's liveliest corners.

"Things that were approved a couple of years ago," said Kollek afterward, "wouldn't be approved now. We've all become more sensitive to Jerusalem."

Kutcher's most dramatic achievement was in single-handedly blocking a plan to construct a massive twenty-five story hotel that would dominate the skyline on a spur of Mount Scopus, two miles north of the Old City. The proposed Hyatt House Hotel had drawn hardly a murmur of public disapproval in the three years since plans for it had been announced—partly because the broad public was unaware of it, partly because its visual impact was not grasped even by those who were aware of it. So unquestioned was the project that the investors held in a cornerstone laying ceremony in November 1971, despite the fact that formal planning approval had not yet been granted. The principal speaker was the tourism minister, who was delighted at such heavy foreign investment in East Jerusalem, where it lent further weight to Israel's claims of sovereignty.

Kutcher, however, was aghast when he studied the hotel's plans and saw how it would impose itself on the landscape. Although he was only a low-level municipal employee, hardly a year on the job, he was determined to torpedo the plan by himself, if necessary. With a telephoto lens he photographed the Scopus ridge from Government House ridge three miles to the south, shooting across the Old City. He was thus able to place the site in its proper visual perspective on the northern rim of hills surrounding the walled city. From the photograph and plans, he drew a sketch of what the hotel would look like if built. The angle he chose showed the hotel looming behind the Dome of the Rock and reducing Jerusalem's most impressive structure to insignificance. The hotel promoters would later claim that the view was telescoped and misleading, but even with allowance made for distortion, the impact was overwhelming.

A week before the District Planning Commission was to give the Hyatt final approval, Kutcher handed the sketch to reporters on *The Jerusalem Post* and the Hebrew daily, *Maariv*. The sketches with accompanying articles appeared in the weekend supplements of the two papers.

A few hours before the planning commission was to assemble, its chairman received a telephone call from the interior minister informing him that political pressure for the hotel had been dropped and that a decision should be made on planning merits alone. Another call came from the chairman of the Knesset's Interior Committee, expressing concern over the project and suggesting that a decision be postponed. His advice was taken. Within four days of publication of Kutcher's sketch, a multimillion dollar international project with powerful political backing had ground to a halt.

As eager as the government was to create political "facts" in East Jerusalem, they did not want to create an aesthetic disaster. Kutcher's sketch put abstract plans into a form public officials could not avoid grasping. When the District Planning Commission next discussed the hotel proposal it was to reject it overwhelmingly and to fix a four-story height limit for any building on the site.

While holding Kutcher in high regard, his colleagues did not find him easy to work with. He could be moody and withdrawn or volatile and acerbic, lashing out impatiently at what he took to be stupidity in high places. When one of Israel's best-known architects submitted a plan to the municipality for approval, the thirty-two-year-old Kutcher had no hesitation in denouncing it to his face as kitsch. He refused to work in the municipality planning office downtown; instead he labored under an old drawing of Berlin that was hung on the wall above his drawing board in his two-room bachelor quarters in the secluded neighborhood of Abu Tor. In his off time, he frequented the Taami Cafe, a student and leftist hangout, where he sometimes helped organize demonstrations against the municipality. Confronted with what he believed to be a mafia of builders and politicians, he determined to set up a countermafia that would mobilize public opinion. Despite the municipality ban on unauthorized employees talking to the press, he became a key source for reporters as planning in the rapidly developing capital city became a major story.

To his immediate superiors, Kutcher's idiosyncrasies were overshadowed by his talent and his devotion, which kept him at his drawing board late into the night, but for Mayor Kollek, Kutcher's outspokenness and defiance of orders grew from a minor nuisance to a major aggravation. When Kutcher's temporary contract expired, the mayor ordered that it not be renewed. Kutcher at the same time announced that he would not seek to have his contract renewed because he could not in good conscience continue to serve the municipality while working to undermine its policies.

Kutcher flew off to London, where he produced in six weeks a book on Jerusalem planning with 183 original sketches and maps. Published by a prestigious English firm, *The New Jerusalem* was a frankly polemical work aimed at inducing change and did not shirk from exaggeration to make a point. But it gave eloquent expression to the increasingly widespread feeling that the building of the new Jerusalem had gotten off to an unfortunate start, that the human scale and divine spirit of Jerusalem was being sacrificed for narrow-visioned political and economic interests.

The authorities favored high-rise buildings, he wrote, because they felt that Jerusalem did not look imposing enough for a capital. ''They of course realize that Jerusalem can never rival Manhattan so they have set their sights a bit lower. Their dream of Jerusalem is a sort of copy of Kansas City.'' To permit intensive commercial development outside the main gates to the Old City, he argued, would lead to increasing commercialization within the walls and turn it into ''a kind of religious Disneyland.'' High-rise buildings, he wrote, shattered the harmony between man-made structures and the landscape that was Jerusalem's distinguishing mark. ''The natural line of the hills is covered with a carpet of buildings and trees of roughly the same height as if the skyline had been raised uniformly. Luxury apartment towers and hotels don't fit the rhythm of the landscape and have social connotations—that there are some groups of people more important than others.''

In retrospect, the most remarkable thing about the building of the new Jerusalem after 1967 was that the results were not worse. Israel had swept through East Jerusalem with the same relentless spirit with which it had forced its own birth against the tide of history. It had created a modern state on the run with little time for agonized reflections—building, fighting, building as if any halt in forward movement would mean a fatal slide into the warm, stultifying embrace of the Levant. The political situation in post-1967 Jerusalem made speedy action even more urgent. Rarely mentioned but ever present was the fear that if Israel did not assert itself on the ground, international pressures would force it back behind the pre-1967 boundaries. In the face of these psychological and political imperatives, it would not have been surprising if the authorities had fastened the Old City to the ground with a girdle of high-rise structures to proclaim beyond any doubt whose sovereignty prevailed.

One such tower, a twenty-story hotel, had in fact been planned shortly after the 1967 war for a site less than fifty meters from the Old City wall near Jaffa Gate.

Somewhere, however, in the headlong drive to clear the rubble and create facts, something clicked in the collective mind of the powers-that-be: the thought that to embrace Jerusalem too tightly with buildings would be to smother it. It took time for the notion to take shape clearly and the toppling of the Jaffa Gate hotel proposal was among its earliest manifestations. Public opinion, tenuously feeling its own strength, played an important part, but the decision-makers themselves, even the high-powered pragmatists among them, were not insensitive men. The passage of time permitted them at some point to lay down their development maps and gaze in tranquillity, if only for a moment, at the landscape they intended to develop. Consciously or not, official thinking began to change.

One morning in 1971, cars carrying Housing Minister Zeev Sharef and Agriculture Minister Haim Gvati drove out along Government House ridge shortly after sunrise. It was the only hour the two ministers could get together at short notice. Their cars stopped near the compound of United Nations Middle East headquarters and the two men got out. Sharef, who had been a confidant of Ben-Gurion's and cabinet secretary at the time of the signing of Israel's Declaration of Independence, was the man who had pushed through the high-rise development at French Hill and the dense development of Ramot in Jerusalem's northern hills against public outcry and aesthetic sense in the name of upbuilding Jerusalem. He had come now to examine the northern slope of Government House ridge for which a large-scale development plan had been drawn up, including hotels, institutions, and villas that only wealthy investors from abroad were likely to be able to afford. The proposal had drawn opposition within the planning community, and Sharef wanted to see the site for himself before another public storm was raised. Gvati was the landlord of the slope since the Israel Lands Administration, which controlled all publicly-owned land, was part of his ministry.

From where the ministers stood, the most superb panorama of Jerusalem lay revealed. Two miles to the north the sun was gilding the golden Dome of the Rock on the Temple Mount. The entire visual basin of the Old City stretched between the horizons, the walled city itself riding a plateau cupped by the surrounding ridges. The two veteran politicians looked out in silence for a few moments. From the slope just below them they could hear the tinkle of bells from a flock of sheep being grazed by a Bedouin boy. According to tradition, it was from this ridge that Abraham had seen the place where he was to sacrifice his son Isaac. After standing in silence for several moments surveying the scene, the housing minister turned to his colleague and said, ''Here we don't build.'' With that one sentence, Sharef, a man for whom the physical development of the country was almost a religious injunction, killed a project involving potential investments of scores of millions of dollars.

In the process of sensitizing the public and the authorities to Jerusalem's special qualities, a central role was played by the young men in the municipality's Urban Planning Unit who first articulated many of the issues and brought them to public view. On the balcony of planner Mike Turner's house in North Talpiot, with its view towards the Old City and the Judean Desert, they would sometimes sit through the night passionately debating high-rise limitations and other issues until dawn silhouetted the desert hills across the valley.

At the heart of these discussions was Art Kutcher, a loner who could afford to take on the establishment and who had the vision and articulateness to do so effectively. He was instrumental in giving the public for the first time a feeling that something could be done, that the juggernaut of government and economic interests could be taken on and defeated by an aroused citizenry. Jerusalem, he said, was experiencing a critical period of growth that would shape the city for hundreds of years and ad hoc planning was no longer sufficient.

''The six square miles around the Old City symbolize the highest ideals of mankind and have inspired hundreds of millions of people,'' he said. ''The way things are going these aspirations will be turned into a joke. But they needn't be.''

In the coming years Kutcher would leave the country, return after a few years, and leave again. With his restless personality, he would probably have packed his bags and moved on even if he had not had his differences with his superiors. But Jerusalem was fortunate that he wandered into town with his sketchbook when he did.

TWENTY-ONE

Twenty Years
in the Life of a City

THE SIDEWALK CAFE on the Ben-Yehuda pedestrian mall was crowded as usual, but a regular patron was able to find a table offering shade and a good view of the passing crowd. From the general babel of conversation around him as he began to read a newspaper and drink his coffee, a sense of something unfamiliar slowly penetrated his consciousness. It was Arabic being spoken at the table behind him.

Discreetly glancing backwards as he turned the pages of the newspaper, he saw three young women, all about nineteen. They were well dressed and attractive, the bloom of youth on their cheeks. They laughed and chatted animatedly in Arabic, pausing only to order sandwiches in Hebrew when the waitress came up. It was a scene seemingly as innocent as a summer morning, but it was one of the most remarkable things he had witnessed in the two decades he had been living in Jerusalem.

Never before had he seen Arabs frequent the cafe in the heart of the Jewish sector, except on very infrequent occasions that were plainly business meetings between an Arab man and an Israeli, usually a contractor or lawyer. Never had he seen Arab women in the cafe. Arab women did not go to cafes in East Jerusalem or most places in the Arab world, certainly not without male escort. That these young women felt free enough to come to Jewish Jerusalem and partake of it as if it were a European city was astonishing. Nor had they any hesitation about sitting out of doors on the busiest street in the city and speaking Arabic.

For a brief period after the Six Day War, East Jerusalem residents had crossed into West Jerusalem in large numbers. On Fridays, the Muslim Sabbath, men in *kheffiyas*, and often whole families, could be seen walking slowly through the crowded downtown streets, staring at faces and window displays like provincial tourists. Then the terrorist bombs started going off, which caused a tightening of security. Arabs walking through the Jewish part of the city would be stopped by security personnel, usually several times in the course of a few blocks. They would be asked for identification papers and questioned about their purpose in being there. Sometimes the checks would be by policewomen, which, for Arab men, added to the sense of humiliation. Whenever there was a bomb explosion, all Arab men in the vicinity would be rounded up and detained for questioning, usually spending at least a night in the police lockup.

One Friday morning, an Israeli journalist saw an Arab lawyer he knew stopped by security personnel on Ben-Yehuda Street. The lawyer, who was with his family, was sharply questioned when he was unable to produce his identity card. The journalist interceded and saved the man from being taken to police headquarters when he assured the police he knew him. The shaken Arab lawyer wanted to head directly home. The Jewish journalist insisted on taking him and his family into a coffee house and talking to them until their composure had returned.

It was not long before Arabs stopped coming to West Jerusalem except to work or conduct business. Some Israeli firms and professionals like lawyers, who had a substantial Arab clientele, deliberately relocated to areas adjacent to former no-man's-land in the knowledge that the Arabs preferred not coming deep into the Jewish city for fear of being arrested if a bomb happened to go off. It would take years for this to begin to change. The sharp reduction in terror incidents led to fewer security patrols and less fastidious checking of Arabs on the street. No less important, a new generation had grown up in East Jerusalem for whom the trauma of the Israeli conquest in the war was not a personal memory. Israel remained a conquerer but not one that terrified; instead it was a place that aroused Arab curiosity and, in some of its aspects, admiration. Arab family groups could be seen on Fridays picnicking in the parks of West Jerusalem or visiting its zoo. The Muslim Sabbath was also the day when East Jerusalemites came to frequent the department stores and specialty shops in the Jewish sector. Toward the middle of the 1980s, small groups of young, well-dressed Arab men could be seen occasionally in popular cafes and restaurants. In the absence of unpleasant experiences, these forays became more widespread.

Other Arabs also began to be seen regularly in West Jerusalem—employees who had come out of the kitchen and storeroom to work behind the counter in pharmacies, hardware stores, and numerous other establishments, dealing directly with the Israeli public in perfect Hebrew. To the clients, these became Arabs with names and familiar smiles. The same feelings were experienced by the Arab employees. In a very small way, in a very real way, the "Arab Problem" now had a human face—years of daily contact had reduced the demon image each side had of the other.

Until the Palestinian uprising at the end of 1987 Jerusalem's Arabs felt themselves at least marginally part of the political process at municipal election time, when they were wooed as avidly as Jewish residents.

Teddy Kollek found the City Hall press corps drinking his brandy and ensconced on his office couches when he arrived from his campaign headquarters at 1:00 A.M. Two hours before, his 1978 election to a third term had been projected on television, this time by the biggest margin yet. His One Jerusalem Party had won sixteen seats on the thirty-one-man city council, giving him for the first time a majority without need of a coalition.

There was a rare mellowness to Kollek as he pulled his chair into the middle of the circle of reporters. He was at peace, floating in the still space between the trial of elections and the trial of his new administration. It was not the Arab vote that had given him the majority, he said, repeating a point made by the television analyst. Would the writers for the afternoon papers please make that clear.

If the Arab vote had given him the majority, the right-wing in the next four years undoubtedly would revive the slogan "Teddy—defender of Islam" whenever he moved to accommodate the Arabs. (Analysis of the final vote would show that the Arab vote *had* given him two mandates, enough for his majority.) Having defended his flank against charges of dependence on the Arab vote, he made a point of protecting the Arabs who voted from charges of political surrender to Israel. The Arab vote, he said, was a vote for a unified city but did not suggest that the Arabs accepted Israeli rule. "I attribute it to the respect we have shown them and to the clear choice between us and the [right-wing] Likud. Beyond that there is no political significance.''

However, the fact that more than 8,000 Arabs of the 43,000 eligible to vote had cast ballots, despite warnings by terrorist organizations, and the vigorous pursuit of the Arab vote by all parties was not without significance in pointing the way to potential political dialogue at the local level. Even the right-wing candidate had campaigned intensively in East Jerusalem, an area his party had ignored in earlier elections. A campaign brochure in Arabic showed the candidate against a backdrop of the Dome of the Rock and called him ''a son of Jerusalem,'' whose family had lived in the city for ten generations. The implication was that he was better suited to talk to the Arabs than, say, a son of Vienna.

Voting day is one of the rare occasions when Jerusalem's collection of populations participate together in the same communal act. The great Hassidic rabbis walk to the polling both in their holiday clothing flanked by clouds of Hassidim. The Arabs of Bait Safafa come to the local schoolhouse early to cast their ballots and relax in the shade of the trees in the courtyard. In Kibbutz Ramat Rachel in southern Jerusalem, a piano tinkles on this work-free day in the room next to the polling station where members cast their ballots. Women in the blue-collar district of Katamon chat with each other about the elections from their balconies across the narrow streets, while Hebrew University professors discuss the likely outcome when they meet on the leafy streets of Rehavia. On this one day, in the secrecy of the polling booth, each person stands alone and is equal to anyone else. By nightfall, when the votes are counted, everyone is back in his tribal encampment.

Jerusalem itself can be viewed as a vast encampment housing tribes some of whom exist in a state of confrontation. To live in Jerusalem means living in casual proximity to ultimate answers and imminent violence. There is little criminal or social violence—old women feel safe walking down dark streets at night. The sense of personal safety in Jerusalem is unmatched in most cities of the world—but the possibility of terrorism or war is something that the authorities prepare for as they prepare for rain runoff or the outbreak of a fire.

Until the early 1970s, by law every new house had to have a cistern, a provision not against drought but against siege. In 1948 it was the city's old cisterns that permitted Jewish Jerusalem to survive the months-long Arab siege and the severing of the city's water lines. Revocation of the municipal cistern ordinance reflected the belief not that Jerusalem would see war no more, only that future battles would almost certainly be over before city roof tanks ran dry. Instead of providing cisterns, builders now had to dig deep to provide mandatory shelters below each house, offering protection against nuclear or chemical warfare.

Visitors to Jerusalem are often puzzled at the absence of litter baskets. They were removed shortly after the Six Day War, when they proved popular depositories for terrorist bombs. The sight of weapons is commonplace in the city, whether held by soldiers stopping off in town, by settlers in from the West Bank for shopping, or by parents escorting a school group to a hike in the territories. Inside banks, civilians with automatic rifles can be seen waiting in line at a teller's window without drawing a glance from the guard. Sometimes, when a storekeeper or passerby leans over to pick up something, a pistol butt can be seen sticking out of the back of his belt.

The two customers entering the sporting goods shop on King George Street in the spring of 1984 carried travel bags. They seemed to the eighteen-year-old clerk to be sweating and nervous. One was about his own age. "We'd like to see jeans," said the older customer in English with an Arabic accent. "Size twenty-eight." The customers took their bags with them when they stepped into dressing cubicles. A few moments later, they emerged holding automatic rifles. The older of the two put the gun to the clerk's head. For several seconds, the Arab looked the young Israeli in the eye, then pushed him aside and ran outside with his partner. A third Arab was awaiting them outside.

The three terrorists opened fire on pedestrians on the crowded street and began throwing grenades. Bedlam ensued as people scattered or fell to the ground amidst the explosions and gunfire. Within moments, Israeli civilians were returning fire.

An insurance agent whose office was on the second floor of a building across from the shop looked out his window and dashed down the staircase. Pulling his pistol from his belt, he began exchanging fire with one of the terrorists. Another, he saw, had been downed by a storekeeper. The third had fled. The insurance agent pursued his quarry and brought him down next to a crowded bus at the corner as the terrorist was trying to arm a grenade. A reporter happening by saw men with drawn pistols along the street looking suspiciously at each other, uncertain whether the others were terrorists or citizens like themselves.

Some forty civilians had been wounded, most of them lightly from grenade fragments. One of the terrorists was killed, another wounded, and the third captured. At least four civilians had fired on the terrorists, hitting two of them. In the absence of police it was clear that they had prevented a massacre.

For Mahmoud Abu al-Nasser and his fellow Arab construction worker, invited by their boss for dinner, it was the first visit to an Israeli home. Since beginning to work for Avraham a few months before, Mahmoud to his surprise had found himself liking the Jewish building contractor, and was touched by the invitation. Avraham's wife greeted the guests warmly. In the course of the amiable conversation over dinner she turned to Mahmoud and with a laugh said, "You've got the the eyes of Fatah." Mahmoud glanced over at Avraham and saw that he was studying him.

"You go to the army," said Mahmoud to Avraham. "I go to Fatah."

Everyone laughed and the conversation moved in other directions although it was clear that the Jewish couple could not be certain whether or not their guest indeed was, as he jokingly suggested, a member of a terrorist organization.

Mahmoud, in fact, was. Not of the mainstream Fatah but of the leftist Popular Front. One of the toughest fighters in the Gaza Strip, he had been dispatched by his organization to Jerusalem with three other residents of the refugee camps. They were ordered to find employment and survey the city for potential targets.

Mahmoud became so caught up in the routine of daily work that he sometimes had to remind himself of the reason he was in Jerusalem. Returning periodically to the Gaza Strip, he helped plan terrorist attacks with his superior. He felt the urge to warn Avraham to avoid going to a certain part of the city on a given day when he knew there would be an explosion there, but he did not warn him.

One day, he took a pistol and grenade that he had brought back with him from Gaza and stationed himself next to the post office on Saladin Street in East Jerusalem to await a target. As he clutched the grenade under the newspaper he pretended to read, an army truck with about 20 soldiers stopped nearby. Mahmoud watched some of the soldiers get off to make purchases in the nearby shops. The first to return to the truck was a girl soldier. She was eating ice cream.

The girl was dark and seemed of Sephardi origin. Mahmoud wanted to wait for others to come back but he could not stand there much longer without someone noticing that he was holding something under his newspaper. Pulling the pin, he casually dropped the grenade under the truck and walked away. He was around the corner when the explosion came. From the paper the next day, he learned that a number of persons had been wounded, including a girl soldier.

A few months later, Mahmoud was in the Gaza Strip hiding from the security services who were searching for him, when he was trapped by an army patrol. Attempting to fight his way out, he was wounded in both legs, one of which had to be amputated. Upon emerging from prison fifteen years later, he would recall the dinner with Avraham and his wife to an Israeli journalist.

It began with the Arab girls teasing the Jewish girls. The Arab girls were sixth-graders from an East Jerusalem school. The West Jerusalem pupils were fourth-graders. The encounter was unplanned. Both classes were visiting the Nature Museum in the city's German Colony. "You're not pretty," said some of the Arab girls with smiles that showed they didn't really mean it.

Dana, who knew she was pretty, walked over with a friend to one of the Arab girls and asked her name. It was Zuza. The girls asked each other what grades they were in, what schools they went to, and how they liked their teachers. Zuza said she liked her teacher. The Jewish girls said they didn't like theirs.

Breaking into small mixed groups, the Jewish and Arab girls moved slowly through the exhibit halls. They spoke with each other a mixture of Hebrew, which the Arab girls spoke unevenly, and English, which both spoke unevenly. Some of the exhibits had no Arabic explanations and the Jewish girls translated the Hebrew to their new companions.

When they exited into the courtyard, the two classes faced each other in the sunlight. The Arab girls wore uniform skirts over slacks. The Jewish girls were mostly in shorts.

There was a feeling, Dana would relate to her parents later, that it shouldn't just end without anything. Then one of the Arab girls said, "Sing us a song."

The Jewish girls huddled amid giggles but couldn't settle on a song. Then one of the Arab girls called: "Sing 'Hai.'" The song had been Israel's winning entry in the annual Eurovision song contest, besting the songs submitted by the score of other nations participating. The Arab girls had watched the contest on television and evidently enjoyed the bouncy music of the Israeli entry without paying much attention to the patriotic thurst of its lyrics.

The Jewish girls began singing the song, at first tentatively, then at the tops of their voices. To their surprise, the Arab girls joined in the chorus "*Hai, hai, hai, am Yisrael hai*" (life, life, life, the Jewish people lives). The Arab girls then sang a song in Arabic, and the Israeli girls listened attentively without understanding. "They had nice clear voices," Dana would relate.

As the teachers called their respective classes to assemble, Dana and Zuza and the other girls exchanged good-byes. The fourth-graders were the first to leave. Dana paused at the gate a moment to look back at the Arab girls, then hurried after her class.

By 1988 the population of Jerusalem had reached about 500,000, almost double the 1967 figure, with Jews constituting 72 percent of the total. No longer a quaint, dead-end town on the country's periphery, Jerusalem was now the largest city in the land and the bustling center of a metropolitan area embracing a good part of the West Bank. Its skyline, punctuated by numerous high-rises, was no longer provincial, and neither was its vibrant cultural life. The Jerusalem Symphony, which drew perhaps two hundred persons to its once-weekly concerts in the YMCA auditorium before the war, would draw full houses several times a week when it shifted concerts to the new nine-hundred-seat Jerusalem Theater. Plays performed by major theater groups from Tel Aviv and Haifa appeared three or four times in half-empty halls before the war. In the postwar era they would appear a dozen and more times before packed houses. The large number of immigrants from the West and the Soviet Union was an important factor in this new cultural vibrancy. So was the infrastructure of theaters provided by Mayor Kollek.

Outdoor cafes, which had never before been a significant part of the Jerusalem scene, began to give the hill city a welcome Mediterranean ambience. Although the Old City remained Jerusalem's focus for visitors, for Jerusalemites it was the pedestrian mall of Ben-Yehuda Street lined by outdoor cafes. New immigrants from the gray, dour uniformity of the Soviet Union would find themselves gripped by the colors of Ben-Yehuda, by the animation and the expressiveness of the faces. Despite these changes, Jerusalem would not presume to challenge Tel Aviv as the nation's cultural capital and only for relatively few would night life last beyond midnight.

Neither would the changes alter other aspects of the city's character. Its beauty survived in the stone facing of Jerusalem's buildings. It remained, too, in the picturesque alleys and courtyards of the older neighborhoods; in the quiet and lushly planted streets of middle-class neighborhoods, rich with the smell of jasmine; and in the sculpted hills surrounding the city. Late afternoon in Jerusalem, when the city is illuminated with golden light, is still a holy time.

The Palestinian upheaval that began in December 1987 would demonstrate once again, however, that neither clenched fist nor outstretched hand can still the demands of a people that feels itself strong enough to demand political independence.

The riots that began in the teeming refugee camps of the Gaza Strip quickly spread to the West Bank and then to Jerusalem itself. Within a few days, neighborhoods that had been peaceful for twenty years became the center of violent protest. In Abu Tor, burning tires sent the black smoke of defiance into the air. In Shuafat, stones—and sometimes petrol bombs—were thrown at Israeli buses. In Bait Safafa, metal barriers were laid across the railway line. Stones broke windows of Jewish apartments a few score meters from Arab families near Government House, and petrol bombs were thrown on houses at the edge of the Jewish Quarter. On A-Tur on the Mount of Olives, the police, exercising emergency powers for the first time since 1967, clamped down a curfew after extensive rioting. A right-wing Israeli minister, Ariel Sharon, threw oil on the fire by demonstratively moving into the Muslim Quarter, ostensibly to provide security along the route to the Western Wall from Damascus Gate. Most Jews, however, preferred to avoid the Muslim Quarter altogether.

Most surprising to many Israelis was the attitude of the Arab merchants in East Jerusalem, who staged a commercial strike that would last intermittently for months. In the past, the pragmatic merchants had relunctantly heeded periodic calls by Arab militants for a general strike, but often asked the Israeli authorities privately to have the police ''force'' them to open so that they could do so without fear of retaliation from the militants. Now, however, most participated in the strike willingly, seeing it as part of an historic national uprising whose time had finally come.

Israeli officials reiterated that Jerusalem would remain united under Israeli sovereignty in any conceivable political settlement. Some, however, began to concede publicly that concessions would have to be made on Jerusalem if a peace agreement were to be signed. Jordan might have started the 1967 war in the hope of destroying Israel, but the Palestinians would not accept relinquishing their claim on Arab Jerusalem as a result of Jordanian military failure.

Between the prospect of Armaggedon and the prospect of the Messiah's Coming, politicians have attempted to weave scenarios of a peace settlement that both Arabs and Israelis could accept—a prospect that often seems no less otherworldly than the first two. It is presumed by most that Jerusalem will be the last item on any peace agenda. If any consensus can be said to have emerged since 1967 about Jerusalem's future, it is that the city should not be physically divided again. President Sadat said so after his visit to the city. Jordan's King Hussein and local Arab leaders have said so, often even publicly. American presidents have said so. Israeli leaders constantly say so. This is, however, a tenuous consensus that could give way.

In 1948 Premier David Ben-Gurion would have accepted Jerusalem even as an internationalized enclave within the Arab part of partitioned Palestine. That was better than an Arab-ruled Jerusalem. The only reason Jerusalem wasn't internationalized was that the Arabs thought they could win it outright by military means. The Israeli government was even happier after meeting the military challenge to see Jerusalem as a divided city, lying partially at least within Israeli sovereignty. That was better than an internationalized Jerusalem. Best of all, of course, was total Israeli sovereignty won after King Hussein made his fatal mistake by attacking Israel in the Six Day War. Today, for Israel, the concept of a divided Jerusalem is unthinkable.

The relativity of politics has been equally apparent on the Arab side. The Arabs have moved from an attempt to conquer Jewish Jerusalem by force of arms in 1948; to delight, in the period from 1948 to 1967, with possession of the half of the divided city embracing the Temple Mount; to adoption of President Sadat's principle for Jerusalem: "Undivided city—divided sovereignty."

It is in the gray political terrain evoked by Sadat's slogan that the battle for Jerusalem's future may eventually be fought. Sadat had pronounced the slogan after being escorted around the city by Teddy Kollek ("The most famous mayor in the world," the Egyptian leader had said upon being introduced to him). One of the major points Kollek had chosen to show him was the park developed in the Hinnom Valley at the foot of the Old City. The flourishing site, teeming with Jews, Arabs, and tourists and dotted with artisan workshops, an amphitheater, a cinema, and a music center, had been an Egyptian minefield in the War of Independence, Kollek told his guest. When the Egyptian army left Jerusalem after the war the Hinnom Valley had remained a grim stretch of no-man's-land for nineteen years thereafter. The mayor was somewhat off in his facts: the Egyptian army had reached the southern outskirts of the city in 1948 but not the Hinnom Valley. Sadat, however, grasped the point. To dissect a city with minefields and fences was to dissect a living organism. The city could remain united physically, he suggested, but the eastern half would be under Arab sovereignty as the western was under Israeli sovereignty.

Kollek was delighted with the first half of Sadat's pronouncement but not the second. "The phrase 'united city—divided sovereignty' is self-contradictory," he said. "If there is divided sovereignty, it is clear there would be two laws. This would mean two police forces and customs. In a month, the minefields would be back. To divide the city would be to kill it."

What then?

Some Arabs, the Vatican, and foreign governments have proposed internationalization but, apart from its dubious practicability, Israel would never accept it. Numerous other suggestions have likewise been made, including Arab sovereignty on the Temple Mount. The concept that has drawn the most attention is the borough system proposed by Kollek and Meron Benvenisti.

The latter spelled it out in a detailed plan he drew up in 1968 at the request of the Foreign Ministry, which wanted a proposal that envisioned continued Israeli sovereignty over Jerusalem while at the same time "satisfying non-Israeli interests (particularly Jordanian)."

The sophisticated plan called for the creation of five boroughs that would include sizeable areas on the West Bank outside the city limits which would fall under Jordanian sovereignty in a peace agreement. The boroughs would form a Greater Jerusalem Council made up of fifty-one delegates, the majority Jewish (reflecting the weight of population.) Two of the boroughs would be entirely Jordanian. Two other Arab-populated boroughs would lie partially within Israeli sovereignty and partially within Jordanian sovereignty, in order to create a deliberate overlapping of interests and blurring of borders. The fifth, and largest, borough would include all the area with a Jewish population.

The boroughs would be responsible for their own education, physical planning, and most other urban affairs, but there would be extensive coordination among them. A metropolitan council would be charged with area-wide concerns, such as sewage, major parks, and interurban roads. Arabs living within the sovereign Israeli area could retain their Jordanian citizenship and continue to vote in Jordanian elections. ''Americans living in Paris can vote for an American president,'' Kollek would note, ''and they don't question that Paris is the capital of France.''

It is a complex plan, subject to numerous variations, but its advocates maintain that only such a complex plan can resolve the problem of Jerusalem to the relative satisfaction of all parties. Despite the economic prosperity the city's Arabs have enjoyed since 1967, they still regard themselves as a conquered people. The concept of Jerusalem as a communal mosaic is workable in the long run only if the communal pieces in the mosaic feel themselves truly equal.

A tale of two cities that became one.

A tale of two peoples who didn't.

Arab *alte zakhen* men reappearing with their sacks in the streets of Jewish Jerusalem in 1967 and singing out in remembered Yiddish for junk. Arab youths not yet born in 1967 challenging the security forces twenty years later with rocks and slogans about Arab Jerusalem, a Jerusalem they had never known.

Arab bombs exploding in the Jewish marketplace. Jewish shoppers thronging the Arab marketplace.

The stony hills drowsing on the approaches to ancient Jerusalem swallowed by a metropolis.

Palestinian Arabs and Israeli Jews living together in the city at the heart of the conflict and doing business with each other each day for twenty years, while the problem of Arab-Jewish irreconcilability is pondered in the major capitals of the world.

Two decades since the removal of the barriers separating East and West Jerusalem caused both Arabs and Jews to fear that the gates of hell had swung open. The fears of rape and massacre did not materialize. Neither did any notion that Ishmael and Isaac would embrace on the Temple Mount. The two had the opportunity, however, to observe, for whatever it was worth, that the other had a human face.

Epilogue

Neighbors Still

"YOU FELLOWS DON'T KNOW what it's all about," said Abu Ali, gesturing at the television screen where American marines were storming ashore at Iwo Jima. "I fought in the Turkish army in the Caucusus against the Russians."

The ninety-one-year-old Arab was talking to his grandson Ziat and Ziat's best friend, Avraham. Avraham would be finding out what it was all about soon enough. In a few months, the seventeen-year-old son of Haim Machsumi would be drafted into the Israeli army.

It was a spring night in 1974, half a year after the Yom Kippur War. Throughout the city, soldiers and reinforced police units patrolled the streets as part of a general alert against terrorist incursions. A mile north of Abu Ali's house, U.S. Secretary of State Henry Kissinger and Prime Minister Golda Meir were locked in negotiations over cease-fire agreements on the Egyptian and Syrian fronts. The journalists at press headquarters in the King David Hotel were filing stories indicating serious snags. But in the Abu Tor Quarter, these portentous events seemed remote. The mothers of Ziat and Avraham chatted in Arabic in one corner as they knitted. Avraham's father sat on the couch drinking mint tea with Abu Ali. As they chatted, they gazed distractedly at the frantic images on the television screen fighting their way through groves of coconut trees.

Since Haim had crossed through the torn barbed wire during the Six

216

Day War seven years before and clasped Abu Ali's hand, the Jewish and Arab families virtually had become one. The relationship had survived the tensions of the Yom Kippur War and periodic outbursts of terrorism.

Every Sabbath afternoon, Abu Ali carried a *finjan* of hot coffee twenty meters up the slope to Haim and Rachel's house. He knew that as observant Jews they did not boil water on the Sabbath. "You drink coffee during the week," he had told them when they protested. "There's no reason why you shouldn't drink it on Saturdays too." Each spring, on the night that Passover ended, Abu Ali and other Arab neighbors would bring freshly baked *pittot* to the Machsumis who, as with all observant Jews, had not eaten bread during the week-long holiday.

On the Muslim feast of Id el-Fitr, Haim and Rachel would likewise call on their Arab neighbors. When there was a wedding in any of the neighboring Arab households, the Jewish couple was always invited.

For a couple of years after the Six Day War, there had still been occasional stone throwing and cursing between Jewish and Arab children in Abu Tor. This had passed. The children now played soccer together in former no-man's-land. The Jewish children spoke Hebrew and the Arab children replied in Arabic. Both sides understood the other perfectly.

Avraham was the oldest of the nine Machsumi children. (Rachel would give birth to two more in coming years.) He and his Arab friend, Ziat, worked together in a book bindery in West Jerusalem, and they spend most evenings in each other's houses. Sometimes they descended to a billiard parlor in the heart of Arab Abu Tor, where other Arab and Jewish youths played. On Saturdays, they went together to the movie house in East Jerusalem, where the subtitles on foreign pictures were in Arabic which Avraham could read. They did not go to the more modern cinemas in West Jerusalem because Ziat could not read the Hebrew subtitles well enough.

Earlier on this spring evening, Haim had walked down into the Arab part of Abu Tor with a visitor. On the main street, the proprietors of two adjacent carpentry shops greeted him warmly and insisted on a round of coffee. As they drank, one of them complained that a municipal inspector had fined him that week for setting up a worktable on the sidewalk. He had probably been fined, said Haim, because the table did not leave room for children to pass. "But they can just step down into the street," said the carpenter.

"That would be dangerous," said Haim, nodding at the parked trucks along the curb.

Haim, who still earned his living cleaning halls in the Finance Ministry, served as an unofficial mukhtar for the residents of Arab Abu Tor. He interceded with the authorities on their behalf—filling out forms for them in Hebrew and often accompanying them to government offices. He made it a point to explain to his Arab neighbors that the burden of taxes and bylaws were shared equally by Jewish residents and were not Draconian measures aimed at Arabs. Under Jordanian administration, there had been little taxation and little public services.

As Haim returned up the slope, Ziat approached with a cousin from Hebron. Haim's five-year-old son, Avner, ran to Ziat and embraced him around the knees. The Arab youth tousled the Jewish boy's hair and invited everyone to his grandfather's house for coffee. The old man was watching the American war movie with one of his young grandchildren. Someone asked Abu Ali if he thought Kissinger could bring peace. "Only Allah can say," he replied in Arabic. "Man without God is nothing."

"He doesn't think much of the modern world," said Haim in Hebrew.

"There is no respect anymore," said Abu Ali. "In the old days when a woman spoke to me she covered her mouth so that I could hardly understand what she was saying." He drew his cloak across his mouth to demonstrate. "Today everyone is walking around naked. Nothing here [patting his arms]. Nothing here [patting his legs]. In the old days, there would be be one thousand people in the mosque on Friday, and they would listen to the imam's every word. Today the coffee houses are full but you're hard put finding ten people in the mosque." (In reality, the mosques were full on Fridays.)

Ziat and Avraham had turned away from the television and were listening to the old man with obvious pleasure. "He doesn't believe in riding buses," Ziat said. "He insists on walking to the Old City and back" (a round trip of six kilometers along steep roads).

Suddenly, Abu Ali roared "*Kief Halak* [Welcome]" and beamed a toothy smile. Haim's sixteen-year-old son, Izik, had come into the room. The boy frequently worked with Abu Ali in the old man's garden and was his favorite. "In Hebron [where he had lived most of his life] we had Jewish neighbors too," Abu Ali told Haim's guest. "We ate together and slept in each other's houses."

The old man had been a farmer and a woodcutter all his life. He had spent that afternoon cutting wood for the primitive outdoor fireplace in which he baked bread. "The children got me angry today," he grumbled. "None of them would help. I had to carry the wood up to the house all by myself."

Suddenly Abu Ali was talking about the recent massacre at Ma'alot in the Galilee, where Palestinian terrorists had killed a score of high school students they were holding prisoner. "When I heard about the killing of those children, I wanted to weep. The people who did it are barbarians. They bring shame on us all."

Nowhere else in Jerusalem had neighborly relations developed between Arab and Jewish families like those between the families of Haim Machsumi and Abu Ali. In part this was a function of proximity—nowhere else were Arab and Jewish houses so close. In larger part it was a function of the attitudes of the two heads of the families—a Jewish janitor and an Arab woodcutter who looked into the faces of the stranger across the line and nodded in recognition.

"There are people who say we can't talk to the Arabs and it's no use trying," said Haim as he left Abu Ali's home. "But that's not right. In our circumstances, we *must* talk to them. We're living among them. There are people who say, 'The only good Arab is one who has been in his grave forty years.' But the opposite is true. Jews can live together with Arabs as well as they can live with other Jews or as well as Arabs can live with Arabs. Before the Six Day War, most of the Arabs in Abu Tor would draw their finger across their throat when they saw me across the barbed wire. Today those same people are my neighbors and friends. Just after the war, Abu Ali told me that he had been sure that I would kill him the first time I came to his house. I told him 'Why should I want to kill you? We both believe in God. We're both human beings.' That's what I believe. We're all human beings."

The Palestinian uprising that began twenty years after the Six Day War appears to have inaugurated a new chapter in Jerusalem's history, one of uncertain direction but likely to be wrenching. Beyond the passions, however, beyond the old scores and exclusionary claims, there will remain for the city's Jews and Arabs the experience of twenty years of coexistence. It was an uneven coexistence born out of a war that burdened one side with the infirmities of defeat and the other with the infirmities of conquest. But its basic lesson for many on both sides of the city will remain that articulated by Haim Machsuni—"We're all human beings."

Index